高校英语选修课系列教材

商务英语口译

主　编　赵　颖
副主编　曲　涛　于红霞
　　　　何志波　刘　欣

清华大学出版社
北　京

内 容 简 介

本书以交替传译技能为主线,将口译技能与商务话题有机地结合在一起,融合多年的商务英语教学与口译实践,旨在培养学生在商务语境中交替传译的能力。每个单元均设有技巧讲解、技巧练习、主题口译、情景口译、句式扩展和口译小贴士几个模块,突出商务英语口译的实战特点,深入浅出地介绍主要的交替传译技巧和练习方法,以丰富的练习延展口译训练的有效性,聚焦口译技巧的提升和语言知识的积累,着力培养学生的跨文化交际能力、自主学习能力和合作学习能力。

版权所有,侵权必究。举报: 010-62782989,beiqinquan@tup.tsinghua.edu.cn。

图书在版编目(CIP)数据

商务英语口译 / 赵颖主编. —北京:清华大学出版社,2018(2025.2 重印)
(高校英语选修课系列教材)
ISBN 978-7-302-47916-1

Ⅰ.①商… Ⅱ.①赵… Ⅲ.①商务–英语–口译 Ⅳ.①F7

中国版本图书馆CIP数据核字(2017)第194159号

责任编辑:钱屹芝
封面设计:子 一
责任校对:王凤芝
责任印制:丛怀宇

出版发行:清华大学出版社
网　　址:https://www.tup.com.cn, https://www.wqxuetang.com
地　　址:北京清华大学学研大厦A座　　邮　　编:100084
社 总 机:010-83470000　　邮　　购:010-62786544
投稿与读者服务:010-62776969, c-service@tup.tsinghua.edu.cn
质量反馈:010-62772015, zhiliang@tup.tsinghua.edu.cn

印 装 者:三河市龙大印装有限公司
经　　销:全国新华书店
开　　本:185mm×260mm　　印　张:17　　字　数:381千字
版　　次:2018年9月第1版　　印　次:2025年2月第8次印刷
定　　价:66.00元

产品编号:073925-01

本书为2016年度大连外国语大学学科建设专项经费资助项目成果，在此致谢！

序

商业活动的活跃和发展是人类社会进步的永动机。在全球化加速发展的今天,中国提出的"一带一路"倡议更是得到了全球许多国家的积极响应,也积极推动了中国与世界各国及国际组织在政治、经济、商务和文化等各领域的广泛交流。国际交流的发展必然会促使社会对高层次、高素质口译人才需求量的增加,这也对高校培养应用型人才提出了要求。

在现行的高校本科专业设置中,商务英语专业发展迅速,究其原因正是该专业的发展顺应了社会对"外语+商务"的复合型人才的需求。同样,自 2007 年国务院学位委员会批准设置翻译硕士专业学位以来,翻译专业硕士也在飞速发展。截至 2016 年 11 月,全国获批翻译硕士专业的高校已达 215 所。翻译专业硕士的设立正是迎合了社会对高层次、应用型、专业性的口笔译人才的需求。但是,翻译专业硕士的发展离不开一定的专业领域。作为商务英语专业重要的专业技能课程和翻译专业硕士主要的选修课程,商务英语口译是在商务背景之下,针对口译技能的专项训练,为高层次的商务口译人才培养奠定基础。

该教材的成形是几位老师在多年教学和工作过程中的一个总结,是针对商务英语口译课程特点精心设计和编排的。该教材以商务知识专题和口译技巧为两条并行的主线,结合商务话题培养学生的口译技巧,力求在真实的场景中提升学生的语言技能和口译技能。

该教材的编写充分考虑到了受众的学习情况,技能训练与情景材料的编排充分考虑到了口译技能培养的渐进性和语言能力提升的循序渐进性,遵循了由简到繁的原则。

《商务英语口译》具有以下特色:

一、口译技能的讲解完整、全面、透彻。从初始阶段的听辩到译后总结均涉猎其中,并针对每个环节的技巧要点和练习方式进行了较为全面和深入的分析,对口译学习者而言,本教材可谓良师益友。

二、材料的选择侧重真实性和代表性。教材凸显了口译的实践性、真实性、知识性相融合等特点,在语料和场景的选择上尽量贴近于真实,多数材料为真

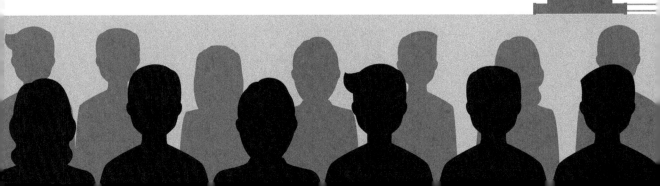

实的语料或依据真实的商务谈判、访谈、演讲等删减转写而来。在商务大背景下，语料尽量涵盖具有代表性的商务类专题，如商业陈述、市场营销、商务谈判等，让学习者在练习的过程中熟悉和了解商务活动的各个环节。

三、内容的设计具有延展性。本教材在每个单元中都设有"句式扩展""情景口译""口译小贴士"等几个具有特色的模块，这些模块具有很强的延展性。"句式扩展"可以作为语言的储备；"情景口译"是课堂话题的有效延伸，可以让学习者自由练习和发挥；"口译小贴士"则是描述口译工作的方方面面，让学习者对口译工作有一个更直观、更全面的了解。

许多年以来，我曾几十次承担各级各类口译任务，包括同传和交传，深知口译工作之艰难。要做好口译，就必须经过艰苦的系统训练。训练一般包括两个大的方面——知识储备和口译技能。知识源于大量阅读和广泛涉猎，这可以通过纸质书籍或网络方式获得。但口译技能则不然。目前，真正将多年积累的口译经验写在教材里的人不多，这也正是该教材的可贵之处。赵颖老师长期从事各类口译，积累了丰富的同传和交传经验，她毫无保留地将口译"秘籍"和大家共享，使有志成为"口译大家"的学生有了"捷径"可走。我为大家有了这样的教材而感到高兴。

杨俊峰

2018 年 5 月

前言

随着中国"一带一路""亚投行""供给侧改革"等长远战略的出台与实施，中国正在零距离地参与世界分工和产品竞争。在这一过程中，经济建设的高速发展，对外开放的日益扩大，全球一体化的迅猛发展，使得对于"商务+外语"人才的需求也到了前所未有的地步。自2006年教育部审批通过全国第一个商务英语本科专业试办以来，该专业得到了快速发展，并于2012年正式被列入《普通高等学校本科专业目录》。截至目前，全国开设商务英语本科专业的普通高校达到323所，该专业已成为国内高等院校学科发展的重点。商务英语的这种大致一年翻一番的开设规模，既反映了教育主管部门积极审慎的态度，也反映了经济社会对商务英语本科专业复合型人才的需求。目前，商务英语已经成为与英语、翻译专业并列的本科专业。

商务英语口译，作为商务英语本科专业的主干技能课，同时又是翻译专业硕士重要的选修课，在培养合格的商务英语口译专门人才方面起到了重要的作用。商务活动的独特性和复杂性对译员工作提出了更高的要求。译员既要熟练运用口译技巧，又要掌握足够的商务知识和谈判技巧。因此，商务英语口译课程的设计既要兼顾口译基本技能的教学，又要在商务英语主题内容的基础上进行反复的强化练习。本教材《商务英语口译》的编写就是为了适应商务英语口译课程的需要。

本教材的主体部分共有15个单元，每个单元均设有技巧讲解、技巧练习、主题口译、情景口译、句式扩展和口译小贴士几个部分。除此之外，本教材还设有"口译导论"部分，对口译的基本概念进行讲解。书后还设有国际口译联合会（AIIC）的职业准则和中国口译服务标准等附录部分，本书的参考答案和录音音频可在网站 ftp://ftp.tup.tsinghua.edu.cn/ 上下载。

本教材具有以下几大特色：

1. **口译技巧与商务话题相辅相成**。商务英语口译课程本身就是口译技巧和商务话题的融合体。本教材从课程本身的特点出发，每个单元详细介绍一种口译技巧，并辅以技巧练习，重点练习该单元介绍的口译技巧；再通过相应的商务话题设计主题英汉/汉英口译练习，反复强化该单元的口译技巧，以期让学生在掌握口译技巧的同时了解商务口译中经常出现的内容。

商务英语口译

2. 实战性为主导。每个单元的主题口译练习前都有主题导入，让学生在口译开始前了解该部分的知识背景，并辅以重点词语的翻译注释，增加口译练习的真实感。

3. 课堂和课后练习丰富。每个单元配有足够的课堂练习，也可做课后练习的辅助材料；每个单元还配有两套根据商务主题设置的情景口译场景，学生可以以小组为单位，根据提示内容进行资料的收集整理，再编写讲话/对话，进行自主口译练习；也可以供教师进行课堂互动教学使用。

4. 注重口译技巧的提升和语言知识的积累。每单元配有"口译小贴士"，全面展示口译基本技巧以外的知识，即口译技巧的练习方法或口译工作中应该注意的方方面面。"句式扩展"则是语言积累的重要组成部分，汇总了该商务话题的主要句式，供学生课后背诵、套用。

本教材是2016年度大连外国语大学学科建设专项经费资助项目，由大连外国语大学高级翻译学院赵颖副教授担任主编。大连外国语大学英语学院曲涛副教授、于红霞副教授、东北财经大学国际商务外语学院何志波副教授及中国工业联合会国际联络部副主任科员刘欣共同编写。具体分工如下：

赵颖负责全书框架设计、修改和终稿的审校，并执笔6、7、8单元；

曲涛负责全书的校对，并执笔13、14、15单元；

于红霞负责执笔4、5、11单元；

何志波负责执笔1、2、3单元；

刘欣负责执笔9、10、12单元。

大连外国语大学高级翻译学院2014级MTI口译方向研究生王梦、金重、于梦心、慕翼蔚、郑丽、郎西贝以及2015级MTI口译方向研究生禹雪艳和宁红曼也为本教材的编写做了很多准备工作。

本教材充分考虑了商务英语口译教学的特点，把口译技能的讲解与商务主题的口译训练内容融合在一起，适合本科院校商务英语专业、翻译专业及英语专业学生使用，也可以作为翻译专业硕士商务英语口译课程的有效补充，同时也可以作为广大口译自学者理想的参考资料。

本教材在编写的过程中，得到了大连外国语大学原副校长杨俊峰教授及高级翻译学院各位领导和老师的大力支持，还得到清华大学出版社的鼎力支持，尤其是钱屹芝编辑对本书出版做了大量细致的工作，大连外国语大学商学院时秀梅教授也为本教材的撰写提出了很多中肯的建议，在此一并表示感谢！同时，本教材在编写过程中，借鉴了很多现有的商务英语口译教材，并引用了很多网站资料作为练习内容，在此向所列参考文献以及由于编者疏漏未能列示的文献作者致以衷心的感谢！

由于编写者水平有限，在编写过程中，受到主客观因素的局限，本教材中难免会存在疏漏和不足之处，恳请广大专家学者、商务口译界同行和读者朋友们谅解并提宝贵意见和建议，以便做进一步修改、补充和完善。

赵 颖

2018年3月28日

序 ……………………………………………………………… 杨俊峰
前言 …………………………………………………………………… iii

口译导论 ……………………………………………………………… 1

第 1 单元　口译的听辨 / 迎来送往 ……………………………… 9

- ✽ 学习目标 ……………………………………………………… 10
- ✽ 技巧讲解 ……………………………………………………… 11
- ✽ 技巧练习 ……………………………………………………… 13
- ✽ 主题口译 ……………………………………………………… 14
  - Text A　机场会面 …………………………………………… 14
  - Text B　代人接机 …………………………………………… 15
  - Text C　宾馆入住 …………………………………………… 16
- ✽ 情景口译 ……………………………………………………… 17
- ✽ 句式扩展 ……………………………………………………… 18
- ✽ 口译小贴士 …………………………………………………… 20

第 2 单元　信息的逻辑分析 / 商务旅行 ……………………… 21

- ✽ 学习目标 ……………………………………………………… 22
- ✽ 技巧讲解 ……………………………………………………… 23
- ✽ 技巧练习 ……………………………………………………… 24
- ✽ 主题口译 ……………………………………………………… 24
  - Text A　大连商务之旅 ……………………………………… 24

  Text B 经济危机与商务旅行 ·· 25
  Text C 客家土楼：世界第八大奇迹 ·· 27
* 情景口译 ··· 28
* 句式扩展 ··· 29
* 口译小贴士 ··· 32

第 3 单元 公共演讲 / 礼仪致辞 ·· 35

* 学习目标 ··· 36
* 技巧讲解 ··· 37
* 技巧练习 ··· 38
* 主题口译 ··· 38
  Text A 王毅部长在外交部 2016 年新年招待会上的致辞（节选） ········· 38
  Text B Queen's Speech at the Welcome Banquet (excerpt) ······················ 39
  Text C 驻新加坡大使陈晓东在慧眼中国环球论坛年会上的发言（节选）··· 40
  Text D Message on Nelson Mandela International Day 2016 (excerpt) ······ 42
  Text E 签约仪式上的讲话 ·· 43
  Text F Matt Damon's MIT Commencement Address 2016 (excerpt) ······· 44
* 情景口译 ··· 46
* 句式扩展 ··· 47
* 口译小贴士 ··· 49

第 4 单元 短期记忆 1/ 公司简介 ·· 51

* 学习目标 ··· 52
* 技巧讲解 ··· 53
* 技巧练习 ··· 54
* 主题口译 ··· 55
  Text A 华为简介 ·· 55
  Text B A Speech of Jack Ma, Chairman of Alibaba (excerpt) ················· 56
  Text C 保利文化集团股份有限公司 ·· 57
  Text D Pfizer Pharmaceuticals Ltd. ·· 58
  Text E 万科企业股份有限公司 ·· 59
  Text F Google Inc. ·· 60
* 情景口译 ··· 61

✽	句式扩展	62
✽	口译小贴士	64

第 5 单元　短期记忆 2/ 商业广告 ······ 67

✽	学习目标	68
✽	技巧讲解	69
✽	技巧练习	70
✽	主题口译	71
	Text A　农夫山泉，甜并快乐着	71
	Text B　Tesla's Advertising Strategy	72
	Text C　"创意"本身真是没有创意：创意广告的小秘密	73
	Text D　How GoPro Is Transforming Advertising	74
	Text E　西安	75
	Text F　Google's Self-Driving Car	76
✽	情景口译	77
✽	句式扩展	78
✽	口译小贴士	80

第 6 单元　口译笔记 1/ 商务陈述 ······ 83

✽	学习目标	84
✽	技巧讲解	85
✽	技巧练习	86
✽	主题口译	87
	Text A　共享经济	87
	Text B　Tips for an Effective Business Presentation	88
	Text C　虚拟智能手机	89
	Text D　Apple Pay	90
	Text E　川菜推介会	91
	Text F　Hermes Scarf	92
✽	情景口译	93
✽	句式扩展	94
✽	口译小贴士	96

第7单元　口译笔记2/ 商业展览 ·············· 99

* 学习目标 ·· 100
* 技巧讲解 ·· 101
* 技巧练习 ·· 102
* 主题口译 ·· 103
  - Text A　预订展位 ································· 103
  - Text B　建立业务往来 ····························· 105
  - Text C　艺术展览 ································· 106
  - Text D　Hong Kong Houseware Fair 2016 ·········· 107
  - Text E　香港美食博览会 ··························· 108
  - Text F　Speech by the Head of German Publishers and Booksellers Association from the Opening Ceremony of Frankfurt Book Fair 2016 (excerpt) ··· 109
* 情景口译 ·· 110
* 句式扩展 ·· 111
* 口译小贴士 ·· 113

第8单元　口译笔记3/ 市场营销 ·············· 115

* 学习目标 ·· 116
* 技巧讲解 ·· 117
* 技巧练习 ·· 118
* 主题口译 ·· 119
  - Text A　跨界营销 ································· 119
  - Text B　Avon in the Chinese Market ··············· 120
  - Text C　中国文化"走出去"的三大战略 ············· 120
  - Text D　McDonald's Market Performance ·········· 121
  - Text E　销售代表年会上的发言 ····················· 122
  - Text F　Management Principle of Starbucks ······· 123
* 情景口译 ·· 123
* 句式扩展 ·· 124
* 口译小贴士 ·· 127

第 9 单元　数字口译 1/ 商务谈判 ······ 129

- ✻ 学习目标 ······ 130
- ✻ 技巧讲解 ······ 131
- ✻ 技巧练习 ······ 133
- ✻ 主题口译 ······ 134
  - Text A　技术引进 ······ 134
  - Text B　冰箱报盘 ······ 135
  - Text C　独家代理 ······ 137
  - Text D　订购汽车 ······ 138
  - Text E　议价 ······ 139
  - Text F　开具信用证付款 ······ 140
- ✻ 情景口译 ······ 141
- ✻ 句式扩展 ······ 142
- ✻ 口译小贴士 ······ 144

第 10 单元　数字口译 2/ 商业投资 ······ 147

- ✻ 学习目标 ······ 148
- ✻ 技巧讲解 ······ 149
- ✻ 技巧练习 ······ 152
- ✻ 主题口译 ······ 152
  - Text A　中国与东盟的经贸合作 ······ 152
  - Text B　China's Outbound Investment ······ 153
  - Text C　金砖国家投资机会 ······ 154
  - Text D　U.S.-China Two-Way Direct Investment ······ 154
  - Text E　外商投资在中国 ······ 155
  - Text F　China's Service Outsourcing Grows in 2015 ······ 156
- ✻ 情景口译 ······ 157
- ✻ 句式扩展 ······ 158
- ✻ 口译小贴士 ······ 161

第 11 单元　信息重组 / 全球采购 ················· **163**

- ✻ 学习目标 ··················· 164
- ✻ 技巧讲解 ··················· 165
- ✻ 技巧练习 ··················· 166
- ✻ 主题口译 ··················· 166
  - Text A　全球采购 ··················· 166
  - Text B　中国制造 ··················· 168
  - Text C　重庆全球采购会 ··················· 169
  - Text D　A Secret to Inditex's Success ··················· 170
  - Text E　海尔的采购战略 ··················· 171
  - Text F　Six Core Purchasing Strategies ··················· 171
- ✻ 情景口译 ··················· 173
- ✻ 句式扩展 ··················· 174
- ✻ 口译小贴士 ··················· 176

第 12 单元　模糊用语 / 商务访谈 ················· **179**

- ✻ 学习目标 ··················· 180
- ✻ 技巧讲解 ··················· 181
- ✻ 技巧练习 ··················· 183
- ✻ 主题口译 ··················· 184
  - Text A　索罗斯访谈 ··················· 184
  - Text B　经济学家罗伯特·希勒的访谈 ··················· 185
  - Text C　瑞德勒的访谈 ··················· 186
  - Text D　对特拉维斯·卡兰尼克的专访 ··················· 187
  - Text E　苹果公司总裁蒂姆·库克访谈 ··················· 188
  - Text F　领英总裁里德·霍夫曼访谈 ··················· 189
- ✻ 情景口译 ··················· 190
- ✻ 句式扩展 ··················· 191
- ✻ 口译小贴士 ··················· 193

目 录

第 13 单元　文化因素的处理 / 企业文化 ········· 195

- ✻ 学习目标 ········· 196
- ✻ 技巧讲解 ········· 197
- ✻ 技巧练习 ········· 199
- ✻ 主题口译 ········· 200
  - Text A　企业文化的意义 ········· 200
  - Text B　Create a Culture with a Passion for Learning ········· 201
  - Text C　腾讯公司人才发展理念 ········· 201
  - Text D　Nurturing Cultural Values ········· 202
  - Text E　中国药膳 ········· 203
  - Text F　A Lesson Learned from the Enron Case ········· 204
- ✻ 情景口译 ········· 205
- ✻ 句式扩展 ········· 206
- ✻ 口译小贴士 ········· 209

第 14 单元　译前准备 / 战略管理 ········· 211

- ✻ 学习目标 ········· 212
- ✻ 技巧讲解 ········· 213
- ✻ 技巧练习 ········· 214
- ✻ 主题口译 ········· 215
  - Text A　集团战略管理概述 ········· 215
  - Text B　The Sunset Rule—A Story of Management in Wal-Mart ········· 216
  - Text C　中久集团总裁在公司年会上的发言 ········· 217
  - Text D　The L'Oreal Group ········· 218
  - Text E　通用汽车战略目标 ········· 218
  - Text F　SWOT Analysis of Vodafone ········· 219
- ✻ 情景口译 ········· 221
- ✻ 句式扩展 ········· 222
- ✻ 口译小贴士 ········· 225

第 15 单元　译后总结 / 交通物流 ·········· 227

* 学习目标 ·········· 228
* 技巧讲解 ·········· 229
* 技巧练习 ·········· 230
* 主题口译 ·········· 231
  - Text A　顺丰速运 ·········· 231
  - Text B　High-Speed Train in China ·········· 232
  - Text C　马士基航运公司 ·········· 232
  - Text D　The Channel Tunnel ·········· 233
  - Text E　世界一流的铁路服务 ·········· 234
  - Text F　Cathay Pacific Airways ·········· 235
* 情景口译 ·········· 236
* 句式扩展 ·········· 237
* 口译小贴士 ·········· 240

附录 1 ·········· 243
附录 2 ·········· 246
附录 3 ·········· 251

口译导论

❋ 口译简史

20世纪初，口译在国际上被认定为正式的专门职业。但是，口译的历史可谓源远流长，可以一直追溯到人类社会的早期。早在人类原始社会时期，原始部落群体的经济和文化活动是一种内部的区域性活动，呈现出各自为政、自我封闭的特点，这种社会形态阻碍了人类经济和文化活动的进一步发展。伴随着部落间跨越疆域、向外发展的愿望，不同语言部落间进行经济贸易、文化交流等活动的需求也被推上了历史舞台，而构筑这种跨文化、跨民族交际活动的桥梁——口译活动也就应运而生。

据考证，中国的翻译职业始于周代，距今已有三千多年的历史。周代的翻译叫做"象胥"，就是通晓四方语言的官吏。虽历经朝代的更替，翻译一直在朝堂之上占有一席之地，"译""寄""象""九译令""译官令""译官丞""译令史""通事舍人""译字生""通译官"等都是为翻译设立的官衔。"舌人"或"重舌"都是对译员的称谓。虽然翻译的官阶不高，有一些朝代的翻译人员甚至没有品级，但翻译作为经济文化交流的中介在中国各个社会发展阶段均扮演着不可替代的角色。

在西方，有关口译的记录最早可以追溯到公元前三千年的古埃及。近代数百年来，西方各国也有专司口译之职的人员。然而，口译在国际上正式被认定为一种专门职业却是第一次世界大战的产物。

在第一次世界大战结束后的1919年，巴黎和会组织招募了一大批专职译员用英语和法语两种语言为巴黎和会做交替传译。巴黎和会结束后，这批译员中的不少人士陆续成为各国翻译学校或翻译机构的创始人。因此，巴黎和会通常被认为是口译职业化的开端。

1927年举行的日内瓦国际劳工组织会议首次使用了同声传译的模式，即采用一种原语和译语近乎同步、不间断出现的传译方式。1945年，第二次世界大战后举行的纽伦堡战犯审判将同声传译列为口译工作的主要模式，专职译员使用英、法、德、俄四种语言提供大规模的同声传译服务。

1947年，联合国正式将同声传译纳入其翻译服务模式，既节约了时间，又降低了费用。随着联合国及其翻译机构的创立以及各类全球性组织和地区性组织的出现，职业会议译员的地位越来越高。1953年，"国际会议口译员协会"（AIIC）在日内瓦成立，口译工作成了一种备受尊敬的职业。

近年来，在中国同世界各国开展的全方位、多层次的交流中，涉外口译工作者成为了中外交往中一支不可缺少的中介力量，是加深中外相互了解的重要窗口。

❋ 口译的特点

口译的英文表达是"interpreting"或"interpretation"。维基百科认为"口译是讲话或手语的口头翻译"。《新牛津英语词典》（上海外语教育出版社，2001）中将"口译"定义为"将一个人的讲话口头翻译成另外一种语言"。由商务印书馆国际有限公司出版的《新华汉语词典》（2016年最新修订版）将"口译"解释为"口头翻译"。

总而言之，口译是翻译的一种，其基本的表现形式是将一种语言所表达的内容用另一种语言及时、准确地口头表达出来。口译是一种跨文化交际行为，在人际交往中起到了桥梁和纽带的作用，对国际政治、经济、文化和科研等交流起到了积极的促进作用。

作为翻译的两种不同形式，口译和笔译有着共同的性质和根本任务，但是两者又具有各自不同的特点。它们的差异主要体现在以下几个方面：

不同之处	笔译	口译
信息输入	文字，可以反复阅读、理解	声音、画面，只能视听一次
信息输出	文字，可以反复修改、润色	声音，几乎不能修改
工作环境	相对封闭、自由的工作空间	现场面对公众
工作模式	随时查阅字典等参考书目或请教相关领域专家	即时、即席完成工作，无法查阅资料或求助他人
反馈形式	几乎不与作者或读者见面	直接面对发言人、观众，根据他们的反应调整口译节奏及用词
质量标准	信、达、雅	准、顺、快

口译与笔译的诸多差异是由各自不同的信息输入和输出方式决定的。就笔译而言，信息来源于书面材料，译者在翻译的过程中不能与作者进行直接的交流，只能通过对原文的反复阅读揣摩作者的意图，再用目的语形成译稿供读者阅读。与之相对，在口译工作中，信息的获取完全依赖于译员对发言人讲话的现场聆听，同时译员要注意发言人的语气、表情、肢体动作等，因为在一定程度上，这些都传达着发言人想要表达的信息，再即时地将这些信息以口头表达的形式传达给目的语听众。

从工作环境来看，译员通常在公共场合，比如：会场、报告厅、礼堂等地方工作，必须面对公众现场翻译，这就决定了口译具有很强的现场性和时限性。口译时，除非发现重大错漏，译员一般不能对自己翻译过的内容进行大量的更正和补充。而在笔译中，译者通常处在自己独立的工作空间中，既不需要面对作者，也不需要面对读者，大多有充足的时间反复阅读原文。译完初稿后，还可以反复修改、润色，直到满意为止。

在工作模式上，译员通常即时、即席独立完成工作。口译过程中一般无法求助于他人，也没有时间查阅词典或其他资料。而在笔译工作中，译者既可以独立工作，也可以和其他译者合作，并且可以随意查阅各种工具书、参考书，甚至可以请教相关领域的专家答疑解惑，反复斟酌，以达到译文的最佳表达效果。

在反馈形式上，口译的即时性和即席性决定了译员要现场面对发言人和听众，随时可以从他们的面部表情、情绪、手势和其他肢体语言中获得反馈信息，并根据现场的情况和听众的反馈及时调整自己的音量、语速、用词等。而笔译工作者在翻译过程中一般没有机会与作者和读者面对面交流,也无法根据他们的反馈进行调整或更正。

在质量标准上,"信""达""雅"是被广泛认可的笔译标准,而这一标准并不能用来衡量口译质量的优劣。口译的即时性和即席性则决定了"准""顺""快"是口译质量的核心。"准"即准确,指准确理解源语信息并即时将其译成目的语。"顺"即通顺,指译员在用译语表达原语信息时要通顺、流畅,符合语言表达规范。"快"即译员反应要快,发言人的话音刚落,译员就要开始翻译。此外,参与交际的各方(如发言人、听众和雇主)从各个角度所认定的交际效果也是衡量口译质量应该考虑的一个重要因素。

❋ 口译的类型

根据信息的传送形式,口译可分为交替传译、同声传译、耳语传译和视译四大类。

交替传译(consecutive interpreting) 也被称连续传译,是指译员在发言人讲完部分内容停下来后立刻将其翻译给听众,译完后发言人再继续讲,译员再译。在这种口译模式中,讲话和口译交替进行,所以将其称为交替传译。交替传译是最常见的一种口译形式,也是口译训练的基础。在口译服务中,交替传译通常应用在日常接见、宴请、谈判、记者招待会、旅游观光等活动中,也应用在对口译质量要求比较高的场合中。

同声传译(simultaneous interpreting) 是指译员在发言人讲话的同时边听边译的口译方式。由于口译与讲话几乎同步进行,同声传译被看成一种高效的口译模式,被广泛地运用在各种国际会议、联合国及欧盟等国际组织中。因此,同声传译又被称为会议口译(conference interpreting)。

译员做同声传译时,听和说同时进行,译员的大脑一直处在高负荷的多任务模式运行中。因此,同声传译是一种高强度、高难度的脑力劳动,要在熟练掌握交替传译技巧的基础上、经过长期的强化训练才能掌握。

同声传译对设备也有一定的要求:译员坐在同传箱(booth)里,利用大会同传设备,通过耳机收听讲话;与此同时,通过话筒将发言人的讲话内容由源语译成目的语,而听众则在会场头戴耳机收听译语。如果听众是多语种的,不同的同传箱中会有持不同语言的译员提供服务,听众可以根据接收设备上的相应按钮选择不同的输出语言。

耳语传译(whispering interpretation) 是指译员将发言人的讲话同步、小声地直接译给身边服务对象的翻译方式。耳语传译也是同声传译的一种,只是服务对象的人数少,通常只针对一至三名听众。

视译(sight interpretation) 是指译员在用阅读的方式获取源语信息的同时,用口头表达的方式将该信息翻译成目的语。视译也是同声传译的一种形式,是一种边看边译的特殊的口译形式。通常将视译作为同声传译训练中的一项基本内容。

此外,根据社会交往的场合,口译又可分为商务口译(business interpreting)、外交口译(diplomatic interpreting)、军事口译(military interpreting)、法庭口译(court interpreting)、医疗口译(medical interpreting)、媒体口译(media interpreting)、社区口译(community interpreting)、电话口译(telephone interpreting)、教学口译(classroom interpreting)等多种类型。

值得一提的是,在2012年1月的国际会议口译员协会(AIIC)大会上,手语(sign language)正式成为AIIC认可的会议口译工作语言,这标志着手语翻译成为一种专业化的口译类型。

✳ 口译的基本过程

在口译的过程中,如果将译员作为研究的主体,口译的基本过程可以用图1进行描述:

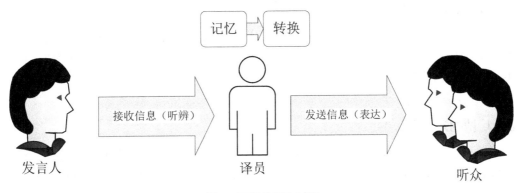

图1 口译的基本过程

译员是发言人和听众之间沟通的桥梁。他接收发言人发出的信息,再用另外一种语言发送给听众,是以传递信息为目的的语言交际活动的核心环节。对于译员来说,口译的基本过程主要涉及听辨、记忆、转换和表达四个环节。虽然这四个环节相对独立,但在实际工作中,它们是一个在瞬间完成的有机整体,相互交错,不可分割。

听辨是口译中信息传递的起始环节。在此环节中,译员主动接收发言人发出的信息,并调动自己所掌握的语言知识(如词汇、句法等)和语言外知识(如主题知识、百科知识等)对源语信息进行分析处理,分清主次,再以自己的方式记忆信息。

在记忆环节中,译员以心记和笔记两种方式对信息进行记忆。心记主要依靠听辨阶段对信息的梳理将输入的信息进行储存和记忆。笔记是对心记的有效补充。当译员面对大量信息的时候,必须依靠口译笔记对重要信息及人名、地名、专有名词、数字等进行记录,以确保信息的完整性和准确性。

在转换阶段,译员将经过分析整理的源语信息进行编码处理,即译员根据自己深厚的语言功底以目的语的表达习惯和表达方式对信息进行解析和重构,以便用目的语听众最易接收的方式将信息传递出去。

表达是指将以目标语编码之后的信息通过口头表达的形式再现出来。译语的表达要即时、迅速：交替传译中，译员通常在发言人话音刚落时即刻开始翻译，停顿时间一般不能超过5秒钟；同声传译中，译员一般滞后原语半句。在表达过程中，译员要发音清晰，音量、语速适中，措辞恰当，与听众保持目光交流。

✳ 译员应具备的素质

口译是一项高难度、高要求、高回报的工作，要成为一名合格的译员，一般都需要经过专门训练，同时还应该具备以下素质：

1. **扎实的双语功底。**

语言知识是口译的立足根本。一名优秀的译员应该具备扎实的双语基本功，良好的双语修养，掌握两种语言的特点，拥有超常的词汇量，具备敏锐的听力和良好的语感，能够快速、准确地遣词造句。

2. **广博的知识面。**

现今的译员不仅要做一个掌握国际常识、法规政策、风土人情等知识的通才，还应该成为某个领域的专才，即在一两个领域具有深入而丰富的知识，这样才能更好地满足市场的需要。

3. **熟练掌握口译技巧。**

要成为一名合格的译员，具有扎实的双语功底和广博的知识面是不够的，最关键的是要掌握口译的基本技巧，比如：公共演讲、短期记忆、口译笔记、数字转换等。

4. **出众的记忆力。**

非凡的记忆力是一名合格译员的必备要素。在口译工作中，译员要调动大量的储存在长期记忆中的词汇、成语、典故和缩略词等，还要把发言人所讲的内容准确详尽地用另外一种语言表达出来，这些都离不开出众的记忆力。

5. **快速学习知识和运用知识的能力。**

译员面临的口译主题多种多样、五花八门，而且通常不能预先拿到资料进行充分准备。这就要求译员必须具有快速的学习能力，包括根据会议议程所做的准备工作和到会议现场后利用周边环境进行学习的能力，以及学以致用地运用知识的能力。

6. 过硬的身体素质和良好的心理素质。

译员的工作强度很大,并且始终处在高度紧张的工作状态;即使连续工作几个小时可能也无法得到充分的休息。所以,译员要学会适应这种高强度的工作,学会调节自己的心态,能够边工作边休息,使大脑能一直在一个轻松的状态下工作,以便充分保证译文的质量。

7. 敏捷、灵活、快速的思辨能力和应变能力。

敏捷的思维能力可以使译员快速、正确地分析和理解接收到的信息;快速的反应能力可以帮助译员迅速完成源语到目的语的准确转换,灵活的应变能力则能在有限时间内使译员妥善处理随时出现的突发情况(包括错误)。

8. 高度的责任心和良好的职业道德。

译员是跨文化交际中必不可少的辅助人员。因此,译员要把双方的语言准确地传递,忠实于发言人的原意,如实地表达发言人的思想,为双方的成功沟通铺平道路。同时,译员要具有良好的职业道德,这主要包括:良好的时间观念、为客户保守秘密等。

✱ 口译小贴士

译员的形象、着装与装备

译员是对外交往的直接参与者,其自身的仪表风度、举手投足都代表着一种民族文化和一种精神文明的特点。在一些公共交际场合,译员的着装已经不仅仅是个人的问题,它与一个公司,乃至一个国家和民族的形象联系在一起。译员的形象和着装应该遵循与中国文化传统相适应的原则。一般来讲,译员要有文明礼貌、热情友好、不卑不亢和"大家风范"的形象;着装应该以庄重得体、美观大方为宜,不必刻意去追求名牌,更不要标新立异,穿奇装异服。女译员的着装不宜过于华贵,也不得过于紧身暴露,这样的装束是与译员的身份和工作性质不相符的。

此外,译员还要准备好必要的装备。参加翻译活动前,译员需要确认自己的装备是否齐全,包括笔记本、笔、译前准备资料、笔记本电脑(如果有需要)、通行证(如果有的话)等。

口译笔记本要准备硬皮、一手可以握住的竖翻笔记本。笔至少准备两支:一支记笔记;另一支备用。译前客户交给译员的准备材料或译员自己准备的材料也可以带在身边,以备不时之需。口译现场出现译员不了解的内容,如果条件允许,也可以用笔记本电脑或手机上网搜索。译员还要事先和客户做好沟通,取得必要的通行证,以防会场严格限制通行,译员无法按时到达会场。

口译的听辨 / 迎来送往

第 1 单元

口译主题 迎来送往

  迎来送往，是商务活动中最基本的形式和重要环节，是表达主人情谊、体现礼貌素养的重要方面。迎接是给客人留下良好的第一印象的最重要工作，也是为双方进一步深入接触奠定基础的重要环节。

  迎接客人要有周密的安排，主人应提前到车站、机场恭候客人的到来，为客人准备好交通工具，将客人送到提前安排好的住处，同时将活动的计划、日程安排交给客人，并在分开时将下次联系的时间、地点、方式等告诉客人。

✱ 学习目标

  了解口译听辨的技巧要领
  了解商务活动迎来送往的主要环节
  掌握迎来送往的常用口译句式

✱ 技巧讲解

听辨是口译的第一步，也是至关重要的一步。译员能否快速而准确地抓住源语信息是成功口译的先决条件。口译中对听辨的质量要求要远远高于一般的外语听力训练，后者通常较多地关注语言层面的信息，能够听懂并完成相应的试题即可；而口译中的听辨则需要译员在听懂的基础上从整体和细节对信息进行全方位地把握，以便能够迅速地用目的语流利、完整地进行表达。

作为口译过程的起始阶段，听辨在口译中的重要性不言自明。巴黎的释意学派认为口译不是简单的语言符号的转换，而是一个"意义"的理解与再表达的过程，包括：语音感知、迅速抛弃语言外壳、保留信息的思维表征、用目的语表达三个环节，是一个"三角形的过程"。语音感知是指译员根据听到的带有一定语义的源语声音流，理解语言并领悟意思；接着，译员谨慎地舍弃源语的词句，记住源语所表达的信息，这就是脱离语言外壳、保留信息的思维表征；再把意思用译语表达出来。

图2完整地表达了释意派所描述的口译过程。口译是一个从源语（听辨）——意义（理解）——目的语（表达）的过程；源语和目的语处在三角形底部的两侧，意义居于三角形的顶端。三角形最下面的虚线代表着从一种语言直接转换为另一种语言的代码转译，而这种对等的转译只适用于术语、数字、名称等语言项的传译；把源语讲话释意后获得的意义用目的语重新表达出来则是一个释意翻译的方式，也是口译的主要方式。

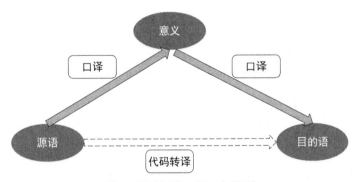

图2 释意派的口译三角模型

从释意派的口译三角模型中不难看出，"听意"是口译听辨环节的核心内容，即源语词语中所传达的信息（message）就是译员要抓住的"意"。"抓住关键词""辨析主干结构""利用预测信息"这三种方法可以帮助译员有效地掌握源语信息。

1. 抓住关键词

关键词是体现发言人意图和中心思想的词语，是发言人强调的对象和传达的信息焦点。从词汇层面来说，由于表达句子中心意义的一般是实词，因此名词、动词和形容词等通常是译员要着重听辨的关键词。从句子的层面来说，主语、宾语或表语都有可能成为关键词。例如：

原文1 Dalian International Conference Center is located in Donggang commercial district with convenient transportation, complete and perfect peripheral service. It is the main venue of summer Davos meeting in China and also one of the China's Top Ten Theatres.

译文1 大连国际会议中心坐落在东港商务区。其交通便利、周边服务配套完善，是夏季达沃斯会议中国区主会场，中国十大剧院之一。

在这段话中，作为主语的"Dalian International Conference Center"指出了信息描述的主要对象，"Donggang"是状语，解释了主语的地点，而"main venue"和"China's Top Ten Theatres"则是作为表语指出了"大连国际会议中心"的作用，抓住这几个关键词，该段落的意思也就一目了然。

从语意层面上看，绝大多数句子都可以看作是"已知信息 + 新信息"的组合，其中"新信息"是发言人引出的新的话题或思想，也是译员需要格外注意的关键词。例如：

原文2 Now let me give the floor to the speaker, Mr. Hammer, CFO of TMNS.

译文2 下面有请 TMNS 公司的财务总监汉莫先生发言。

此句中前半句是固定的主持词，对听众和译员来说都属于已知信息，而发言者的名字、职位等信息则是关注的焦点，也就是该句的关键词。

2. 辨析主干结构

对于译员来说，光抓住关键词还不够，还要听辨出这些关键词是如何组织起来表达发言人思想的，也就是说，听辨出句子的主干结构也同样重要。

以英语为例，最常用的是以主谓结构为核心衍生出的主谓宾、主谓表、主谓宾补状等结构。听辨出句子的基本结构也就掌握了关键词的组织方式，译员也就可以借此顺序储存关键信息，组织译语表达。例如：

原文3 Korean pop and rock music artists have gained popularity in Japan, China and
　　　　　　主语　　　　　　　　　谓语　　宾语　　　　　状语
throughout South East Asia.

译文3 韩国的通俗和摇滚艺术家在日本、中国及整个东南亚颇受欢迎。
　　　　　　主语　　　　　　　　状语　　　　　　　谓语 宾语

3. 利用预测信息

预测信息是指译员根据口译的交际场合和背景，结合语法知识和主题知识所进行的有利于口译听辨理解的预测。听辨中的预测主要分为言内预测和言外预测两种。大多数情况下，有效的预测是两种方式的结合。

言内预测是依据语言内信息，即固定搭配、表达方式、语篇衔接、连贯手段等进行的。例如：当听到"comparison"这个词的时候，译员自然会期待之后"with"引导的成分，预测出两者之间比较。当听到"difference/relations"等词时，译员自然会预测其后会出现诸如"between...and..."之类的限定成分。再比如：听到"importance""significance""necessity"等表示属性的抽象名词时，译员能预测到后面会出现限定成分来补充完整要表达的实际意义。例如："the importance of diplomatic relations""confidence in the administration"等。

言外预测主要是根据文体风格、交际场合、主题知识等做出的预测。言外预测只有在积累了足够的主题知识和文体知识以后才能将听到的信息与大脑中已储存的知识建立联系，快速理解分析，做出合理的预测。换言之，长期的知识积累是言外预测的基础。

此外，译员也可以充分利用语言中的冗余现象预测出关键信息或分析关键词的意思。对于发言人反复提到的信息，毫无疑问就是其强调的要点；而很多意思相近或相对的词语通常都会成对出现，理解了其中一个词的意思也就很容易推测出另一个词的意思。这也是译员常用的技巧。

✻ 技巧练习

🎧 听录音，将下列段落用源语进行复述，注意体会听辨技巧。

1. 世界卫生组织曾指出走路步行是世界上最好的运动。中国的养生学家也提出"百练不如一走"，长期坚持步行运动，其健身养生之效绝不比苦练死打的习武功夫为差。步行有助于强化心肌功能、帮助控制血糖、降低坏胆固醇、使硬化血管恢复弹性及促进新陈代谢和增强免疫力。常年坚持步行还有助于体内释放一种化学物质，不仅令人精神欢愉，而且可预防老年痴呆。

步行的要领是：每天的步行时间不少于半小时，距离不少于三千米。身体健康的中青年人步速可达至每秒两步；而慢性病患者及长者宜每秒钟一步或每分钟80步。步行运动忌穿紧身衣裤，忌在夜深、浓雾及空气欠佳的环境中进行。

2. There are many reasons why we buy too much clothing, and affordable pricing is one. But new research also points to other factors that can sneakily influence our shopping behaviors—and we actually have more control over those causes. Neuroscience research shows that being mentally fatigued can make you an impulsive shopper. Just a day at work can burn out our limited resources of self-control, and nearly turn off the brain areas in charge of evaluating decisions. In other words, the person who walks out of the office and into the shops downstairs is simply not your best version of yourself, and probably shouldn't be making decisions involving money and future planning.

主题口译

Text A　机场会面

主题导入

海昌集团的公关部经理王晓晓在大连机场迎接巴黎大学的威尔逊教授。以下是他们的对话。

请先熟悉列出的词汇与短语再听录音，并在录音停顿时将下列对话口译成英语或汉语。

词汇与短语

公关部	Public Relations
倒时差	to get over the jet-lag
中国民乐表演	Chinese folk music show
活动安排	schedule

A: 先生，请问您是从巴黎来的威尔逊教授吗？//

B: Yes, I'm John Wilson from the University of Paris. You must be Miss Wang, if I'm not mistaken. //

A: 是的，我叫王晓晓，海昌集团公关部经理。威尔逊教授，我一直在此恭候您的到来。//

B: Thank you for coming to meet me at the airport. //

A: 我很高兴能在大连接待您。我们非常高兴您能成行啊，非常感激您不辞辛劳，在百忙中抽空来我海昌指导。//

B: I've long been expecting to learn about the famous Haichang Group. I really appreciate this opportunity, for it is also a good opportunity for me to learn about Chinese enterprises at close distance. //

A: 旅途顺利吧？十几个小时的飞行一定很辛苦吧。//

B: Not too bad. But we were later than expected. Our flight delayed taking off as there was a mechanic breakdown. We were held up for several hours at the airport, waiting for a new plane. But we had good flying weather and we enjoyed a good attending service. //

A: 嗯，长途旅行之后您一定很累了吧，您还得倒时差呢。行李都齐了，我们直接回宾馆吧。//

B: Yes. I'm a bit tired. I'm very bad with a jet-lag. But I'll be all right in a couple of days. //

A: 好的，先回宾馆下榻，好好休息一下。明天不必早起。明天的安排是这样的，我们中午设宴为您洗尘，下午会见集团总裁，晚上我们去看一场中国民乐表演。不知威尔逊教授意下如何？//

B: I like that. I've heard Chinese people are very friendly and hospitable. You're very considerate,

Miss Wang. I'll soon be spoiled, I'm afraid. //

A: 我们希望您在这里过得愉快，希望您与海昌集团合作愉快。东西齐了，车已在外等候，我们走吧。//

B: Sure. //

Text B 代人接机

主题导入
王明是 HB 贸易公司的销售经理，他代替公司的刘经理去机场迎接英国来的帕森斯先生，并安排相关事宜。以下是他们的对话。

请先熟悉列出的词汇与短语再听录音，并在录音停顿时将下列对话口译成英语或汉语。

词汇与短语

formality	礼节
turbulence	气流
多功能厅	multi-functional hall

A: 请问您是罗伯特·帕森斯先生吗？//

B: Yes, I am. And are you Mr. Liu? //

A: 不，我不是。我是王明，HB 贸易公司的销售经理。刘先生要我来接您，因为他今早突然有事，无法分身。他非常想见您，要我代他向您致意。//

B: I see. Well, it's very nice to meet you, Wang Ming. And please feel free to call me Robert. I'm not used to formalities. //

A: 好的。罗伯特，一路还算顺利吧？我以前也坐过横渡大西洋的航班，我知道那有多累。//

B: This one was very uneventful, except for a little turbulence now and then. In fact, I feel much more energetic than I had expected. //

A: 很高兴听你这么说。刘先生让我问一下你今晚是否愿意和我们一起吃顿便饭。//

B: It's very nice of him, but truthfully I'd rather just spend a quiet evening in the hotel getting ready for the coming conference. Mr. Liu won't mind, will he? //

A: 当然不会。他想到你可能需要稍作休息。跟你确认一下，明天的会议是上午 9:30 在我们公司的多功能厅举行。我明早 9:00 到酒店接你。//

B: That'll be wonderful. Thank you so much. //

A: 别客气。对了，会议结束后，你是否想去参观一些地方呢？我可以带你四处逛逛。//

B: Well, I have instructions not to mix pleasure with business on this trip. But could we walk around the Xinghai Square? I've heard a lot about it! //

A: 没问题，这周晚些时候我会安排。//

B: Thank you very much. //

Text C 宾馆入住

主题导入

爱德华·亚当先生入住香格里拉酒店，但预订信息出了问题。最终在前台接待的帮助下得到了有效的解决。以下是他们的对话。

请先熟悉列出的词汇与短语再听录音，并在录音停顿时将下列对话口译成英语或汉语。

词汇与短语

确认函	confirmation letter
双人间	double room
豪华套房	deluxe suite
总台	front desk
餐饮部	catering service
商务中心	business center
楼层服务台	floor service desk
morning call	叫早

A: 下午好，欢迎光临香格里拉饭店。先生，您有什么需要？//

B: Yes, I'd like to check in, please. //

A: 好的，先生，请问尊姓大名？您有没有预订房间？//

B: Yes, it's Edward Adam. I suppose someone has made a reservation for me. //

A: 稍等，我查一下预订记录。让您久等了，先生。不过，恐怕这里查不到您的预订记录。您是在哪里订的？有确认函吗？//

B: That's very strange. I made the reservation about a week ago through a travel agency at home. But I don't have the confirmation letter with me, except a copy of the itinerary. I wonder whether it is possible for the accommodation for just three days. //

A: 别着急，我查一下有没有空房间。太好了！我们还有一个双人间和一套豪华套房，都没有人入住。不知您要哪一套呢？//

B: Many thanks. I prefer the double room. How long can I keep it? Is there any extra charge besides the regular rate? //

A: 好的，先生。请出示您的护照。双人间最多可供您住上 5 天。我们不多收费，入住最后一套豪华套房，您还可以享受 7.5 折优惠呢。//

第 1 单元　口译的听辨 / 迎来送往

B: The double room is fine. Could you please tell me some services provided here? //

A: 当然啦。请问您有什么要求吗？//

B: Yes. I'd like to have an 8 o'clock morning call, and breakfast could be sent up to my room. I'd also like to book a taxi heading to Dalian International Conference Center at 9 o'clock. //

A: 没问题。请分别打电话给总台、餐饮部和商务中心就可以了。您也可以直接与楼层服务台联系。//

B: Thank you very much. //

A: 不用客气。//

✱ 情景口译

提示：

学生三人或四人一组，根据下面的主题提示进行模拟口译，注意使用本单元介绍的技能和句型。

 机场送别

参与人： 1. 王芳女士，某集团海外部经理

　　　　2. 布莱尔女士，法国某红酒集团公关部经理

　　　　3. 译员

地　点： 大连机场

内　容： 1. 王女士再次感谢布莱尔女士的来访

　　　　2. 布莱尔女士表示此次来访很成功，合作前景广阔

　　　　3. 布莱尔女士邀请王经理访法，进一步商讨合作事宜

　　　　4. 王女士接受并感谢布莱尔女士的邀请，祝布莱尔女士返程顺利

 机场迎接

参与人： 1. 孙晨先生，大连某贸易公司销售经理

2. 史密斯先生，英国某投资有限公司投资部经理

3. 译员

地　点： 大连机场

内　容： 1. 孙先生表达了对史密斯先生的欢迎

2. 孙先生询问史密斯先生旅途情况，获知史密斯先生乘坐的飞机因大雾耽误了几个小时

3. 孙先生对史密斯先生表示关心，并告知史密斯先生在大连的行程和安排

4. 孙先生将史密斯先生送到预订的酒店

✲ 句式扩展

1. I've heard so much about you. How wonderful to meet you here!

   久仰大名。很荣幸在此见到您。

2. Wish you a pleasant journey back home.

   希望您返程愉快。

3. The journey was pleasant and the service on board was excellent.

   旅途很愉快，飞机上的服务也很周到。

4. I'd like to introduce you to Mr. Paul Rice, CEO of the E-Tech Company.

   我想把您介绍给易泰科技公司总裁保罗·赖斯先生。

5. The past week in Dalian has been truly enjoyable and memorable.

   在大连度过的这周真的非常愉快，而且令人难忘。

6. The hotel is conveniently located, just beside the subway.

   旅馆所处位置交通很方便，就在地铁旁。

7. The conference center is not far from here, just about a 10-minute drive.

   会议中心离这里不远，也就是10分钟的车程。

8. If there's something you need, please call the reception.

   如果您有什么需要，请拨打服务台电话。

9. I would like to have a quiet room away from the main street if it is not too much trouble.
   如果不麻烦的话,我想要一个远离主街的安静的房间。

10. I'm pleased that we are able to accept your extension request.
    很高兴我们可以接受您延长住宿的要求。

11. 王先生因不能前来迎接您而感到抱歉。
    Mr. Wang regrets that he is not able to come to meet you personally.

12. 有朋自远方来不亦乐乎。
    It's a delight to have friends coming from afar.

13. 这是我为您拟定的活动日程安排,请您过目。
    Here is a copy of the itinerary for you. Would you please have a look?

14. 我很愉快地以我个人的名义,对来宾致以热烈欢迎。
    I am very delighted to extend this personal warm welcome to all the guests.

15. 我喜欢轻装出行。
    I'd love to travel light.

16. 我给您介绍一下行程吧。如果有必要,您可以做改动。
    Let me introduce the schedule for you. Please feel free to make any changes if necessary.

17. 考虑到您需要时间克服时差,今天的安排相对宽松。
    Considering that you need some time to get over the jet lag, you have a light schedule for today.

18. 我很高兴和你再次相聚。
    I am very happy to have this second chance of joyful gathering with you.

19. 我为此次能访问这座美丽的城市,再次表达我的愉悦之情。
    I wish to say again that I am so delighted to visit this lovely city.

20. 今晚我们设宴为您洗尘。
    We'll host a reception dinner in your honor this evening.

口译小贴士

英语听辨能力的练习方法（上）

俗话说"熟能生巧"，这同样也适用于英语听辨能力的训练。很多同学对英语听辨不仅缺乏自信，还有恐惧、抵触等情绪，其实通过一定的训练，听辨能力是完全可以大幅提升的。

首先，要改变习惯性的"被动听辨"为口译中的"主动听辨"。比如：在听辨训练的初级阶段，练习者可能还做不到"听"与"辨"同时进行，那么可以采取提问的方式对所听内容进行分析，即关注五个"W"和一个"H"（What, Who, When, Where, Why and How），从而对所听语篇进行准确理解。

其次，在材料的选择上，难度和长度都要循序渐进。初始阶段可以选择语速较慢的英语音频、视频或请训练伙伴模拟现场发言，再过渡到正常语速的英文现场发言。同时，随着熟练程度的增加，练习材料的长度也应该逐步增加，由最初的几句话，逐步过渡到几段话。中心思想就是要在训练的过程中把注意力从源语的词句表达上转移到其表述的意思上。在进行源语复述练习时，不要拘泥于原文词句，而是要用自己的语言将原文的内容和逻辑关系表述清楚。在练习的过程中不应该记笔记。

最后，材料的选择要注重多样性，主要体现在三个方面。在内容上，可以从比较熟悉的领域开始，逐步扩展到比较生疏的领域，以培养临场适应能力和综合分析能力。在文体上，应该尝试各种不同风格的讲话，以锻炼迅速理解分析信息的能力。在语音上，训练则应从标准语音入手，因为练习的初始阶段要尽量降低听力方面的障碍，将更多的精力放在分析、梳理讲话内容上。在掌握了听辨的主要技巧之后，可以逐步引入带有各种口音的英文视听资料，为在实际工作中遇到"非标准"英语做好充分的准备。

信息的逻辑分析 / 商务旅行

第 2 单元

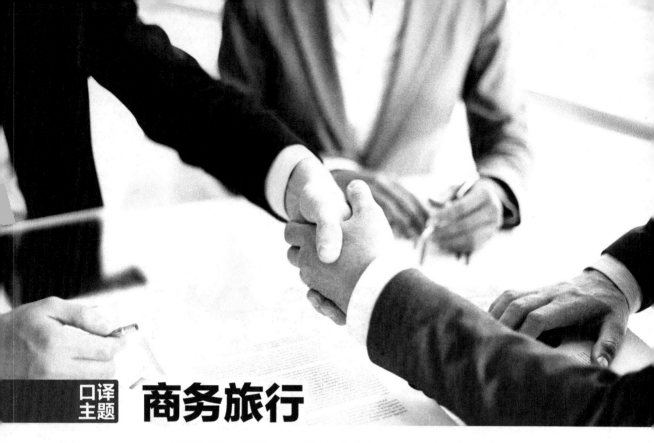

口译主题 商务旅行

  商务旅行是指商务旅游者以商务为主要目的，离开自己的常住地到外地或外国进行的商务活动及其他活动。

  商务旅行活动通常包括谈判、会议、展览、科技文化交流活动以及随之带来的住宿、餐饮、交通、游览、休闲、通信等活动。总之，几乎与商务旅行者发生的所有活动相关的活动都可称为商务旅行活动。

✻ 学习目标

  了解口译中信息逻辑分析的基本方法

  掌握商务旅行中的常用口译句式

✽ 技巧讲解

在译员所处的交际场合中，发言人提供的信息呈密集式发布状态，语速通常保持在150词/分钟。在这样的语速下，如何迅速抓住信息是口译成功与否的关键。因此，在听辨过程中对听取的信息进行逻辑分析是非常必要的。

听辨中的逻辑分析主要分为纵向分析和横向分析两种。纵向分析是指分清关键信息和辅助信息，也就是找出讲话的逻辑层次；横向分析是指明确各信息点之间的逻辑关系，如因果关系、总分关系、对比对照等。打个比方，纵向分析就好比描绘出一棵大树主要的枝干走势，而横向分析则是要弄清楚每条枝干上树叶的分布状况。

纵向分析要求译员对所听到的内容进行结构上的梳理：首先概括出讲话的中心内容，这是逻辑的最上层；再围绕该中心问题分析出第二层逻辑关系，即发言人从哪几个方面阐述该问题；接着再分析每个方面又从哪些角度做了具体的论述，这是逻辑的下一个层次。通过这样的分析，就会形成一个原文的清晰逻辑线路图，有利于译员快速对全篇内容进行有效地把握和理解。

横向分析则要求译员找出信息之间的逻辑关系。一般的信息结构都遵从一定的逻辑关系模式，比如：概括（generalization）、分类（classification）、因果（cause-effect）、对比对照（compare & contrast）、按照时间、空间、步骤、重要性的顺序排列（sequencing）、列举（simple listing）、提出问题—解决问题（problem-solution）等。

英文中，逻辑关系的判定可以根据一定的线索词汇来完成，例如：

概括关系：to sum up, in summary, in conclusion, in brief, in short, on the whole 等；

顺序关系：first, second, furthermore, before, preceding, during, when, finally, meanwhile 等；

对比关系：likewise, as well as, in common with, both, similarly, compared to 等；

对照关系：on the other hand, on the contrary, otherwise, instead, still, yet, whereas, differently 等；

因果关系：so, since, thus, because, as a result, consequently, lead to, therefore 等。

此外，话语标记词也可以帮助译员梳理逻辑关系。话语标记词体现了语篇内部的衔接和连贯，暗示了发言人对话语内容的态度或情感，从而辅助说话人构建语篇。例如："as we all know""as you know""as is known to all"这些标记词虽然既不能构成话语的基本内容，也不能对讲话内容产生实质的影响，但是这些词语属于评论性标记，说明即将出现的话语内容是发言人和听众都十分熟悉的。选择这种标志词通常是要强调或突出即将说出的内容，译员听到这样的词，就要对下文即将听到的信息有所准备。

听辨中的逻辑分析要求译员在全神贯注听取信息的同时，结合自己对口译主题和发言人背景的了解，进行合理的分析和预测，积极理清讲话的逻辑主线，这样才能更好地跟上发言人的思路，缓解"听"的压力。

✱ 技巧练习

🎧 请根据下列段落的录音对其进行逻辑分析,指出段落的主题思想和逻辑结构。

1. 人们通常认为红、黄、橙色为暖色,而蓝、绿则为冷色。但是当你用手触摸一片绿叶,并不会觉得它比一片黄色的叶子冷,那么为什么人们会有以上的冷暖色之分呢?

众所周知,太阳光能给人带来温暖。久而久之,当人们看到红色、橙色和黄色也相应地产生温暖感;海水和月光使人感觉清爽,于是人们看到青和绿之类的颜色,也相应会产生凉爽感。由此可见,色彩的温度感不过是人们的习惯反映,是人们长期实践的结果。色彩的冷暖还和明暗度有关。含白的明色具有凉爽感,含黑的暗色具有温暖感。同时色彩的冷暖与物体的表面光滑度有一定的联系。一般来说表面光滑时色彩显得冷;表面粗糙时,色彩就显得暖。总的说来,色彩的温度感是相对的,绝对地说某种颜色是冷色或暖色是不准确的。

2. Being a mechanic is a lot like being a surgeon. First, the mechanic has to examine an engine just as carefully as a surgeon examines a patient when something is wrong. After finding out the problem, both the surgeon and the mechanic have to take on the intricate and complicated job of fixing it. Mechanics use expensive instruments and tools, just as surgeons do, and both are required to know everything about their profession, otherwise the operation could be a failure. The job is difficult and time-consuming; however, the mechanic and the surgeon both feel a certain satisfaction when the job is completed.

✱ 主题口译

Text A　大连商务之旅

主题导入

某公司的销售部经理约翰逊先生到大连出差,要在大连逗留几天,大连分公司负责接待工作的张欣女士对大连进行了简要的介绍,希望可以使他的大连之行更加愉快。以下是他们的对话。

🎧 请先熟悉列出的词汇与短语再听录音,并在录音停顿时将下列对话口译成汉语或英语。

ⓦ 词汇与短语

达里尼	Dalny
跨海大桥	Bay Bridge
城堡酒店	Castle Hotel
大连国际会议中心	Dalian International Conference Center
圣亚海洋世界	Sun Asia Ocean World
金石滩度假区	Golden Pebble Beach Resort

第 2 单元　信息的逻辑分析 / 商务旅行

A: I'm really lucky to have the chance to come to Dalian, the romantic city of North China. It's magnificent, indeed! //

B: 是的。大连位于中国东部沿海地区，是中国北方重要的港口城市。"大连"的名字是来自俄语"达里尼"，意思是"远东的城市"。我敢说你此行一定很棒，因为大连真的是个迷人的城市，它常被昵称为"北方明珠"。//

A: I am told that Dalian was formerly an unimportant fishing village. But now it has grown into one of the most important seaports and a famous tourist city in China. Amazing changes! Would you please tell me more about it? //

B: 好的。大连在 19 世纪末开始逐渐发展起来。自 20 世纪 80 年代以来，它更是加快了向世界敞开大门的步伐。现在大连已经成为中国最富有活力的国际化城市之一。//

A: I read from a tourist information guide that, as you walk through Dalian, especially around Zhongshan Square, you may feel as though you were entering a fair of world architecture or an art gallery of human civilization. Do you think the words are an exaggeration? //

B: 哦。我认为这些话并没有夸张。事实上，大连的建筑风格多种多样，中山广场周围的建筑更是受到了俄式和日式建筑的影响，颇具特点。这种多样性反映了国内外建筑师、工程师、工人们的智慧和努力，是全世界的珍贵遗产。//

A: I see. Would you recommend some scenic spots worth visiting in Dalian? //

B: 当然。首先，我要向你推荐星海广场。它是亚洲最大的广场，就坐落在海边，也是欣赏跨海大桥和城堡酒店唯美夜景的好去处。//

A: Thank you very much for your detailed introduction. //

B: 不用谢。还有很多地方不能错过呢，比如：大连国际会议中心、圣亚海洋世界、金石滩度假区等。//

A: I am sure I will have a good time in Dalian. //

B: 希望你的大连之行愉快！//

 **Text B** 经济危机与商务旅行

主题导入

受经济危机影响，全球消费平均水平下降。为了减少日常开支，很多公司都在出差差旅费，特别是机票方面，减少开支。美国航空公司业务部经理汉斯接受《中国日报》记者的采访，主要谈及尽管企业都在缩减差旅开支，但是商务旅行却在逐步发展的情况。以下是他们的对话。

商务英语口译

> 🔊 请先熟悉列出的词汇与短语再听录音，并在录音停顿时将下列对话口译成英语或汉语。
>
> 📝 **词汇与短语**
>
> | | |
> |---|---|
> | 机票连续涨价 | successive fare increases |
> | 习惯性地航班延误 | chronic delays |
> | 紧缩差旅开支 | to tighten their belts |
> | 高速公路 | expressway |
> | American Express | 美国运通公司 |

A: 汉斯先生，作为业内人士，您一定感受到了目前航空业存在的一些现象，比如：机票连续涨价，航班和座位数量巨幅减少，习惯性地航班延误等。// 表面上看，这些现象似乎都在表明商务旅行正走向衰退。然而，我们调查发现，尽管企业都在紧缩差旅开支，但是商务旅行仍然在稳步发展。//

B: That's true. Though the economic crisis has led to cutting down on travelling expenses in most companies, the majority of our clients are still traveling as much in terms of frequency. // However, most companies are figuring out some methods to do things less expensively. They prefer to pay less, but not at the cost of not going. The companies are just getting more creative. //

A: "创意"这个词用在关于企业差旅管理的表述中，恐怕会使一些商务旅行者感到不安。这种"创意"是否意味着他们很快就要收到通知，告知他们和别人共住一间酒店客房的好处呢？或者要在高速公路上搭便车去与新客户会面呢？//

B: Not quite. At least not yet. A recent survey conducted by *Business Traveler* magazine found that more than 3 quarters of over 500 business travelers said they were now staying at less expensive hotels or, when possible, leaving and returning on the same day to avoid accommodation expense. //

A: 用这个办法节省开支，确实不错。//

B: However, arranging a same-day trip to save money is tricky since the airlines have revived the Saturday night and other minimum-stay requirements. These make it far more difficult to get a cheap fare without spending the weekend on the road. //

A: 我想没有多少员工愿意这样浪费周末吧。//

B: Of course not. A survey conducted by American Express showed that most respondents expected to get "more from their travel dollars" by tightening controls on spending. //

A: 这很符合情理。//

B: The survey also revealed that companies were tightening spending for first-class and business-class travel on long-haul flights. Those companies that used to allow premium-class travel on flights over six hours have extended the flying hours to eight or nine hours or even more. //

A: 天啊，公司都这样吗？//

B: No, 21% of companies in the United States said they expected their international business travel to increase over the next 6 months, and 38% said they expected it to remain the same. //

A: 非常感谢您与我们分享这些信息。//

B: You are welcome. //

Text C 客家土楼：世界第八大奇迹

主题导入

客家土楼是福建省西部的传统民居建筑，被称为"世界第八大奇迹"。来自英国的格雷森先生到福建洽谈合作项目，闲暇之余向当地人何伟经理了解客家土楼的相关知识文化。以下是他们的对话。

请先熟悉列出的词汇与短语再听录音，并在录音停顿时将下列对话口译成汉语或英语。

词汇与短语

客家土楼	Hakka Earth Buildings
联合国教科文组织	UNESCO
古罗马竞技场	the ancient Roman Coliseum
防潮抗震	anti-humidity and anti-earthquake
中原	central China
防卫御敌	defensive function
水平的木栓	horizontal wooden bar
室外环状走廊	open round hallway

A: Mr. He, I've heard one of the landmarks in Fujian Province is the famous Hakka Earth Building. Could you please tell me about it? //

B: 没问题。客家土楼是坐落在中国南方福建省西部的传统民居建筑，被联合国教科文组织惊叹为"世界第八大奇迹"。//

A: Why is it so unique? //

B: 看到土楼，不禁会让人联想到古罗马竞技场，也有人认为很多现代体育场馆的设计也是受了土楼的影响。// 总的来说，土楼有造型独特、结构庞大、防潮抗震三大优势，因此它被誉为世界上独一无二的神奇民居。//

A: I bet those characteristics must be closely related to its history. //

B: 没错。客家人原来居住在中原地区，一千年前，一些客家人为了躲避战乱和饥荒，迁移到福建和两广地区。// 由于文化习俗上的差异，客家人与当地人产生了摩擦，为了保护自己，客家人修建了以防御为主的土楼。//

A: So originally the Earth Building was used for defending? //

B: 是的。也是从防御的角度出发,土楼被设计成多层的圆形结构,可供整个家庭或家族居住。最大的土楼能住千户人家。//

A: It is really amazing! But I'm sure it must have other functions since it is both a defending and habitable architecture. //

B: 当然。防卫御敌只是土楼的一个功能,它还具有防火、防潮、防震、宽敞及通风好等特点。此外,土楼形状多种多样,有方形、长方形、半圆形和圆形等。//

A: Round? How is that possible? //

B: 圆形的土楼是最为著名的。大部分圆形土楼都是三层结构,直径在七八十米。土墙通常有一米厚,整幢土楼只有一个大门。大门用铁皮包裹并用两根水平的木栓锁门。开门时,这两根木栓可以推进两边的土墙里。//

A: It is a miracle. No wonder it is regarded as a wonder in the world. But does it have any realistic value? //

B: 土楼是建筑史上的一个奇迹,也是一种具有高度历史价值的建筑形式,它所蕴含的客家文化影响了世世代代遍布在全球的客家人。//

A: If time permits, I must go and see it. //

B: 不如明天签约仪式结束后我们一起去吧。//

A: Sounds great! //

情景口译

提示:
学生三人或四人一组,根据下面的主题提示进行模拟口译,注意使用本单元介绍的技能和句型。

主题一　大连滨海路风光

参与人: 1. 约翰逊先生,澳大利亚某成衣制作有限公司总裁

2. 谢露女士,大连某服装有限公司总裁

3. 译员

地 点：大连滨海路上

内 容：1. 谢女士介绍大连滨海路的发展历史

2. 约翰逊先生提起他在旅游指南上读到的老虎滩风景区，谢女士向他讲述老虎滩的传说

3. 谢女士介绍燕窝岭婚庆公园和主要的建筑特色，约翰逊先生问起中国的婚礼习俗

4. 约翰逊先生感叹星海湾跨海大桥美丽的夜景

5. 谢女士介绍星海广场及在此举行的主要大型活动，并带约翰逊先生参加啤酒节活动

主题二　北京颐和园

参与人：1. 罗格先生，德国某电器制造公司销售部经理

2. 赵欢女士，北京某电器销售公司外联部经理

3. 译员

地 点：北京故宫颐和园

内 容：1. 赵女士介绍颐和园的设计理念和建造原则

2. 罗格先生询问颐和园的建造过程，赵女士进行讲解

3. 赵女士介绍颐和园的建筑分布

4. 罗格先生询问颐和园在中国历史上的地位和作用

✲ 句式扩展

1. Attracted by the natural beauty of New Zealand, tourists also find a thriving urban culture and a society very much in touch with global trends.

除了被新西兰的自然美景吸引，游客们还发现新西兰不仅拥有日益繁荣的都市文化，而且也是一个紧随国际潮流的国家。

2. Because of the sparse population and vast territory, it is always possible to find a peaceful spot to be alone with nature.

由于地广人稀，要想找一个与大自然独处的宁静之地永远不成问题。

3. Many of the world-renowned attractions in Australia are specific, such as the Great Barrier Reef, Ayer's Rock, Kakadu National Park and Sydney Opera House.

   澳大利亚许多举世闻名的旅游胜地都具有独特的景观,比如:大堡礁、阿叶尔斯石柱山、卡卡杜国家公园和悉尼歌剧院。

4. London, the capital of the United Kingdom, has a population of about 7 million and an area of 1,580 square kilometers. Although it no longer ranks among the world's most populous cities, London is still one of the world's great centers for classical and popular culture.

   伦敦是英国的首都,人口700万,面积1 580平方千米。今天的伦敦虽然已不再是世界人口最多的城市之一,但仍然是世界上主要的古典文化和通俗文化中心之一。

5. Away from the noise and bustle of the city you can enjoy outdoor activities such as fishing, walking and swimming.

   远离城市的喧嚣和忙碌,你可以尽情享受各种室外活动,例如:钓鱼、散步和游泳等。

6. York is a major tourist city for many reasons. The city boasts one of the most famous cathedrals in the world. It has a number of interesting museums and the architecture within the city covers different periods of history.

   约克成为旅游重镇有很多原因。该市拥有世界上最为著名的教堂之一。它有很多有趣的博物馆。另外,城里的建筑反映了不同历史时期的风格。

7. Canada, which is larger than the United States in terms of territory, is the second largest country in the world. The distance from the east to the west is over 5,500 kilometers and the country covers six of the world's 24 time zones.

   加拿大的领土面积比美国大,是世界上占地面积第二大的国家。从东部到西部的距离超过5 500千米,而且加拿大覆盖了世界上24个时区中的6个。

8. Australia is a land of exceptional beauty. It is the world's smallest continent and largest island, and a relatively young nation established in an ancient land.

   澳大利亚是一个异常美丽的国家。这是世界最小的洲,也是最大的岛,是在古老的土地上建立起来的较为年轻的国家。

9. Bali, probably the most seductive island on earth, is the place for indulgent spa treatments, like floral baths and all kinds of massages.

   巴厘岛可能是世界上最具诱惑力的岛屿,也是尽情享受水疗护理的好地方,比如:花浴和各种按摩。

10. The jewel in the British cultural crown is the British Museum, with 4 kilometers of galleries and more than 4 million exhibits.

   大英博物馆是镶刻在英国文化皇冠上的一颗宝石，拥有 4 千米长的展廊和 400 余万件展品。

11. 西安是中国黄河流域古代文明的重要发源地之一，也是世界四大文明古都之一。

   Xi'an is one of the birthplaces of the ancient civilization in the Yellow River Basin, and it is also one of the world's four great ancient capitals.

12. 当地人把九寨沟的湖泊叫做"海子"。九寨沟有 108 个"海子"，虽大小不一，形状各异，却都清澈见底。

   The local people of Jiuzhaigou call these lakes "haizi" (meaning "little sea"). There are 108 "haizi" of various sizes and shapes in Jiuzhaigou, but of invariant limpidity to the bottom of the lakes.

13. 杭州是浙江省的省会，是驰名中外的旅游城市，也是历史文化名城和中国七大古都之一。

   Hangzhou is the capital of Zhejiang Province. It is a world-famous tourist destination, a city with a long history and profound culture, and also one of the seven ancient capitals in China.

14. 杭州也是著名的旅游城市，风景秀丽，与苏州共享"上有天堂，下有苏杭"的美誉。

   Hangzhou is also a famous tourist city in China. With its beautiful scenery, it shares with Suzhou the reputation of "the paradise on earth".

15. 海南岛在中国南部，面积 3.4 万多平方千米，它北隔琼州海峡，同雷州半岛相望，是中国第二大岛。

   Facing the Leizhou Peninsula across the Qiongzhou Strait to the north, Hainan Island, the second largest island in China, lies in the far south of China, with an area of over 34,000 square kilometers.

16. 初访上海的游客第一个印象必然是那些象征着这座大城市财富和魅力的高楼大厦。

   First-time visitors to Shanghai will invariably first be captivated by the soaring skyscrapers that symbolize the metropolis' wealth and glamour.

17. 四川素有"天府之国"的美称。这是个盆地，四周群山环绕。古时候，四川称为蜀国，交通十分不便。唐朝著名诗人李白在他的诗中叹道："蜀道难，难于上青天！"现在的四川水陆空交通四通八达，蜀道难的时代已经一去不复返了。

   Sichuan has always enjoyed the reputation of "Heavenly Land of Plenty". It is a basin surrounded by huge mountains. In ancient times, Sichuan was called Shu Kingdom, where the transportation was greatly inconvenient at that time. Li Bai, one of the most famous poets in Tang Dynasty, exclaimed in his poem: "Walking on the narrow paths of Shu Kingdom is more difficult than climbing up to Heaven!" Now the transportation by water, land and air in Sichuan extends in all directions. The times when walking on the narrow paths of Shu Kingdom are gone forever.

18. 众所周知，北京是世界文化名城，有三千多年的历史，有着众多的名胜古迹和丰富的文化底蕴。北京保存着世界上最完整的宫殿群——故宫，以及被称为"世界七大奇迹"之一的长城。

    Beijing is known as a famous historical and cultural city in the world. As a city with a history of over 3,000 years, Beijing has numerous sites of interests and a brilliant rich culture. It has preserved the Forbidden City, the most complete palace complex, and the Great Wall, which is known as one of the seven wonders in the world.

19. 中国园林可分为御花园和私家花园两类。前者多见于北方，后者则多见于南方，尤以苏州、无锡和南京三地为甚。

    Chinese gardens can be divided into two categories, the imperial and the private. The former are seen most frequently in northern China, while more of the latter can be found in the south, especially in Suzhou, Wuxi and Nanjing.

20. 上海是美食家的乐园，全市数以千计的餐馆汇集了国内外各大名菜，尤其是上海的本帮菜，特别受到海外人士的青睐。

    Shanghai is a paradise for gourmets, boasting thousands of restaurants serving a complete list of well-known Chinese and international cuisines, among which the Shanghai food enjoys particular popularity among overseas visitors.

口译小贴士

英语听辨能力的练习方法（下）

口译听辨能力的提升不是一蹴而就的，而是要经过长期的反复训练，可以从以下几个方面着手训练：

1. 培养沉着冷静、高度集中的听辨习惯。无论在何种情况下，都要保持冷静和自信，不要因为个别词句或是发言人的某种口音没反应过来而慌了手脚，良好的心理素质对提高临场的听辨能力有一定的帮助。

2. 听辨练习与口语表达齐头并进。复述是听辨练习的主要模式，复述练习又可以分为源语复述和目的语复述。练习时可以从源语复述入手，逐步过渡到目的语复述。无论进行哪种形式的训练，对复述进行录音是非常有必要的。回听录音可以检查复述中是否有信息遗漏、错误或逻辑混乱之处，也可以对语音、语言质量、表述方式等进行监控。

3. 泛听练习与精听练习相结合。听辨能力的提升与综合听力的提升是相辅相成的，这就需要将泛听练习与精听练习结合起来。复述练习是一种泛听练习，而在复述练习之后对原文进行字字对应的听写练习就是精听练习。通过精听练习可以更加全面细致地把握文体特征、增加词汇量、解析各种语言现象（如爆破、连读等），这些都是提升听辨能力的基础。

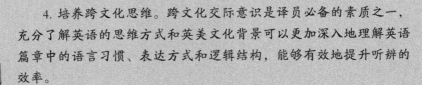

4. 培养跨文化思维。跨文化交际意识是译员必备的素质之一，充分了解英语的思维方式和英美文化背景可以更加深入地理解英语篇章中的语言习惯、表达方式和逻辑结构，能够有效地提升听辨的效率。

公共演讲 / 礼仪致辞

第 3 单元

口译主题 礼仪致辞

  礼仪致辞通常是在欢迎仪式、答谢宴会、开闭幕式等社交场合中发表的用以表达赞美、感谢、欢迎、欢送等情感的致辞。礼仪致辞的用语清晰生动,情感表达真挚委婉,开头和结尾通常都有相对固定的表达模式。

  礼仪致辞要体现发言人的真情实感,在听众中创造亲切感、熟悉感和认同感。礼仪致辞的语言在很大程度上直接影响着听众对该主题的看法和情感。

✻ 学习目标

    了解公共演讲的技巧要点

    了解礼仪致辞的语言特点

    掌握礼仪致辞的常用口译句式

✴ 技巧讲解

著名口译实践家让·艾赫贝尔在其所著的《口译须知》一书中指出:"要想成为一名优秀的口译人员,首先必须是一位好的演说家。"无论是站在"台前"完成交替传译的译员,还是坐在幕后成为"看不见的发言人"的同声传译译员,公共演讲技巧都是至关重要的。

总体说来,口译中的公共演讲技巧主要包括口头表达和肢体语言两部分,译员要将二者有效地融合在一起,才能做好台前幕后的"演说家"。

口头表达通常是指音量、音高、语速、停顿、发音和吐字几个要素的综合运用。

音量是指发言人声音的大小和强弱程度。译员的声音要响亮有力,既不声嘶力竭,也不低声细语,要确保每一位听众都能够听清。口译时,译员可以关注听众的表情,尤其是最前排和最后排听众的反应,以此进行音量调节。

音高指声音的高低程度。一般来说,中音沉稳可信,可以让听众充分感受到亲切、友好、温和、诚恳之感,因此也是译员在口译过程中最常使用的音高。当然,译员也可以根据口译内容的变化恰如其分地运用高音和低音来传情达意。

语速是口译表达中的重要因素,语速过快或过慢都不利于听众把握讲话内容。译员应根据讲话的内容特点和所采用的速度来确定自己的传译节奏,做到速度适中,但可以在重要信息点,比如:数字、专门用语等关键点上放慢速度。

停顿是指信息传递过程中的短暂间隙。这既是译员正常换气的生理需要,也是表情达意的需要。在口译过程中,适当的停顿有利于显示信息的层次感、调节语言节奏。不恰当的停顿则往往会影响语意的表达。

发音是译员呈现给听众的首要印象,是译员的"门面"。因此,译员要在中英双语表达上不存在任何障碍,发音到位,符合标准,正确掌握两种语言的语音、语调和节奏。这是译员最基本的语言素质之一。

吐字强调的是口齿清楚、发音准确。吐字要圆润、饱满,克服发音含糊不清、过度吞音,更要避免加入"嗯""啊""这个"等不必要的填充词。

肢体语言与口头表达同样重要,主要包括眼神交流、面部表情和手势等要素。

眼神交流尤为重要。译员不能只"埋头苦译"而不去关注听众的反应。而且,适当的眼神交流是自信的表现,也会加强与听众的沟通效果,及时了解听众对译文的反馈,对传译进行适度的调整。

面部表情要保持轻松自然,时刻向听众传达友好信息。即使在口译过程中有困难出现,译员也不应该皱眉、瞪眼、吐舌头或流露出其他沮丧、无奈的表情。

手势也要适度。在非正式的日常工作口译中,译员可以适当在交流中辅以手势;但在正式场合,译员一定要保持端正持重,切忌手舞足蹈。

此外,由于大多数情况下译员是通过麦克风传递声音,因此译员要学会正确使用麦风的方式，即嘴巴与麦克风保持适当的距离以确保适当的音量，防止声音失真；要控制好呼吸，以防传出喘气声、咳嗽声、吸鼻子等刺耳的声音。

❋ 技巧练习

根据以下话题进行演讲，注意公共演讲的技巧。

1. 我的中国梦
2. My Ideal Boyfriend/Girlfriend

❋ 主题口译

Text A 王毅部长在外交部 2016 年新年招待会上的致辞（节选）

主题导入

新年之际，中国外交部都会在钓鱼台国宾馆为各国驻华使节和国际组织驻华代表举行新年招待会。以下节选自外交部部长王毅在 2016 年新年招待会上的致辞。

请先熟悉列出的词汇与短语再听录音，并在录音停顿时将下列篇章口译成英语。

词汇与短语

国务委员	State Councilor
民族复兴	national renewal
大国外交	major-country diplomacy
小康社会	a society of initial prosperity
使团事务办公室	an office for handling affairs relating to diplomatic missions
礼宾和领事事务职能	protocol and consular functions

尊敬的杨洁篪国务委员和夫人，

尊敬的各位使节、代表和夫人，

女士们，先生们，朋友们： //

很高兴与各位新老朋友欢聚一堂，喜迎新年。我谨代表中国外交部，对各位嘉宾出席今天的招待会表示热烈的欢迎，向各位驻华使节、代表一年来为促进中外友好合作做出的宝贵贡献致以诚挚的谢意，对各兄弟部门给予外交工作的大力支持表示衷心的感谢！//

2015年是中国外交的全面推进之年。我们牢牢把握坚持和平发展、促进民族复兴这一主线，聚焦和平与发展两大主题，统筹推进丰富多彩的全方位外交活动，凸显了中国特色，取得多方面积极成效。//

2016年是中国"十三五"规划开局之年。我们将在以习近平同志为总书记的党中央领导下，认真践行中国特色大国外交理念，积极承担相应国际责任，为全面建成小康社会、营造更加有利的国际环境，为世界和平与发展事业续写新的篇章。//

中国与世界各国友好关系的深入发展，离不开各位使节、代表的辛勤付出，我愿再次向你们表示衷心的感谢！借此机会，我愿向大家通报，外交部将设立使团事务办公室，整合礼宾和领事事务的职能，为各国驻华使、领馆和各国际组织驻华代表机构提供更优质和更专业的服务。// 新的一年，外交部期待同各位使节、代表进一步加强交流合作，同各有关部门进一步加强协调配合，共同推动中国与世界各国的友好合作不断向前迈进！//

现在，我提议：

为中国人民同各国人民的友谊，

为世界和平与繁荣，

为各位来宾的健康，

干杯！//

Text B Queen's Speech at the Welcome Banquet (excerpt)

主题导入

2015年10月20日，国家主席习近平和夫人彭丽媛出席了英国女王伊丽莎白二世在白金汉宫举行的盛大欢迎晚宴。伊丽莎白二世女王强调要不断发展中英全面战略伙伴关系。以下节选自女王在欢迎晚宴上的致辞。

请先熟悉列出的词汇与短语再听录音，并在录音停顿时将下列篇章口译成汉语。

词汇与短语

Buckingham Palace　　　白金汉宫
Terra Cotta Warriors　　　兵马俑

Mr. President,

Prince Philip and I are delighted to welcome you and Madame Peng to Buckingham Palace this evening. //

Your visit to the United Kingdom marks a milestone in this unprecedented year of cooperation and friendship between the United Kingdom and China, as we celebrate the ties between our two countries and prepare to take them to ambitious new heights. //

The United Kingdom and China have a warm and longstanding friendship. Prince Philip and I recall with great fondness our visit to China almost thirty years ago, where we were privileged to experience your country's rich history and culture, including the Great Wall, the Forbidden City and the Terra Cotta Warriors: all unforgettable memories of China's ancient civilization. //

Yet it was China's desire to shape a new future which captivated us the most. We were struck by the energy and enthusiasm with which China's leaders were forging ahead with a new and ambitious future for the Chinese people. //

Mr. President, the relationship between the United Kingdom and China is now truly a global partnership. We have much reason to celebrate the dynamic, growing economic relationship between our countries as well as our success in working together to address pressing international challenges. //

This global partnership is supported by an expanding network of links between the people of our two countries, which are essential in building mutual understanding and friendship, while we welcome the increasing numbers of Chinese tourists, students and business visitors to the United Kingdom. //

Mr. President, your visit is a defining moment in this very special year for our bilateral relationship. I am confident that it will serve to highlight the sincerity and warmth of our friendship and to strengthen relations between our countries for many years to come. //

Ladies and gentlemen, I ask you to rise and drink a toast to the President and Madame Peng and to the people of China. //

Text C 驻新加坡大使陈晓东在慧眼中国环球论坛年会上的发言（节选）

主题导入

慧眼中国环球论坛致力于深入探讨中国的经济发展，剖析中国各级政府和社会的各个层面，同时研究政治、社会、经济各种重大因素的形成和交互影响，让与会者洞悉中国变迁因素、掌握中国脉动规律。以下节选自驻新加坡大使陈晓东在慧眼中国环球论坛2016年年会上的发言。

第 3 单元　公共演讲 / 礼仪致辞

> 请先熟悉列出的词汇与短语再听录音，并在录音停顿时将下列篇章口译成英语。
>
> **词汇与短语**
>
> | | |
> |---|---|
> | 慧眼中国环球论坛 | Future China Global Forum |
> | 厄尔尼诺 | El Niño |
> | 英国脱欧 | Brexit |
> | "黑天鹅"事件 | "Black Swan" incidents |
> | 新常态 | new normal |
> | 一带一路 | the Belt and Road Initiative |

女士们、先生们：

大家早上好！很高兴出席慧眼中国环球论坛 2016 年年会。我谨代表中国驻新加坡大使馆预祝论坛年会取得圆满成功。//

2016 年以来，受"厄尔尼诺"现象影响，全球极端天气事件频发。同样让人感到乱象纷呈的还有世界经济，主要经济体政策分化明显，全球贸易低位徘徊，英国脱欧等"黑天鹅"事件更不约而至，加剧全球金融市场震荡。//

中国经济迈入"新常态"后，面临着多重困难和挑战，下行压力依然较大，经济走势分化，金融风险有所增加。// 2016 年上半年中国经济数据几天前刚刚出炉，中国 GDP 同比增长 6.7%，增速是同期世界经济平均增速的 2.8 倍，对世界经济增长的贡献率达 26.3%。这些数据再次印证了中国经济"总体平稳、稳中向好"的基本态势。//

大家都很关心"一带一路"倡议进展。三年来，共有 70 多个国家和组织参与"一带一路"建设，中国同"一带一路"参与国双边贸易额突破 1 万亿美元，占中国外贸总额的 25%；// 中方对"一带一路"沿线 49 个国家的直接投资额近 150 亿美元，同比增长 18%。总之，"一带一路"倡议在纵深推进中，不断为中国和沿线国家经济发展带来新的机遇。//

回顾中国改革开放 30 多年的历史，中国经济正是在克服一个又一个困难、战胜一个又一个挑战中走到今天，也是在部分西方媒体的质疑和唱衰声中成长为全球第二大经济体。// 新加坡总理李显龙曾在去年的慧眼中国环球论坛年会上表达了对中国经济发展的信心，新加坡各界的有识之士也在为中国经济的转型升级之路积极建言献策。这些独到的视角和深度的观察正是慧眼中国环球论坛年会的价值所在，也让我们坚信中国经济的前景必将更加光明！谢谢大家！//

Text D: Message on Nelson Mandela International Day 2016 (excerpt)

主题导入

纳尔逊·曼德拉（1918.7.18—2013.12.5）出生于南非特兰斯凯，曾任非国大青年联盟全国书记、主席。于1994—1999年任南非总统，是首位黑人总统，被尊称为"南非国父"。2009年11月，联合国大会为表彰南非前总统纳尔逊·曼德拉对和平文化与自由的贡献，宣告7月18日为"纳尔逊·曼德拉国际日"。以下节选自联合国秘书长潘基文在2016年"纳尔逊·曼德拉国际日"发表的致辞。

请先熟悉列出的词汇与短语再听录音，并在录音停顿时将下列篇章口译成汉语。

词汇与短语

Madiba	马迪巴（曼德拉的族名）
2030 Agenda for Sustainable Development	《2030年可持续发展议程》
Mandela Foundation	曼德拉基金
Nelson Mandela International Day	纳尔逊·曼德拉国际日

Nelson Mandela International Day is an opportunity to reflect on the life and work of a legend who embodied the highest values of the United Nations. //

Madiba was a model global citizen whose example continues to guide us in our work to build a better world for all. Today, we remember a man of quiet dignity and towering achievement who worked tirelessly for peace and human dignity. //

Nelson Mandela gave 67 years of his life to bring change to the people of South Africa. His accomplishments came at great personal cost to himself and his family. His sacrifice not only served the people of his nation, but made the world a better place for everyone, everywhere. //

As the United Nations sets out to implement the newly adopted *2030 Agenda for Sustainable Development*, let us seek to continue building on Nelson Mandela's legacy of selflessness and deep sense of shared purpose. // The United Nations joins the Mandela Foundation in inviting people around the world to devote at least 67 minutes on 18 July to a community service activity. //

The heart of Nelson Mandela International Day is volunteer work for people and the planet. Its theme—"Take action, Inspire change"—is meant to mobilize the human family to do more to build a peaceful, sustainable and equitable world. // Tutor a child. Feed the hungry. Clean up a site or care for your environment. Volunteer to serve at a hospital or community center. Be part of the Mandela movement to make the world a better place. // This is the best tribute to an extraordinary man who, with his steadfast belief in justice and human equality, showed how one person can make a difference. Let us all continue being inspired by Nelson Mandela's lifelong example and his call to never cease working to build a better world for all. //

Text E 签约仪式上的讲话

主题导入

随着互联网的迅速发展，许多传统行业已经突破了原有的营销模式，利用"互联网+"不断拓宽市场和品牌影响力。以下是大连百纳瑞信息技术有限公司张总经理在与宁夏沃福百瑞枸杞产业股份有限公司合作签约仪式上的讲话。

请先熟悉列出的词汇与短语再听录音，并在录音停顿时将下列篇章口译成英语。

词汇与短语

大连百纳瑞信息技术有限公司
Dalian Binary Information Technology Co., Ltd.
宁夏沃福百瑞枸杞产业股份有限公司
Ningxia Wolfberry Biological and Food Engineering Co., Ltd.
国际互联网大会　World Internet Conference (WIC)
工控智能　industrial control intelligence
系统集成　system integration

尊敬的郭副市长，

尊敬的王总经理，

女士们、先生们：

正当第三届国际互联网大会召开之际，我们迎来了大连百纳瑞信息技术有限公司和宁夏沃福百瑞枸杞产业股份有限公司的合作签约仪式，这是宁夏特色枸杞产业与互联网应用结合的里程碑。//

"十三五"时期，中国将大力实施网络强国战略、国家大数据战略、"互联网+"行动计划，发展积极向上的网络文化，拓展网络经济空间，促进互联网和经济社会融合发展。我们的目标就是要让互联网发展成果惠及13亿多中国人民，更好造福各国人民。//

互联网+，通俗来说，就是"互联网+各个传统行业"，但这并不是简单的两者相加，而是利用信息通信技术以及互联网平台，让互联网与传统行业进行深度融合，创造新的发展生态。//

这次国际互联网大会以"创新驱动、造福人类——携手共建网络空间命运共同体"为主题，更是强调互联网+的合作精神，只有合作得好，融合得好，经济才能大幅度增长。// 今天，我们大连百纳瑞信息技术有限公司以自己的软件开发与测试、工控智能化及系统集成、国际化 IT 产业人才团队，与宁夏沃福百瑞枸杞产业股份有限公司的枸杞系列产品开发、生产相结合，就是要运用信息技术提升宁夏枸杞产品的价值和信誉，利用互联网拓展国际市场，把品牌做响，把产业做大，成为宁夏互联网+的样板，为宁夏的经济发展做出应有的贡献。//

最后，感谢各位来宾见证我们的签约仪式，衷心祝贺大连百纳瑞信息技术有限公司与宁夏沃福百瑞枸杞产业股份有限公司合作成功。

谢谢！//

Text F Matt Damon's MIT Commencement Address 2016 (excerpt)

主题导入

1998年马特·达蒙凭借《心灵捕手》斩获影帝，2007年被《人物》杂志评为"全球最性感男人"。不过，这位有着非凡成就、实打实的演技派甚至没有真正从大学毕业。2016年马特·达蒙受邀为麻省理工大学（MIT）2016届的毕业生做一场演讲，他告诉毕业生们——失败是走向成功的最好盔甲！以下节选自马特·达蒙的演讲。

请先熟悉列出的词汇与短语再听录音，并在录音停顿时将下列篇章口译成汉语。

词汇与短语

commencement	毕业典礼
Simulation Theory	模拟理论
to postulate	假定
Zimbabwe	津巴布韦

Thank you, President Reif—and thank you, Class of 2016! It's an honor to be part of this day—an honor to be here with you, with your friends, your professors, and your parents. But let's be honest—it's an honor I didn't earn. //

Look, I don't even have a college degree. As you might have heard, I went to Harvard. I just didn't graduate from Harvard. I got pretty close, but I started to get movie roles and didn't finish all my courses. I put on a cap and gown and walked with my class; my Mom and Dad were there and everything; I just never got an actual degree. You could say I kind of fake graduated. //

So you can imagine how excited I was when President Reif called to invite me to speak at the MIT commencement. Then you can imagine how sorry I was to learn that the MIT commencement speaker does not get to go home with a degree. So yes, today, for the second time in my life, I am fake graduating from a college in my hometown. //

You're working on some crazy stuff in these buildings. I'll tell you one that's been on my mind: Simulation Theory. There's a philosopher named Nick Bostrom at Oxford, and he's postulated that if there's a truly advanced form of intelligence out there in the universe, then it's probably advanced enough to run simulations of entire worlds—maybe trillions of them—maybe even our own. //

The basic idea is that we could be living in a massive simulation run by a far smarter civilization, a giant computer game, and we don't even know it. What if this—all of this—is a simulation? //

But then again: what if it isn't a simulation? Either way, what we do matters. What we do affects the outcome. MIT, you've got to go out and do really interesting things. Important things. Inventive things. Because this world has some problems. We need you to drop everything and solve. //

But before you step out into our big, troubled world, I want to pass along a piece of advice that Bill Clinton offered me a little over a decade ago. What he said was "Turn toward the problems you see. Engage with them. Walk right up to them. Look them in the eye. In my experience, there's just no substitute for actually going and seeing things."//

There was a refugee crisis back in 2009 that I read about in an amazing article in *The New York Times*. People were streaming across the border of Zimbabwe to a little town in northern South Africa called Messina. I was working in South Africa, so I went up to Messina to see for myself what was going on. Human beings will take your breath away. They will teach you a lot, but you have to engage. There are a lot of trouble out there, MIT. But there's a lot of beauty, too. I hope you see both. //

The point is to try to eliminate your blind spots—the things that keep us from grasping the bigger picture. But looking at the world as it is, and engaging with it, is the first step toward finding our blind spots. There are a few more things I hope you'll keep in mind. //

First, you're going to fail sometimes, and that's a good thing. Not having an answer isn't embarrassing. It's an opportunity. Don't be afraid to ask questions. //

The second thing is that you've got to keep listening. Even outside your work, there are ways to keep challenging yourself. Listen to online lectures. I love what President Obama said at Howard University's commencement last month: he said, "Democracy requires compromise, even when you are 100 percent right". //

The third and last thought I want to leave you with is that not every problem has a high-tech solution. We need to be just as innovative in public policy. //

So, graduates, let me ask you this in closing: What do you want to be a part of? What's the problem you'll try to solve? Whatever your answer, it's not going to be easy. //

Here you are alive at a time when science and technology may not hold all the answers, but are indispensable to any solution. //

So I hope you'll turn toward the problem of your choosing. Because you must. I hope you'll drop everything. Because you must. And I hope you'll solve it. Because you must. Your game begins now. Congratulations and thanks very much！//

情景口译

提示：

学生两人一组，根据下面的主题提示进行模拟口译，注意使用本单元介绍的技能和句型。

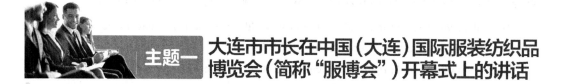

主题一 大连市市长在中国（大连）国际服装纺织品博览会（简称"服博会"）开幕式上的讲话

参与人： 1. 肖盛峰先生，大连市市长
2. 参加服博会开幕式的中外嘉宾
3. 译员

地　点： 大连服博会开幕式现场

内　容： 1. 肖市长对海内外嘉宾的到来表示热烈欢迎
2. 肖市长祝贺服博会开幕
3. 肖市长回顾服博会的历史和作用
4. 肖市长对本届服博会提出展望和期望
5. 肖市长祝本届服博会圆满成功

主题二 晚宴致辞

参与人： 1. 赫尔曼先生，德国某大型电器制造公司大中华区执行总裁
2. 某电器销售公司考察团及参加欢迎宴会的中外嘉宾
3. 译员

地　点： 某酒店宴会厅

内　容： 1. 赫尔曼先生对考察团的到来表示热烈的欢迎
2. 赫尔曼先生对该电器销售公司长久以来给予的支持表示感谢

3. 赫尔曼先生讲述两家公司共同发展的事例

4. 赫尔曼先生向全体嘉宾祝酒，并致以新春的问候

✳ 句式扩展

1. I would like to express my deepest appreciation to the people and Municipal Government of Dalian for the hospitality and excellent arrangements of this important event.

   我想向大连人民和市政府表达深深的谢意，感谢你们的热情款待及为本次重要活动所做的精心安排。

2. I want to begin by thanking the U.S.-Canadian Business Council for hosting this seminar and reception.

   首先我要感谢美加商务委员会主办这次研讨会和招待会。

3. Since we arrived, the gracious hospitality with which we have been received has been truly heartwarming. A Chinese proverb best describes my feeling: "When the visitor arrives, it is as if returning home".

   我们在这里一直受到你们的热情款待，让我们倍感温暖。中国有句老话最能表达我的感受，那就是"宾至如归"。

4. On behalf of all the members of my delegation, I would like to take this opportunity to express our sincere gratitude to our host for their earnest invitation and the gracious hospitality we have received since we set foot on this charming land.

   我愿借此机会，代表我们代表团的全体成员，对我们东道主的诚挚邀请，对我们一踏上这块充满魅力的土地便受到的友好款待，向东道主表示真诚的感谢。

5. In the name of myself, I would like to convey our heartfelt appreciation to your gracious hospitality.

   我以个人的名义，对你们的盛情款待表示衷心的感谢。

6. On behalf of the Australian delegates, I'd like to thank our Chinese colleagues for your invitation and your excellent program.

   我谨代表澳方代表，感谢中方的盛情邀请和精心安排。

7. I'd like to express my deep appreciation to Mr. Chairman for this opportunity to address the topic of world peace and development.

我为有机会就世界和平与发展问题进行发言,向主席先生致以深深的谢意!

8. It is my privilege and great pleasure to host this banquet in honor of Mr. Johnson and other distinguished guests.

   我为能在此设宴招待约翰逊先生以及其他贵宾而深感荣幸和愉快。

9. In closing, I would like you to join me in a toast! To the health of the President and Mrs. Williams! To the health of all our distinguished guests. To the lasting friendship and cooperation between our two countries!

   在我结束讲话之际,我请各位与我一起举杯!为威廉姆斯总统和夫人的身体健康!为所有贵宾的健康!为我们两国之间的持久友谊与合作!

10. This is a very happy and memorable occasion for me personally and the members of the Board to host you here in New York.

    对我本人以及董事会的全体成员来说,能在纽约接待您是非常愉快和令人难忘的。

11. 请允许我代表中国政府,对卡塔尔政府为筹备WTO第四届部长级会议所做的大量工作表示感谢。

    Please allow me, on behalf of the Chinese government, to express our appreciation to the Qatari government for its tremendous work in organizing the 4th Ministerial Conference of the WTO.

12. 首先,我谨代表我的夫人和同事们,并以我个人的名义,对怀特总统和夫人给予我们的周到安排和盛情款待表示衷心的感谢。

    First of all, I wish to express on behalf of my wife and my colleagues and in my own name, my sincere thanks to you, Mr. President and Mrs. White, for your thoughtful arrangements and gracious hospitality.

13. 我谨代表中国政府,向前来参加博览会的海内外嘉宾表示热烈的欢迎!并向所有支持本次博览会的朋友们表示真挚的谢意!

    On behalf of the Chinese government, I would like to extend my warmest welcome to all distinguished guests who joined this fair from home and abroad and express my sincere gratitude to those who have been supporting the fair.

14. 特别要感谢上海加拿大商会和加中贸易理事会共同主办今晚的活动。

    Special thanks go to the Canadian Chamber of Commerce in Shanghai and the Canada-China Business Council for co-hosting this evening's event.

15. 首先,我想对日内瓦外交与国际关系学院授予我名誉博士学位表示诚挚的感谢。

Let me begin by expressing sincere thanks to the Geneva School of Diplomacy and International Relations for awarding me this honorary doctorate.

16. 祝首轮中美战略与经济对话圆满成功。

    I wish the first round of China-U.S. Strategic and Economic Dialogue a complete success.

17. 首先，我代表中国政府和全国各族人民，向在座各位，并通过你们向全体澳门市民，致以诚挚的问候和良好的祝愿！

    Let me begin by extending, on behalf of the Central Government and people of all ethnic groups in China, warm greetings and best wishes to all of you here and through you, to all the citizens of Macao.

18. 祝大家身体健康，事业成功，合家欢乐，万事如意！

    I wish you good health, successful career, happy family and good luck in everything!

19. 现在我提议，为了大会的圆满成功，为了各位来宾的身体健康，干杯！

    Now I propose a toast, to the success of the conference and to the health of all the distinguished guests here, cheers!

20. 现在我宣布第14届妇女儿童权利保障论坛正式开幕！

    Now I declare the opening of the 14th Forum on the Protection of Children and Women's Rights!

口译小贴士

译员如何克服"怯场"心理

无论是经验不足的新译员，还是身经百战的老译员，每个译员在口译现场都会感到紧张，毫无例外。适度的紧张情绪有助于帮助译员保持一定的兴奋性，也有利于提醒译员从战略和战术上重视口译工作。但是，如果在口译工作中，总是"怯场"，总是因为紧张而发挥不出应有水平，是件非常令人可惜的事。

克服"怯场"最佳的方法就是全面提升口译实力，对口译任务做好充分的译前准备。试想一个有丰富会议经验而且对所译内容胸有成竹的译员与零经验且对所译内容知之甚少的译员相比，哪个更容易"怯场"？答案是显而易见的。所以，要想在口译工作中沉着应战、挥洒自如，就必须平时加强口译训练的强度，做好点滴积累、译前准备和译后总结，全方位地提升口译实力。

克服"怯场"还需要调节心理。一般而言,越重视某件事,心理负担就会越重,也就越有可能表现得不尽如人意。新译员虽然应该在战术和战略上充分重视每一项口译任务,譬如有针对性的练习语音、语调、语速、与听众的目光交流等公共演讲技巧,但是也要适度地通过心理暗示鼓励自己。例如:译员可以暗示自己"这只是一次口译练习""我已经做了充分的准备,不会有问题的"等。

克服"怯场"也可以通过"模拟会议"练习进行训练。在"模拟会议"中,练习伙伴可以相互找问题,挑毛病,甚至"鸡蛋里挑骨头",互相出难题。经过这样"魔鬼训练"的人,到了真正的口译现场上反而会觉得轻松自如。如果没有进行"模拟会议"的机会,在平时的训练中,练习者可以用诸如电脑、手机等电子设备为自己录像,通过回看评估自己在公共演讲方面的表现。此外,还可以采取一些其它的练习方式,比如:在一些集会或是公园、广场等公共场所发表即兴演讲,其目的就是把自己暴露在"众目睽睽"之下,锻炼自己的胆量。长此以往,真正到了实战时就不会感到"怯场"了。

俗话说:"熟能生巧"。大多数"怯场"都是经验不足造成的。坚持不懈地进行口译练习,适度调节心理,不断积累口译经验,"怯场"自然会不辞而别。

短期记忆 1/ 公司简介

第 **4** 单元

口译主题 公司简介

  公司简介是对公司或企业的介绍,一般包括公司概况、发展状况、公司文化、主要产品、销售网络等信息。在公司举办的新闻发布会、产品推介会或是公司参加的各类展会中,免不了要对公司的品牌进行推广和营销,公司简介在这样的场合中就会发挥巨大的作用。

✲ 学习目标

  了解短期记忆的类型和特点

  了解提高短期记忆效率的方法

  了解公司简介的文体特点

  掌握公司简介中的常用口译句式

✼ 技巧讲解

记忆的分类

通常有三种记忆参与到口译活动中,即瞬时记忆、短期记忆和长期记忆。

瞬时记忆,又称为"感觉储存",是人们对外界刺激的真实拷贝,保持时间非常短,约2秒。

短期记忆存储时间短,记忆容量有限。一般来说,普通人一次可以记住 $7±2$ 个信息单位。通常认为短期记忆保持的时间约为 5~20 秒,最长超不过 1 分钟。

长期记忆是指在头脑中能够保持 1 分钟以上的记忆。此类记忆在头脑中存储时间长,能保持几个月、几年,甚至终生不忘。人的大脑像一个拥有无限容量的信息库,存储着人们对这个世界的一切认知。

工作记忆是指人脑对信息进行暂时加工和存储的、容量有限的记忆。它在口译过程中起着重要的作用。人脑从瞬时记忆中筛选出有用的话语信息,并从长期记忆中激活并提取相关部分,然后将两者结合,对信息进行进一步加工并储存成短期记忆为主的记忆。在长期记忆中容易被激活和提取的信息通常是人们平时反复使用、非常熟悉的信息。这部分信息容易被激活,并且提取速度快,更容易与新的信息结合,并进一步存储到短期记忆中,甚至长期记忆中。

合格的译员应该具备较好的瞬时记忆和短期记忆来存储听取到的信息,较强的长期记忆在具体语境中提供相关信息。由于口译信息发布的即时性和一次性的特点,在信息存储和加工的过程中,短期记忆更显重要。由于存在个体差异,不同人的短期记忆能力天生不同,有的人能过耳不忘,有的人则边听边忘。然而,绝大多数人的短期记忆能力比较相近。而且,通过一定的方法和训练,短期记忆能力也是可以提高的。

提高短期记忆效率的方法

逻辑记忆和形象记忆是最常用的提高短期记忆的方法。

逻辑记忆主要是通过对语言信息的纵向及横向的逻辑分析,找出信息点(具体的信息内容)、线(各点之间的联系)和面(整体概念)之间的逻辑层次和联系,以便减少记忆单位的数量,达到提高记忆效率的目的。

语言信息中的"路标词",比如:演讲中经常出现的"第一""第二""首先""其次""再次"等,都是逻辑分层的明显标志。译员可以利用类似的"路标词"将听取的信息划分出大的层次,作为记忆的首要信息单位,再根据第一、第二单元中介绍的听辨技巧,抓到每个层次的关键词和逻辑线索,提高记忆的效率。

译员也可以将已经掌握的相关背景知识作为参考,纵横联想、合理扩展。译员的联想可以激活与听取信息相关的背景知识，再将已知的知识与新接受的信息进行对比，找出其中的联系与区别，以此缩短信息理解和提取的时间，提高记忆效果。

形象记忆，也可以被称为图像记忆，是指以感知过的事物的形象或画面为内容进行记忆。比如：在描述地理位置或所处环境时，发言人会描述其地理方位、空间结构、路径路线等。如果译员结合自己的背景知识，把这样的信息想象成一幅地图或路线图，记忆也就不难了。再比如：对于某些场景、故事情节、事件发展、某种流程的描述，译员如果把它们想象成一个动态的画面，储存在短期记忆中，在口译时通过整个画面的回放，也可以快速地回想起记忆的内容。

总之，提高短期记忆效率的方法有很多，可以根据个人的情况，边练习边摸索。

✲ 技巧练习

🎧 请听录音，听的过程中不要记笔记。听完后用源语进行复述，想想可以用哪些方法提高短期记忆效率。

1. 台风于今天凌晨在汕头沿海登陆，大约有 50 万人不得不紧急撤离。大风将树木连根拔起，许多房屋的屋顶被掀掉，一些不牢固的房子甚至被完全摧毁了。台风带来的强降雨使得路面大量积水，不少私家车进水，无法前行，横七竖八地停在马路中央。大街上空无一人，只有在一些没有被吹断的电线杆上飘着的五颜六色的广告海报的"残骸"才让人看得出这里曾经是一个繁华的小镇。

2. The basic ingredients of the economic system of any country are its natural resources, labor supply, and technology and management expertise. The United States is the fourth largest country in the world and it is rich in natural resources. It has a climate favorable for agricultural exports with rich deposit of industrial materials, such as oil, coal, natural gas, iron ore and other metal and minerals. The American labor force is also large by world standards. Most importantly, since World War II America has led the world in technological innovation and scientific discovery, which is most clearly seen in transportation and communications.

第 4 单元　短期记忆 1/ 公司简介

主题口译

Text A　华为简介

主题导入

华为公司是一家生产销售通信设备的通信科技公司,总部位于深圳市。华为的产品主要涉及通信网络中的交换网络、传输网络、无线及有线固定接入网络和数据通信网络及无线终端产品,为世界各地通信运营商及专业网络拥有者提供硬件设备、软件、服务和解决方案。2014年《财富》世界500强排行榜华为位列全球第285位。以下是对华为公司的简介。

请先熟悉列出的词汇与短语再听录音,并在录音停顿时将下列篇章用源语复述出来,再用目的语进行复述。

词汇与短语

信息与通信技术	information and communication technology (ICT)
云计算	cloud computing
大数据	Big Data
研究院 / 所	R&D institutes and centers
联合创新中心	joint innovation centers
5G 创新	5G innovation
未来数据中心领域	future data center domain
人工智能	artificial intelligence

女士们、先生们:

上午好!

首先,我代表华为技术有限公司,并以我个人名义,对在座的各位朋友表示最热烈的欢迎和最衷心的感谢。下面我简单介绍一下华为公司的基本情况。//

华为科技公司成立于1987年,总部设在中国深圳,是全球领先的信息与通信技术(ICT)解决方案供应商。// 自创建以来,华为专注于信息与通信技术领域,坚持稳健经营、持续创新、开放合作,为运营商客户、企业客户和消费者提供有竞争力的ICT解决方案、产品和服务。// 目前,华为的员工数量超过17万,业务遍及全球170多个国家和地区,服务全世界三分之一以上的人口。//

当前,以云计算、大数据为特征的技术正在成为引领和促进ICT行业创新和发展的核心技术。// 为适应这一变化,华为公司围绕客户需求和技术领先持续创新,与业界伙伴开放合作,持续为客户和全社会创造价值,同时也成为消费者喜爱和信赖的、全球领先的智能终端品牌。//

华为在全球范围内拥有16个研究院/所和36个联合创新中心，在ICT的前沿领域，如5G创新领域、未来数据中心领域、人工智能领域等取得丰硕成果。//

基本情况我就介绍到这里，祝各位在华为参观愉快！//

Text B | A Speech of Jack Ma, Chairman of Alibaba (excerpt)

主题导入

阿里巴巴集团创立于1999年，是目前中国最大的互联网公司。美国纽约当地时间2014年9月8日，阿里巴巴集团在纽约华尔道夫酒店开始首次公开募股的首站路演。以下节选自马云为阿里巴巴上市路演准备的致辞。

请先熟悉列出的词汇与短语再听录音，并用源语对所听到的信息进行复述练习。然后重新听录音，在录音停顿时将下列篇章口译成汉语。

词汇与短语

ecosystem	生态系统
to ignite innovation	激发创新
entrepreneur	企业家

Hello, I'm Jack Ma, founder and chairman of Alibaba Group. 15 years ago, 18 founders in my apartment had a dream that someday we can build up a company that can serve millions of small businesses. Today, this remains our mission to make easy to do business anywhere. //

At Alibaba, we fight for the little guys, the small businessmen and women and their customers. Our role is simple. Through our ecosystem, we help merchants and customers find each other and conduct business on their terms and in ways that best serve their unique needs. We help merchants to grow, create jobs and open new markets, in ways that were never before possible. //

Today, 15 years passed. We've grown so significantly and have become a household name in China. And soon, we are ready for the world to know us. //

With Alibaba's platforms, people are improving their lives today, and have hope for a better tomorrow. From our humble beginnings and throughout the past 15 years, Alibaba has changed commerce in China. Our business has grown, but we never lost sight of our customers, focusing on solving their problems, leading to the best outcome for our business. //

Alibaba has come a long way, but we want to be a company that can last 102 years. We still have 87 years to go, and we believe one thing—"Today is difficult. Tomorrow is more difficult, but the day after tomorrow is beautiful". So we have to work very hard in order to survive the long journey. //

第 4 单元 短期记忆 1/公司简介

Text C 保利文化集团股份有限公司

主题导入

保利文化集团股份有限公司成立于 2010 年 12 月，隶属于中国保利集团公司。前身是 2000 年 2 月成立的保利文化艺术有限公司，是国有中央企业中唯一的专业文化产业企业集团。以下是该公司的简介。

请先熟悉列出的词汇与短语再听录音，并在录音停顿时将下列篇章口译成英语。

词汇与短语

保利文化集团有限公司	Poly Culture Group Corporation Limited
保利剧院管理有限公司	Poly Theatre Management Co., Ltd.
（在……）上市	to be listed (on)
产业格局	an industry layout
产业升级	industry upgrade
子公司	subsidiary
自治区	autonomous region
直辖市	municipality
大使剧院集团	Ambassador Theatre Group
美国布什诺艺术中心	U.S. Bishnoi Art Center
阿姆斯特朗国际音乐艺术公司	Armstrong International Music and Art Company
战略合作伙伴关系	strategic partnership
领事馆	consulate

保利文化集团股份有限公司隶属于中国保利集团公司，其前身是成立于 2000 年的保利文化艺术有限公司，2010 年完成股份制改造，2014 年在香港联交所上市。//

成立 17 年来，保利文化已形成演出与剧院管理、艺术品经营与拍卖、影院投资管理三项主业并举的产业格局，其中演出与剧院管理、艺术品拍卖等业务稳居行业领先地位。// 立足三项主业，保利文化积极开拓艺术教育、文化金融、文化旅游、文化资产运营管理四项新业务，寻求产业升级。//

北京保利剧院管理有限公司是保利文化集团股份有限公司的主业子公司之一。它是全国最大的剧院管理和演出运营企业。// 截至 2017 年 6 月，公司业务涉及全国 18 个省、自治区及直辖市的 46 座城市，经营管理国内一流剧院 54 家，共上演剧目 36 800 场，接待观众总数超过 4 000 万人。仅 2016 年，演出量就达到了 6 800 场，接待观众突破 750 万人次。//

北京保利剧院管理有限公司也是"一带一路"的文化使者。公司的海外发展战略不断深化，先后与英国大使剧院集团、美国布什诺艺术中心、阿姆斯特朗国际音乐艺术公

司等海外机构建立了战略合作伙伴关系,与法国、波兰、德国、西班牙等国家的驻华领馆文化处开展了深入的合作。//

Text D Pfizer Pharmaceuticals Ltd.

主题导入

辉瑞公司创建于1849年,迄今已有160多年的历史,总部位于美国纽约,是目前全球最大的以研发为基础的生物制药公司。辉瑞公司的产品覆盖了包括化学药物、生物制剂、疫苗、健康药物等诸多广泛而极具潜力的治疗及健康领域,同时其卓越的研发和生产能力处于全球领先地位。以下是对辉瑞公司参观者的欢迎词。

请先熟悉列出的词汇与短语再听录音,并在录音停顿时将下列篇章口译成汉语。

词汇与短语

pharmaceutical company	制药公司
cardiovascular disease	心血管疾病
Alzheimer's	老年痴呆症
schizophrenia	精神分裂症
initiative	倡议
trachoma	沙眼
infectious	传染性的
to be committed to	致力于

Welcome to Pfizer—the world's largest, most valuable and fastest-growing pharmaceutical company. Ours is a noble purpose: to help realize humanity's quest for longer, healthier, happier lives. // Our mission is to become the world's most valued company in serving patients, customers, colleagues, investors, business partners and the communities where we work and live. We now employ 78,000 people worldwide, turning well over 5 billion USD a year on research and development. Our products are available in more than 150 countries. //

We currently have nearly 100 new medicines in various stages of development, and are working on dozens of new uses for our current medicines. Our targets include many of humanity's most feared illnesses, including cardiovascular disease, diabetes, Alzheimer's, cancer, HIV/AIDS, depression and schizophrenia. //

We have pioneered numerous initiatives to improve access to medicines including the international Trachoma Initiative, aimed at the world's greatest cause of preventable blindness, and a program aiming at HIV/AIDS patients in developing nations. Through the Pfizer Foundation, we are building with our partners an advanced infectious disease treatment and medical education center in Kampala, Uganda. //

We demand of ourselves and others the highest ethical standards, and our products and processes will be of the highest quality. We are deeply committed to meeting the needs of our customers, and we constantly focus on customer satisfaction. // We play an active role in making every country and community in which we operate a better place to live and work. I hope you will enjoy your visit for the rest of the day. Thank you. //

万科企业股份有限公司

主题导入

万科企业股份有限公司成立于 1984 年，1988 年进入房地产行业，经过近 30 年的发展，成为国内领先的房地产公司，目前主营业务包括房地产开发和物业服务。以下是对万科企业股份有限公司的简介。

请先熟悉列出的词汇与短语再听录音，并在录音停顿时将下列篇章口译成英语。

词汇与短语

万科企业股份有限公司	China Vanke Co., Ltd.
城市配套服务商	an integrated urban service provider
住宅开发	housing development
物业服务	property service
物流仓储	logistic storage
长租公寓	long-term rental apartments
珠三角	the Pearl River Delta
长三角	the Yangtze River Delta

万科企业股份有限公司成立于 1984 年，1988 年进入房地产行业，经过近 30 年的发展，已成为国内领先的房地产公司。2016 年公司首次跻身《财富》"世界 500 强"，位列榜单第 356 位；2017 年再度上榜，位列榜单第 307 位。//

公司定位于城市配套服务商，坚持"为普通人盖好房子，盖有人用的房子"，坚持与城市同步发展、与客户同步发展的两条主线。公司核心业务包括住宅开发和物业服务。// 近年来，公司积极拓展业务版图，进入商业开发和运营、物流仓储、冰雪度假、长租公寓、养老、教育、"轨道＋物业"等领域。//

公司聚焦城市圈带的发展战略。截至 2016 年年底，万科地产已经进入中国大陆 65 个城市，分布在以珠三角为核心的南方区域、以长三角为核心的上海区域、以北京为核心的京津冀区域，以及中西部区域。//

Text F Google Inc.

主题导入

谷歌公司是全球知名的互联网公司，创建于1998年。谷歌在互联网搜索、云计算等领域为世界翘楚。2016年谷歌的品牌价值超越苹果，成为全球第一。以下是关于谷歌产品及企业文化的介绍。

请先熟悉列出的词汇与短语再听录音，并在录音停顿时将下列篇章口译成汉语。

词汇与短语

cloud computing	云计算
acquisition	并购
to nominate	提名
attraction index	吸引力指数

Google Inc. is an American multinational corporation that provides Internet-related products and services, including Internet search, cloud computing, software and advertising technologies. //

The company was founded by Larry Page and Sergey Brin while both attended Stanford University. Google was first incorporated as a privately held company on September 4, 1998, and its initial public offering followed on August 19, 2004. //

The company's mission statement from the outset was "to organize the world's information and make it universally accessible and useful" and the company's unofficial slogan is "Don't be evil". //

Rapid growth since incorporation has triggered a chain of products, acquisitions, and partnerships beyond the company's core web search engine. The company offers online productivity software including emails, office suite, and social networking. //

Google's products extend to the desktop as well, with applications for web browsing, organizing and editing photos, and instant messaging. Google leads the development of the Android mobile operating system, as well as the Google Chrome OS browser-only operating system. //

Google is known for having an informal corporate culture. On *Fortune* magazine's list of best companies to work for, Google ranked first in 2007, 2008 and 2012 and fourth in 2013 and 2014. Google was also nominated in 2015 to be the world's most attractive employer to graduating students in the Universal Communications Talent Attraction Index. //

第 4 单元　短期记忆 1/公司简介

情景口译

提示：
学生三人或四人一组，根据下面的主题提示进行模拟口译，注意使用本单元介绍的技能和句型。

主题一　SDL 公司介绍

参与人： 1. 孙睿女士，SDL 公司发言人

2. 参加语言服务业年会的中外嘉宾

3. 译员

地　点： 某酒店多功能厅

内　容： 1. 孙女士简要介绍 SDL 公司的成立背景

2. 孙女士利用大数据介绍 SDL 公司在全球语言服务业所处的地位和作用

3. 孙女士解析 SDL 公司的理念及相关产品等

主题二　某手机公司基本情况介绍

参与人： 1. 陈晓诺女士，某手机公司人力资源部主管

2. 海外人才招聘会的参会人员

3. 译员

内　容： 1. 陈女士讲述该公司的创办背景

2. 陈女士介绍该公司的理念和企业文化

3. 陈女士简述该公司手机主要的功能和特点

4. 陈女士介绍该公司旗下的其他主要产品

5. 陈女士展望公司发展方向及 2020 年发展目标

✲ 句式扩展

1. Now, I'd like to move from these timely initiatives to our timeless values, values that bind us together and make this company work unlike any institution in the world.

   现在我要从这些当前的计划转向我们公司永恒的价值观，就是这些价值观将我们紧紧联系在一起，使我们与世界上其他任何公司都不相同。

2. As the first professional banquet catering service company in Beijing, our goal is to provide access to delicious food, large selections of beverages and excellent service.

   作为北京第一家专业宴会餐饮服务公司，我们致力于为社会各界提供美味的食品、大量可供挑选的特色酒水及优质的服务。

3. So I made the decision to switch gear and become a consumer-oriented search site.

   所以我决定将公司转型成为一家客户导向型的搜索网站。

4. For Citibank, credit cards are essential to our success and leadership in global consumer banking.

   信用卡业务对于保证花旗银行在全球个人银行业各方面的领导地位和成功来说至关重要。

5. Our diversity, our shared culture and our unified purpose are the defining element that enables our company to touch lives and improve life every day.

   我们的多元化、共享文化以及一致的目标是我们的基石，使我们公司每天都在走进生活、改善生活。

6. McDonald's multi-national, multi-billion dollar business and standardized products and procedures have come to symbolize globalization and the American way of life.

   麦当劳跨国经营，拥有数十亿美元资产。其标准化的产品和业务流程体现了全球化和美国式的生活方式。

7. The market capitalization of our company is greater than the GDP of many countries, and it serves consumers in more than 180 countries and regions.

   我们公司的市场资本额超过许多国家的国内生产总值，消费者遍布180多个国家和地区。

8. Stature comes both responsibility and opportunity. Our responsibility is to be an ethical corporate citizen, but our opportunity is something far greater, and is embodied in our purpose.

   这种规模带来的是责任和机遇。我们的责任是做一个符合社会道德要求的企业公民，我们的机遇更是高瞻远瞩，与我们的目标息息相关。

9. So what we try to do in every place we've gone is to make sure that the fundamental foundation of what has built the company around the cultural values is in place first.

   因此我们无论到哪一个市场都要确定最基本且首要的事情，就是在公司的价值和文化的准绳上来建立每一个市场。

10. Together, we represent around 145 nationalities. Our recruiting and development philosophy to "build from within" fosters a strong culture of trust and shared experiences.

    我们的员工来自近 145 个国家。"内部提升"的招聘和培养理念营造了信任与共享的强大企业文化。

11. 我们公司是目前中国最大的互联网综合服务提供商之一，也是中国服务用户最多的互联网企业之一。

    Currently our company has grown into one of the largest Internet comprehensive service providers, and one of the Internet companies serving the most users in China.

12. 面向未来，坚持自主创新，梳理民族品牌是我们公司的长远发展规划。

    Looking forward, our company remains committed to enhancing its development and innovation capabilities while strengthening its nationwide branding for its long term development.

13. 我们是中国最大的食品零售企业之一，在这个世界上人口最多的国家拥有逾 3 000 家门店，销售网络比与它旗鼓相当的西方竞争对手家乐福和沃尔玛大得多。

    We are now one of the largest food retailers in China, with more than 3,000 stores and a much wider network in the world's most populous country than close western rivals Carrefour and Wal-Mart.

14. 中国最大图书销售网站当当网本周二在纽约证交所上市，融资 2.72 亿美元，比目标融资额多出近四分之一。

    Dangdang, China's leading online bookseller, raised 272 million USD, almost a quarter more than originally planned, in its New York Stock Exchange IPO on Tuesday.

15. 我们集团创立于 1990 年，创业 27 年来坚持创新精神，创立了世界级的品牌。

    Founded in 1990, our Group has been dedicated to innovation and creating a world famous brand over the past 27 years.

16. 我们集团从一个濒临破产的集体小厂发展成为全球拥有 7 万多名员工的国际集团，2016 年营业额达到 2 468 亿元人民币。

Originally a small collective plant on the verge of bankruptcy, our group has now grown into an international group which has more than 70,000 employees around the globe and realizes a turnover of 246.8 billion RMB in 2016.

17. 美国服装零售商 GATE 今年将在中国开设四家门店和一个电子商务业务单位,这是其十多年来最大规模的海外扩张。

    GATE, the U.S. clothing retailer, is to open four stores and an e-commerce operation in China this year in its most significant overseas expansion in more than a decade.

18. 中国是瑞银的战略重点。

    China is a strategic priority for UBS Group.

19. 我们成功的基础源自企业价值和企业文化。

    The foundation of our success has been our cultural values of the company.

20. 我们公司在中国拥有 16 个研发中心,分布在北京、南京、杭州、上海和深圳,共有 2 500 多名合格的工程技术人员,几乎占公司在中国雇员总数的 8%。

    Our company now has 16 Research and Development centers in China, located in Beijing, Nanjing, Hangzhou, Shanghai and Shenzhen, with over 2,500 highly qualified engineers comprising almost 8% of the total workforce in China.

✵ 口译小贴士

宴会上的口译

由于工作需要,译员经常需要随同他人参加各类宴会,有时是非常隆重的晚宴、大型招待会,有时也可能是小型冷餐会或是工作餐。与会议、谈判相比,宴会通常没有那么正式,气氛更加轻松活泼,话题也可能包罗万象。因此,宴会场合对译员来说仍是极具挑战意义的战场。

首先,在宴会上,译员要尽量选择有利于翻译的就座位置。如果译员负责为一位主要人物翻译,译员需要紧随其左右。如果被安排的位置与该人物距离较远,不便于做口译工作,译员可酌情要求移到靠近翻译对象的位置。

如果译员被要求在酒会上帮助有需要的人,那么在餐桌上,译员要承担临近人员的翻译任务,不能只为一两个人翻译,要兼顾其他人员的需求。

其次，译员在宴会上需要格外注意饮食方面的翻译，需要清楚：翻译内容可能与饮食有关或由饮食引起。曾流传这样一件翻译尴尬事。在一次晚宴上，一位嘉宾说"这不是小葱拌豆腐——一清二白吗？"译员未加思索翻译成"It is as clear as crystal"。这时，这位来宾又饶有兴致地对外宾说"你们国家有豆腐吗？"译员一愣，只好硬着头皮接着翻译："Do you produce crystal in your country?"（你们国家有水晶么？）外宾十分干脆地说"Yes"。译员明知不妙，但无奈"Yes"一词尽人皆知，只好照实翻译为"有啊！"谁知来宾接着追问道："是南豆腐，还是北豆腐？"这时，译员才明白撑不下去了。

另外，译员须注意在宴会上吃东西时要谨慎，不能因为吃饭耽误了翻译。尽量小口、多餐、饮料配合。不要吃带骨头的、有刺的，难以吞咽的东西。译员要有心理准备，在宴会上可能会常常吃不上饭，或吃不好饭。所以需要随身带些可补充能量的吃食，以备不时之需。过好吃饭这一关，对译员来说既有利于工作，又有利于健康。有人总结："三流的译员吃不好也翻不好；二流的译员吃得好也翻得好；一流的译员既吃得好又翻得好，还能帮忙把领导吃不了的给消灭掉。"

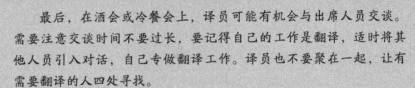

最后，在酒会或冷餐会上，译员可能有机会与出席人员交谈。需要注意交谈时间不要过长，要记得自己的工作是翻译，适时将其他人员引入对话，自己专做翻译工作。译员也不要聚在一起，让有需要翻译的人四处寻找。

短期记忆 2/ 商业广告

第 5 单元

口译主题：商业广告

商业广告是通过大众传媒所进行的有关商品、劳务、观念等方面信息的有说服力的促销活动。

商业广告可分为商品广告、劳务广告以及声誉广告。

商品广告又称产品广告。它是以销售为导向，介绍商品的质量、功能、价格、品牌、生产厂家、销售地点以及该商品的独到之处等有关商品本身的一切信息。

劳务广告是一种服务广告，比如：介绍银行、保险、旅游、饭店、车辆出租、家电维修、房屋搬迁等内容的广告。

声誉广告又称公关广告、形象广告，它是指通过一定的媒介，把企业有关的信息有计划地传播给公众的广告。这类广告的目的是为了引起公众对企业的注意和好感，获得合作机会，从而提高企业知名度和美誉度，树立良好的企业形象。

✻ 学习目标

　　了解短期记忆的训练方法
　　了解商业广告的文体特点
　　掌握商业广告中的常用口译句式

✴ 技巧讲解

逻辑记忆和形象记忆是口译过程中提高记忆效率的方法，在平时的训练中，译员也可以运用多种训练手段提升自己的短期记忆力。以下是几种常用的口译记忆训练方法。

逻辑训练

逻辑训练可以提高短期记忆的容量、速度和准确度，也是逻辑记忆的前提和基础。逻辑训练要求训练者在听清讲话内容的同时，快速确定讲话的中心思想和信息点及其关键词，同时分清信息点的主次，以及各信息点之间的逻辑关系。该训练的目的在于通过练习，训练者可以更好地把握信息的逻辑关系，使信息规整有序，以增加短时记忆的容量。在翻译产出阶段，训练者只要依照逻辑关系，利用关键词去激活相关信息，就能复原所有主要信息来完成忠实翻译。分析、论证、推理性语篇最适合培养训练者的逻辑思维能力。

练习中，训练者听完讲话后，让其说明讲话的中心内容、从几个方面进行说明、几个方面关系如何等。另外，也可以让训练者听一些缺乏语篇连贯性或语言次序颠倒的材料，听过后按正常语篇的要求，梳理成一段主题明确、语义连贯的发言。

复述练习

复述练习可以分为源语复述练习和目的语复述练习，前者是后者的基础。

在源语复述练习中，训练者选取一段大约 200 个词的音频，材料的难度和长度可根据自己的水平而定。听的时候不要记笔记，听完后用同种语言复述材料的内容。要首先把握材料的主要内容，体会各个信息点之间的逻辑关系，然后尽可能记住细节。训练起始阶段应尽量使用源语的字词进行复述。由于训练者的英文水平一般不及母语，因此建议多选用英文材料进行记忆练习，同时可以提高听力理解能力。

在目的语复述练习中，训练者选取一段大约 200 个词的音频，材料的难度和长度可根据自己的水平而定。在听的过程中不记笔记。听完材料后，用目的语进行复述。该练习把记忆训练和语言转换有机地结合在了一起。

影子跟读

影子跟读是指听到发言人的讲话后用源语同步或晚几秒进行跟读。跟读时需要耳朵、嘴巴、脑子同时工作，听、说、记同步进行。它是用来提升训练者短期记忆能力以及听说同步能力和改进语音语调非常有效的训练方法，也是训练者练习同声传译技巧的常用方法。

影子跟读可以分成两个阶段：第一个阶段，用源语几乎同步地跟读发言人的讲话。刚开始练习可能比较难，训练者可以边看文字边跟读，但要把注意力放在"听"上，而不是"看"上。内容熟悉之后，不看文字，再练习跟读。这样一点点跟上发言人的讲话，做到同步跟读。第二个阶段，迟于原文两个词或 3~5 秒，乃至一句话的时间跟读。

经过上面两个阶段的练习后，可以在跟读训练中加入干扰因素，比如：边跟读边写数字或英文 26 个字母，来进行多任务协作练习，训练耳、口、手、脑同时工作的协调性。

影子练习需要注意力非常集中。在高语速条件下，边跟读边完全理解语义是有相当难度的，但这种训练可以提升短期记忆能力，为口译打下扎实的基础。

✻ 技巧练习

🎧 1. 请听录音并同步跟读，然后复述。

这是一个健康至上的年代。无数专家不止一次地表示睡眠对于人体健康的重要性。一个良好的睡眠将是每日工作的良好开端。作为一个日理万机的成功人士，需要时刻保持精力充沛，而一张好床就如引擎一般，将带来无限动力。历史悠久的海丝腾是全球奢华床具的传奇，定义着最高品质，其所带来的完美睡眠体验，能让人更加健康、强壮、充满魅力、容光焕发。海丝腾是品味非凡、眼光独到之者的最佳之选。

🎧 2. 下面 8 段录音是 2016 年 12 月驻英国大使刘晓明在华为冬季音乐会上的致辞，但语序已经被打乱。请听录音，将 8 段录音排序，并说明理由。

① In Huawei UK, we see a fine example of Chinese company doing business in this country.

② Ten years on, Huawei UK is highly acclaimed for its devotion to charity and strong sense of corporate social responsibility.

③ I hope Huawei UK will continue to work for sustainable development. I hope your business will grow stronger and I hope you will continue to give back to the local community.

④ But much more than that, Huawei UK is also a proud leader in the construction, research and development of high-speed broadband network in Britain.

⑤ It is a pleasure to join you again for the winter concert of Huawei Technologies UK. This is the 7th consecutive winter charity concert that Huawei has hosted in London. Ten years ago, Huawei UK became a member of the Prince's Trust.

⑥ I am sure your continued success in this country will help build stronger business relationship between China and the UK.

⑦ Thank you!

⑧ Huawei's success in Britain is a microcosm of the overall China-UK business cooperation. It also heralds a future of even stronger business ties between our two countries.

主题口译

Text A　农夫山泉，甜并快乐着

主题导入

广告即"广而告之"之意。作为一种传递信息的活动，广告是企业应用最广的促销方式和营销手段。提起农夫山泉，不免会让人想到那句脍炙人口的广告语"农夫山泉有点甜"。以下是农夫山泉广告策略的解析。

请先熟悉列出的词汇与短语再听录音，并在录音停顿时将下列篇章口译成英语。

词汇与短语

乐百氏	Robust
饮用水	drinking water
农夫山泉	Nongfu Spring
净化	purification
代名词	to be synonymous with

　　1998年，娃哈哈、乐百氏以及其他众多的饮用水品牌大战已是硝烟四起，而且在娃哈哈和乐百氏面前，刚刚问世的农夫山泉显得势单力薄；另外，农夫山泉只从千岛湖取水，运输成本高昂。//

　　农夫山泉在这个时候切入市场，并在短短几年内抵抗住了众多国内外品牌的冲击，稳居行业三甲，成功要素之一在于其差异化营销之策。而差异化的直接表现来自于"有点甜"的概念创意——"农夫山泉有点甜"。//

　　农夫山泉真的有点甜吗？非也，营销传播概念而已。农夫山泉的水来自千岛湖，是从很多大山中汇总的泉水，经过千岛湖的自净、净化，完全可以说是甜美的泉水。但怎样才能让消费者直观形象地认识到农夫山泉的"出身"，怎样形成美好的"甘泉"印象？这就需要一个简单而形象的营销传播概念。//

　　"农夫山泉有点甜"并不要求水一定得有点甜，甜水是好水的代名词，正如咖啡味道本来很苦，但雀巢咖啡却说"味道好极了"，说明是好咖啡。一样，中文有"甘泉"一词，解释就是甜美的水。"甜"不仅传递了良好的产品品质信息，还直接让人联想到了甘甜爽口的泉水，喝起来自然感觉"有点甜"。//

Text B Tesla's Advertising Strategy

主题导入

特斯拉是一家美国电动车及能源公司，产销电动车、太阳能板及储能设备。特斯拉生产的电动汽车因其漂亮的外形、简单的操作、充沛的动力受到了消费者的欢迎。它的销售模式更是突破了传统销售方式。以下是特斯拉广告战略的分析。

请先熟悉列出的词汇与短语再听录音，并在录音停顿时将下列篇章口译成汉语。

词汇与短语

Chief Marketing Officer	首席营销官
to subscribe	订购
newsletter	简报
to strike a chord	引起共鸣
advocate	支持者
buzz	网络口碑

Quickly, name one advertisement you've seen recently from Tesla Motors themselves? OK, name any advertisement you've seen from the company, ever? Tesla's marketing strategy is as disruptive as its business model. It lets you and me advertise for them, for free. //

Tesla does not spend millions of dollars in a traditional ad campaign. The company has no advertising, no ad agency, no Chief Marketing Officer, no dealer network. And that's no problem. //

If you drop by the Tesla forums, you'll see a community of passionate fans discussing how to market Tesla better. There are over 55,000 people subscribing to the newsletter. The brand has clearly struck a chord with its fans. //

Tesla fans are crazy advocates. They attach deep emotional significance to the car. They're not just paying for a mode of transportation. They're paying for a slice of the future. //

Alexis Georgeson, the spokeswoman of the company once said: at the moment, the stores are their advertising. Tesla is very confident that 20,000-plus cars a year can be sold without paid advertising. Paid advertising may be something the company will consider. But it's certainly not something crucial for sales at present. //

She has also mentioned that Tesla has no plans to hire agencies or run ads in the near future. The in-house marketing team has only seven staffers and an internal team runs the website, where customers order directly. By contrast, Nissan, GM, Toyota, and Ford have deep marketing budgets that allow them to run some of the most creative advertising campaigns to date. //

However, Tesla Motors doesn't have that luxury, yet. Tesla's capital investment is used to lay down the foundation for tomorrow's success. One thing Tesla does well with a minimum cash flow is to create a buzz. Without spending any money on direct advertising campaigns, Elon Musk and the creative minds behind the company know how to generate buzz, and in this modern age, that means using social media. //

Text C "创意"本身真是没有创意：创意广告的小秘密

主题导入

广告创意，简单来说，就是通过大胆新奇的手法来制造与众不同的视听效果，最大限度地吸引消费者，从而达到品牌声名传播与产品营销的目的。其实，广告创意不是天马行空的，而是有章可循的。以下揭示了创意广告中的常用模式。

请先熟悉列出的词汇与短语再听录音，并在录音停顿时将下列篇章口译成英语。

词汇与短语

转发	to forward
模板	template
形象化类比（模板）	Pictorial Analogy Template
极端情景（模板）	Extreme Situation Template
呈现后果（模板）	Consequences Template
制造竞争（模板）	Competition Template
互动实验（模板）	Interactive Experiment Template
改变维度（模板）	Dimensionality Alteration Template
鞋柜	shoe cabinet
头皮	scalp
头皮屑	dandruff

大家都知道，"创意"对广告来说非常重要。实际上，在互联网时代，"有趣的创意"更加重要——既然你无法像电视广告那样强迫别人关注，那么依靠"好玩的创意"来引起大量的转发和关注就尤其关键。//

大部分人的理解是：把一群人放到会议室里奇思妙想、发散思维，然后就可以得到"伟大的创意"。很多人甚至把"广告创意"想象成了"不经过专业的学习和训练就能自动掌握的东西"。//

但是实际上，"创意"的过程并没有大多数人想象得那么有"创意"：很多的创意是遵循规则的产物，是大量学习的结果，而不是漫无方向的发散思维。研究发现，大量的创意广告实际上遵循了6大模板，即形象化类比、极端情景、呈现后果、制造竞争、互动实验和改变维度。巧妙地使用这6大模板可以在广告中"人为地制造惊叹"。//

长城是中国的象征，超人是正义的象征，子弹是速度的象征……总之，几乎任何一个抽象的概念你都可以找到不止一个"象征物"。把它同自己产品的某个方面（比如：形状、

LOGO、包装)结合起来,你就得到了一个"形象化类比"的创意广告。//

极端情景模板指的是找到一个情形,在该情景下,产品的一个卖点重要到了不切实际的程度。比如:宜家为了突出"鞋柜不够用了,你需要买个好鞋柜",呈现一张因为鞋子放不下而不得不把一只鞋塞到另一只鞋的图片。//

让消费者根据广告的描述,完成一个行动,或者让消费者想象完成行动的情景,这就是利用互动实验模板进行广告创意。比如:洗发水广告用一个黑色的纸贴头皮,让人看到后就会这么做(或者这么想),从而对自己的头皮屑问题更加敏感。//

从以上的例子不难看出,如果利用好这6个模板,你也可以设计出一个创意十足的广告!//

Text D How GoPro Is Transforming Advertising

主题导入

GoPro 公司是生产可佩戴照相机和其配件的公司。该公司将客户拍摄的内容发布到网络社交媒体中,无形中帮助公司打出了广告,扩大了公司影响,获得了优厚的利润。以下是这种营销方式的介绍。

请先熟悉列出的词汇与短语再听录音,并在录音停顿时将下列篇章口译成汉语。

词汇与短语

to harness	利用
to dispel	消除、驱散
to affix to	贴上
BASE jumper	定点跳伞运动员
footage	录像
financial disclosure	财务披露
public offering	公开发售
Wall Street Daily	《华尔街日报》
vanguard	先锋
compelling	引人注目

GoPro's rising stock prices just show that harnessing content created by the user is not just an affordable marketing strategy; it's also pretty powerful stuff. //

Some people still think of user-generated content as shaky videos or filtered photos, only good for sharing with family or friends on social media. But that is an outdated concept, and one which GoPro would dispel. //

Many media platforms are proving that user-generated content has the quality to captivate audiences. Video cameras affixed to the helmets of skiers, snowboarders, and BASE jumpers generate footage for the slickest television commercials, and Instagram photos from fashion fans are now the center of online catalogues for major fashion brands. //

第 5 单元　短期记忆 2/ 商业广告

Everyone got a glimpse of the power of user-generated content, thanks to GoPro's recent financial disclosures leading up to its public offering. The company more than doubled its net income from 2010 to 2011 to $24.6 million but only spent $50,000 more in marketing costs to do it, according to *Wall Street Daily*. // And GoPro repeated the feat in 2013, increasing marketing costs by only $41,000, but making $28 million more in net income. //

Embedded in those numbers is the multi-million-dollar marketing and advertising value of user-generated content. In place of an art director, acting cast, and team of videographers, GoPro simply hands a wearable camera to an amazing athlete and gets back advertising and marketing gold. // Regular customers have become advertisers on a smaller scale, shooting high-quality video, loading it onto YouTube and social networks, and advertising the capabilities of the cameras to friends, family, and complete strangers. //

Technological advancements have made user-generated content both compelling and high-quality, and GoPro proves that a tiny camera, in the hands of the right people, can create captivating content that will gain an audience no matter what purpose it is used for: social media marketing, advertising, or television programming. //

Text E　西安

主题导入

西安，古城"长安"，是陕西省省会，著名的旅游城市。西安是中国历史上建都朝代最多、时间最长、建都最早、影响力最大的都城。中国历史上最为强盛的周、秦、汉、隋、唐等朝代都建都于此。著名的秦始皇兵马俑、华清池、大雁塔等都坐落于此。以下是西安城市宣传片的解说。

请先熟悉列出的词汇与短语再听录音，并在录音停顿时将下列篇章口译成英语。

词汇与短语

丝路	the Silk Road
名胜古迹	historical sites
周礼	rites of the Zhou Dynasty
秦制	institutional make-up of the Qin Dynasty
汉风唐韵	charm of the Han and Tang dynasties
大明宫	Daming Palace
大雁塔	Buddha Dayan Pagoda

华夏元脉、千年帝都、丝路起点、龙的故乡。西安，这座有着 3 100 年建城史和 1 100 年的建都史的中国城市，和雅典、开罗、罗马并称为世界四大文明古都。// 它浓缩了

5 000年华夏文明的遗传基因,印记着华夏民族生生不息的奋斗精神,是亿万中华儿女的精神家园。//

走进西安就是走进中国历史博物馆。名胜古迹星罗棋布,稀世文物灿若星辰,金匾丹青赏心悦目,古槐青砖意境深邃。西安的每一寸土地都沉淀着厚重的传统文化,都承载着久远的中华文明。// 从蓝田猿人、仓颉造字到周礼秦制、汉风唐韵。无数史书典籍,出土文物和古迹遗址,深情地述说着这座中华人文之都的辉煌和沧桑。//

今天,千年古都的西安正依托深厚的人文资源,引领着城市文化复兴之路。大雁塔北广场欢快的音乐喷泉,曲江池荡漾的画舫游舟,大明宫国家遗址公园,檐牙高啄的丹凤门楼,中国"博物馆之城"的宏伟构想,无不体现出西安在城市化和现代化进程中对历史的尊重和文化的敬仰。// 保护文化遗产,延续中华文脉,滋养现代文明,西安成功开创了一种古城保护与发展的崭新模式。//

Text F Google's Self-Driving Car

主题导入

谷歌无人驾驶汽车是谷歌公司的Google X实验室研发的全自动驾驶汽车,不需要驾驶者就能启动、行驶及停止。以下是谷歌无人驾驶汽车的相关介绍。

请先熟悉列出的词汇与短语再听录音,并在录音停顿时将下列篇章口译成汉语。

词汇与短语

autonomously	独立自主地
minus	没有
mishaps	灾祸
prototype	原型;雏形
steering wheel	方向盘
pedal	踏板
from scratch	白手起家;从头做起
hitch	故障
intersection	十字路口
sonar	声呐
stereo camera	立体照相机

Google has been long working on self-driving cars that would autonomously take the passengers to their desired destination minus any road mishaps. As a part of Google X project, this prototype of a self-driving car will have no steering wheel or pedals, unlike their previous self-driven versions that were actually normal vehicles made by Toyota and Lexus. // This self-driven vehicle, however, is an independent prototype that has been built from scratch and can take the responsibility of driving even in crowded streets without a hitch. //

This self-driving prototype vehicle is capable of detecting objects even at a distance of two full length football fields which is vital on interstate highways and cities with a lot of intersections. //

The current prototype version has a top speed of 25 miles per hour, is a two-seater car, is started by a start/stop button, has a screen showing the route/map and looks like a very basic design with no craving for luxury or looks. That is fully justified as Google is developing this vehicle keeping in mind road safety and mobility for millions of people on the road. //

Google's driverless car tech uses an array of detection technologies, including sonar devices, stereo cameras, lasers, and radar. All these components have different ranges and fields of view, but each serves a particular purpose according to the patent filings Google has made on its driverless cars. //

In Google's current process, a human driver would take control, and (so far) safely guide the car. But fascinatingly, in the circumstances when a human driver has to take over, what the Google car would have done is also recorded, so that engineers can test what would have happened in extreme circumstances without endangering the public. //

❉ 情景口译

提示：

学生三人或四人一组，根据下面的主题提示进行模拟口译，注意使用本单元介绍的技能和句型。

主题一　某品牌巧克力的广告创意

参与人： 1. 任星先生，某国际食品（中国）有限公司广告部经理

2. 参加营销大会的国内外来宾

3. 译员

地　点： 某酒店多功能厅

内　容： 1. 任先生介绍该品牌巧克力的特点

2. 任先生讲述该品牌巧克力背后的故事

3. 任先生简述该品牌巧克力的 4P 营销策略

4. 任先生详细解析该品牌巧克力的几款广告创意

 **主题二　某品牌最新运动手环**

参与人： 1. 斯威夫特女士，某体育用品公司的技术总监
2. 参加产品发布会的中外嘉宾
3. 译员

内　容： 1. 斯威夫特女士介绍该款运动手环的研发理念
2. 斯威夫特女士利用实物介绍该运动手环的外观和材质
3. 斯威夫特女士介绍并演示该运动手环的技术支持和新增性能
4. 斯威夫特女士详细分析该运动手环的独到之处

✲ 句式扩展

1. The company has enough cash and investments in hand to fund its losses for at least the next few years.

   该公司还有足够的现金和投资去对冲至少未来几年的损失。

2. Y company's most recent quarter shows that it has not lost the ability to surprise.

   Y公司最新一季度的财务报表显示，其仍未失去创造惊喜的能力。

3. One school of thought says brands succeed mainly by inspiring loyalty.

   一种学派认为品牌的成功主要依靠激发消费者的忠诚度。

4. We ran advertising to remind people of the joy of toys. But mostly it was just being straight with people.

   我们通过广告提醒人们玩具带来的快乐，但最主要的是，对消费者坦诚。

5. For marketers who are looking to advertise to Chinese consumers, the social platform WeChat is attractive.

   对于希望对中国消费者投放广告的商人来说，微信这个社交平台无疑是极具吸引力的。

6. The company now owns a 9.3% market share and the number two spot in China's online ad market.

第 5 单元　短期记忆 2/ 商业广告

该公司拥有 9.3% 的市场份额，在中国互联网广告市场上占据着第二把交椅。

7. A massive 60% jump in online advertising sales to a record of 6.5 billion RMB means that T company's ad revenue is now equivalent to 39% of B company's.

   T 公司的网络广告收入飙升 60%，达到创纪录的 65 亿元人民币。这表明 T 公司现在的广告收入已经达到了 B 公司的 39%。

8. Advertising and subscription revenues were in danger of burning to the ground amid the proliferation of digital media.

   在迅猛发展的数字媒体的包围下，传统媒体的广告和订阅收入面临荡然无存的危险。

9. The company is planning its largest global marketing campaign to support the launch of the phone.

   该公司正在酝酿一场史上最大规模的全球营销战来推广该款手机。

10. At about 3.8 million USD for a 30-second spot, an ad on this year's Super Bowl was easily the most expensive ad buy on television.

    30 秒广告时段收费约 380 万美元，今年"超级碗"（美国橄榄球联盟年度冠军赛）决赛广告时段，轻松成为美国有史以来最昂贵的电视广告。

11. 无论是大使馆、各类社会组织、公司、家庭宴客或举办各类宴会活动，我们公司都会竭诚为您提供高品质服务。

    Our company wholeheartedly provides high-quality service for embassies, social organizations, companies and families that entertain guests or hold different types of banquets.

12. 智慧电讯集团将推出更多汇聚顶尖科技的新产品。

    Telewise Group will launch more new products that boasts cutting-edge technology.

13. 一种获得免费广告的方法是写一篇与企业产品相关的文章，提交给所有专门发布有关信息的出版物和媒体。

    One way to get free advertising is to write an article relative to your particular products and submit it to all the publications and media dealing in the dissemination of related information.

14. 该酒店信奉的商业价值使其不仅成为员工理想的工作场所，也是旅客满意的下榻之处。

    The hotel believes in a set of business values that make it a desirable place for employees to work in and a satisfying place for travelers to stay in.

15. 促销组合的四个可能存在的要素是：广告、个人销售、公关及促销。

    The four possible elements of a promotion mix are advertising, personal selling, public relations, and sales promotion.

16. 对零售商们来说，真正可以提高生意利润的重要因素，不是价格战，也不是花样繁多的促销战，而是服务与品类管理。

    To the retailers, the important factors to improve their profit are not price war or war of promoting sales, but service and category management.

17. 欢迎各位光临本公司数码摄像机新品发布会。今天这个发布会也是本年度第一次和媒体朋友交流沟通的盛会。

    Welcome to our new DV products release ceremony. It's also the very first communication between our company and the media friends this year.

18. 我们的产品深受世界各地人们的欢迎，因为他们品质优良、风格新颖、技术精湛、设计时尚、价格合理。

    Our products are well received over the world for their excellent quality, unique style, sophisticated technology, modern design and competitive price.

19. 我们的产品远销英国、美国、日本、意大利和东南亚，深受消费者好评。

    Our products are sold in Britain, America, Japan, Italy and Southeast Asia and well appreciated by the purchasers.

20. 该品牌的耳机在国际市场上极具竞争力，属同类产品中的畅销品。

    Earphones of this brand are competitive in the international market and are the best-selling products of their kind.

✲ 口译小贴士

商务考察中的口译礼仪

译员经常需要陪同外商来华参观或陪同企业的相关人员进行境外考察。考察通常包括对工厂或公司的视察，了解当地的自然和人文环境、政策法规等。在陪同期间，需要做好以下准备：

第5单元 短期记忆2/商业广告

1. 熟悉中外双方人员的口音。要争取尽快适应外方人士的口音。因为商务活动中的外商往往来自世界各地，所说的英语也会带有各国各地的口音，给听力造成障碍。因此，尽量争取在实地考察之前就多与外方接触，熟悉他们的口音和表达习惯。同时，译员也要留意中方人员口音。由于中国方言差异较大，用词和表达方式差异较大。即使中方人员说普通话，若带着浓重的口音，也不容易让人听懂。因此不仅要事先了解外方人员的口音特点，也要了解中方人员的口音，做到万无一失。

2. 事先了解参观工厂的环境，掌握可能涉及的术语。参观工厂时往往工人在工作，噪音非常大，加上大家边走边说，译员有时很难听清对方说的话。这时译员必须多问，不要一知半解地胡乱翻译。另外，了解参观的目的、要协商的问题以及参观流程都会帮助译员克服因陌生术语和技术等带来的紧张感。

3. 在陪同旅行期间，要有良好的服务意识和组织协调能力。在完成口译工作之外，还要根据情况协调同行人的吃、住、行、用、玩等事务性工作。

4. 要对旅游路线、旅游景点可能涉及的历史、典故、诗词、风俗、宗教、天文、地理、政治、经济、人文、美食等领域做好充分准备。针对不同层次的客人采取灵活的方法，像讲故事或聊天一样介绍景点、食物或人文等。

口译笔记 1/商务陈述

第 6 单元

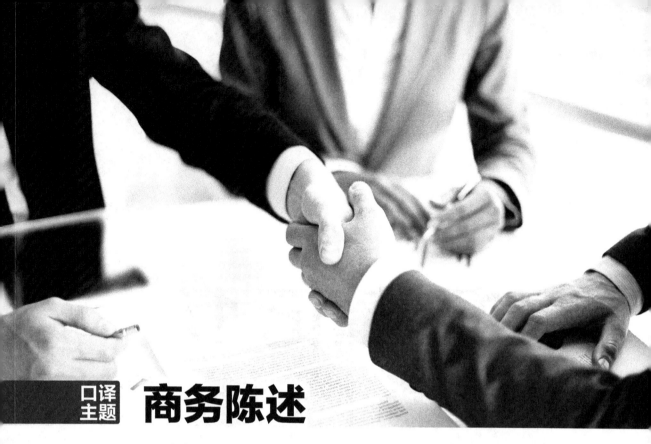

口译主题 商务陈述

商务陈述是一个比较宽泛的概念，它可以指代任何商务场合中进行的介绍性陈述。人们在陈述商业提案时，多数情况下并不是在单纯地传达信息，而是在说服别人，促使客户签订协议或者进行投资。比如：某公司的研发主管做出提案，希望得到高层主管的授权，向某个关键项目投入更多资金；设计师展示公寓概念的设计；广告公司总监向潜在客户展示新的市场创意；销售人员进行新产品介绍等，这些都是商务陈述的范畴。

商务陈述通常属于介绍性演讲，要简明扼要地描述产品、项目、设计、提案等的特性、特点等要点。在多媒体的广泛应用下，幻灯片、视频、音频等声光电集一体的表达方式通常也运用在商务陈述中。

✱ 学习目标

    了解口译笔记的基本原则和基本要求

    逐步了解口译的笔记符号，并开始建立自己的笔记系统

    了解商务陈述的文体特点

    掌握商务陈述中的常用口译句式

✲ 技巧讲解

口译笔记是一项重要的口译技能。在很多口译场合中,发言人为了使自己的意思表达得完整、连贯,通常要持续发言几分钟、十几分钟,甚至几十分钟才会停下来。在这种情况下,单纯依靠短期记忆,译员是无法完全记住讲话内容的。而且,如果在讲话过程中,出现数字、人名、地名、专有名词等,全凭短期记忆进行口译的难度就更大了。因此,熟练地运用口译笔记可以帮助译员有效地补充短期记忆,提高口译质量。

口译笔记的功能和作用

口译笔记是短期记忆的有效补充,可以减轻译员的记忆负担。口译笔记是对讲话内容逻辑的梳理和意思的高度概括,可以帮助译员回想起所听到的信息,组织译语,进行表达。此外,口译笔记可以有效记录数字、人名、地名、专有名词等难以准确记忆的信息,保证口译的质量。

口译笔记可以提高译员工作的耐久度。译员的工作通常要持续一整天或是连续几天,有时甚至要从大清早工作到午夜,工作的强度大、时间长,全凭脑力。有效的口译笔记可以帮助译员减轻大脑负担,提高工作的耐久度,从而保证口译质量始终如一。

口译笔记的特点

1. 简约性。由于时间的限制,口译笔记不可能、也不需要做到面面俱到、词句分明。译员要边听边记,记录的是能够提示内容的关键信息点,还要理顺逻辑关系。为了最大限度地节省时间和精力,译员使用简洁易懂的符号进行记录,这也体现了口译笔记的简约性。

2. 个性化。口译笔记既不同于课堂笔记,也不同于速记。课堂笔记通常是用一种语言系统地记录完整的课堂内容以便课后复习使用;而速记则是用特别简单的记音符号和词语缩写符号迅速记录语言的方法,可以快速地,一字不漏地记录完整的内容,拥有系统、完整的体系。而口译笔记只是为译员自己服务,是因人而异的,没有标准的笔记可供效仿,只有一些原则和建议可供参考。

3. 即时性。口译笔记仅供译员在口译该语段的讲话时使用,只要当时能够辨认出所记录的内容并结合短期记忆将该部分译出即可,随后笔记也就失去了作用。

口译笔记的方法

口译笔记的方法可以从笔记结构和笔记语言两方面入手。

口译笔记的结构是指笔记记录的格式,即将信息置于笔记纸上的组织方法。掌握正确的记录格式非常重要,原则是要简单明了、一目了然,一般有以下几个要点:

1. 纵向分页:在记录纸上纵向画一条中线,将其分割成左右两半以充分利用纸面。记录时先用左边,后用右边。有的译员习惯在页面的左右两侧各留出1~2厘米的边距,用于记录逻辑线索或补充、连接前后信息。

2. 阶梯式排列:信息的记录以意群为单位进行分割,每个意思或层次要单独成行,信息的先后、从属顺序可以通过缩进的形式体现出来。而并列信息或是连续、对立等信息则可以通过条例式方法进行记录。这样的阶梯式排列有利于译员区分信息之间的并列、从属等逻辑关系，获得清晰的视觉效果。

  3. 重复借用：发言中的重复信息不必重复写出，只需用箭头或连线表示即可。这既可以最大限度地节省时间，又可以体现信息间的逻辑关系。

  4. 明确结束：当发言人结束一段讲话时，译员应该画一条贯穿该栏的横线以区分已译和未译部分，使译员能迅速地找到每一部分的起始位置。

  口译笔记的语言既不特指源语，也不特指目的语（虽然建议使用目的语进行记录）。对大多数译员来说，口译笔记是图像、符号、缩写词、字母或文字（源语和目的语的组合）的综合运用，以表达口译信息的内容结构。口译笔记中大量地运用图像、符号、缩写词等，其最大优点在于用它们做记录省时省力，也便于用目的语进行解读。例如：数学中的"="，无论是用中文还是用英文，译员都可以很快地读出"等于"或"相当于"。有关口译符号的具体分类和应用将在下一章中详细介绍。

  以下的笔记案例清晰地反映出上述口译笔记的特点。

原文：

  For years, America's automakers have faced serious challenges—burdensome costs, a shriking share of market, and declining profits. In recent months, the global financial crisis has made these challenges even more severe. Now some U. S. auto executives say that their companies are nearing collapse—and that only way they can buy time to restructure is with help from federal government.

笔记：

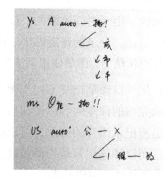

✳ 技巧练习

🎧 请根据录音将下列段落口译成英语或汉语，尝试以口译笔记作为辅助。

  1. 女士们，先生们，进入 21 世纪的上海正在迅速发展为世界经济、金融和贸易中心之一。// 上海金融业的发展尤为引人注目，现已逐渐形成了一个具有相当规模与影响的金融市场体系。// 浦东新区的崛起使这块黄金宝地成了海外投资的热点，投资总额已达 830 亿美元。// 上海这颗璀璨的东方明珠以其特有的魅力召唤富有远见卓识的金融家和企业家来此大展宏图。//

  2. Ladies and gentlemen, I regard it as a great honor and a sign of good business that you come to this official launch of IBM of Shanghai and show so much interest in IBM products. // As the world leader in personal computers, IBM would like to share with Chinese customers our successes. // Among other things, IBM products enjoy an excellent performance and high quality, which I believe, are very

important to our Chinese customers. // We are looking forward to a long-term relationship with our clients and strategic partners which will help further strengthen our position we enjoy as the leader in the world's computer market. //

主题口译

Text A　共享经济

主题导入

"没有一个房间也可以开酒店,没有一辆车也可以开租车公司,没有一件商品也可以开商场。"这句话充分描述了当下最流行的"共享经济"的模式。以下是对"共享经济"和常见的"共享经济"现象的描述。

请先熟悉列出的词汇与短语再听录音,并在录音停顿时将下列篇章口译成英语。

词汇与短语

共享经济	sharing economy
闲置资源	idle resource
共享单车	shared bike
分时租赁	periodic lease
绿色出行	green commuting
移动支付	mobile payment
充电宝	power bank
共享睡眠仓	shared sleep cabin
紫外线消毒	ultraviolet disinfection

女士们、先生们:

大家上午好!很荣幸有机会和大家聊聊目前最为火爆的共享经济。//

"共享经济"一词最早是由美国社会学教授提出的。共享经济的本质是将拥有闲置资源分享给他人,提高资源有效利用,进而获得收益。// 提供者通过在特定时间提供物品或服务获得一定经济回报,需求者则通过租、借等共享方式使用物品。目前,共享经济大多是在互联网作为媒介的基础上实现的。主要有以下几种常见的形式://

最常见的就是"共享单车"了。大家不难发现:在校园、公交站、地铁、商业区、居民楼等地方都可以看到共享单车,它采用分时租赁模式,可以给人们解决"最后一公里"的难题,同时也给"绿色出行"带来了不错的效果。//

随着互联网技术的发展及移动支付的普及,人们生活中越来越离不开手机,而手机使用离不开电池供电,如果出门在外手机没电了,或许"共享充电宝"是你的不错的选择。

据说，共享充电宝整个租借过程不到20秒，大大地方便了出行在外，手机没电的用户。//

在大城市里，应该有不少工薪阶层都需要在晚上加班。如果加班太晚，离家又远的话，一般会选择附近旅馆住一晚。随着共享经济的发展，人们可以睡觉的地方又多了一个——"共享睡眠舱"。// 据报道，共享睡眠舱里面有空调、阅读灯、Wi-Fi、插座，用户用微信扫码打开舱门开始计费。睡眠结束后，从微信上点击"解锁舱门"，门就会自动打开。结束入住后，共享睡眠仓会自动开始紫外线消毒。另外，一次性床单、枕巾、毯子使用后会分类回收。//

总的来说，共享经济在为人们出行、娱乐、健身、居住等多个方面提供便利的同时，也带来了挑战。挑战主要集中在行业发展规范、公共服务、政策环境、保障措施等方面。//

Text B Tips for an Effective Business Presentation

主题导入

生动而有效的商务陈述是信息传达的重要途径。但是，在商务陈述中，单单依靠幻灯片是不够的，还要讲究一定的方式和方法。以下是对有效商务陈述的几点建议。

请先熟悉列出的词汇与短语再听录音，并在录音停顿时将下列篇章口译成汉语。

词汇与短语

credibility	可信度
initiative	计划
thought-provoking	发人深思的
Q&A session	问答环节
to drive home	把（论点、问题等）讲得透彻明白

Ladies and gentlemen,

Good morning! You might have discovered that a successful business presentation is much more than the slides you have created. Today I would like to give you some tips on how to deliver an effective business presentation. //

First of all, start your presentation by establishing credibility. You can use a short story about your background related to the topic, share an experience that shaped the presentation or conclusion, or even reveal references that support your information and is directly related to what you are about to tell them. //

Secondly, include a goal early in the presentation. If your audience knows the purpose or goal of the presentation from the start, they are more likely to relate what you say with that purpose as you present your materials. // This makes it easier at the end to get the action you want, whether it's funding, approval to proceed with an initiative, to change their minds, or simply get agreement and understanding. //

第 6 单元　口译笔记 1/ 商务陈述

Thirdly, use supporting materials effectively. Instead of just presenting the material, accompany it with information that supports it and gives it credibility. // For instance, you can tell a story, give statistics, or even provide quotes from well-respected figures that support your message. //

Moreover, for more impact, you may introduce each separate topic or idea with a relevant quotation or full-screen image that evokes the topic instead of using a stock title slide. Please notice that asking thought-provoking or rhetorical questions is an effective way to convey information. // If there is a Q&A session after the presentation, you need to consider all the objections the audience might have or questions they may raise about your points and information, and be fully prepared. Also a second or a short closing after the Q&A session that drive home your key messages and points may make your presentation more impressive. //

Hopefully these tips may help you to deliver a more powerful presentation. Thank you! //

Text C　虚拟智能手机

主题导入

虚拟现实技术是一种可以创建和体验虚拟世界的计算机仿真系统。它利用计算机技术生成一种模拟环境，是一种多源信息融合的、交互式的三维动态视景和实体行为的系统仿真，可以使用户沉浸到模拟的环境中。以下是对全球首款虚拟智能手机的介绍。

请先熟悉列出的词汇与短语再听录音，并在录音停顿时将下列篇章口译成英语。

词汇与短语

虚拟现实	virtual reality
氢 1	Hydrogen One
安卓操作系统	Android operating system
VR 头盔	VR helmet
高端的	high-end
电影摄像机	cinematic camera
《阿凡达》	*Avatar*
身临其境的	immersive
计算程序	algorithm
立体声	stereo
全息的	holographic

虚拟现实，简称 VR，是指通过技术手段所创造的世界。身处其中，人们会近距离感受到现实世界所拥有的体验。如今，在虚拟现实科技世界中，多家知名公司提供了精彩的游戏、视频、样片以及 360 度相机所拍摄的图像，让我们沉浸其中。//

虚拟现实技术使体验虚幻的事物，漫游未知的世界，探索新的情感和感悟成为可能。因此，虚拟现实技术在提供惊人的游戏体验这方面保持了较高的水准。// 此外，虚拟现实技术也进入不同的领域，这对促进和扩大日益发展的平台来说是一种绝佳方式。令人兴奋的是，它不仅仅限于创造出更好的产品，更是创建前所未见的平台。//

2017年7月，一家名为RED的美国公司推出了全球首款VR智能手机"氢1"。这款手机基于安卓操作系统，可以迅速地将2D内容转换成3D内容，甚至无须佩戴VR头盔即可传送精彩的游戏。RED公司早已经制造出高端的电影摄影机，用于拍摄电影《阿凡达》。//

设计这款VR手机花费了三年时间。公司将通过自有途径提供身临其境的纪录片、游戏和电影。同时，"氢"用户也可以插入自有的内容。由于RED公司的特殊计算程序，用户可以在这款智能手机的音乐功能中将立体声转换为高端音频。//

这款VR智能手机可以使人们有机会捕捉到静态、动态及全息图像。仅凭借"氢1"这一种产品就开启了虚拟现实技术的新模式。//

Text D Apple Pay

主题导入

Apple Pay 是苹果公司在 2014 年发布的一种基于近场通信技术（NFC, near field communication）的手机支付功能。用户可用苹果手机进行免接触支付，免去刷信用卡支付步骤。用户的信用卡、借记卡信息事先存储在手机中，用户将手指放在手机的指纹识别传感器上，将手机靠近读卡器，即完成支付。以下是关于 Apple Pay 的介绍。

请先熟悉列出的词汇与短语再听录音，并在录音停顿时将下列篇章口译成汉语。

词汇与短语

Apple Pay	苹果支付
Apple watch	苹果智能手表
mobile payment	移动支付
digital wallet service	数字钱包服务
debit card	借记卡
magnetic stripe	磁条
point-of-sale terminals	销售终端
dynamic security code	动态安全码
Touch ID sensor	触摸式传感器
American Express	美国运通公司

Ladies and gentlemen,

Are you still paying in cash or swiping cards when you buy something? Then you are out. Now, with "Apple Pay", you can pay for many things with your iPhone or your apple watch. //

As a mobile payment and digital wallet service by Apple Inc., Apple Pay lets users make payments using the iPhone 6, 6 Plus, and later, Apple Watch-compatible devices (iPhone 5 and later models), iPad Air 2, iPad Pro and iPad Mini 3 and later. // Apple Pay digitizes and replaces the credit or debit card chip and PIN or magnetic stripe transaction at point-of-sale terminals. It is represented by the following advantages. //

First of all, Apple Pay is safe. The service keeps customer payment information private from the retailer, and creates a "dynamic security code generated for each transaction". // Apple added that they would not track usage, which would stay between the customers, the vendors, and the banks. Users can also remotely halt the service on a lost phone via the "Find My iPhone" service.//

Secondly, Apple Pay is very convenient. To pay at points of sale, users hold their authenticated Apple device to the point-of-sale system. IPhone users authenticate by holding their fingerprint to the phone's Touch ID sensor, whereas Apple Watch users authenticate by double clicking a button on the device. // To pay in supported iOS apps, users choose Apple Pay as their payment method and authenticate with Touch ID. It will only take users two or three seconds to complete the payment. // In addition, users can add payment cards to the service in any of three ways: through their iTunes accounts, by taking a photo of the card, or by entering the card information manually. //

Thirdly, Apple Pay provides a wide coverage. Apple partnered with American Express, MasterCard and Visa in America. Besides, Apple Pay has been put into practice in China since Feb. 18, 2016, and it has partnered with 19 banks and could be used in many places including McDonald's, Seven-Eleven (in Beijing), Carrefour, etc. //

Join us in the new trend of Apple Pay! //

Text E 川菜推介会

主题导入

川菜作为中国汉族传统的四大菜系之一、中国八大菜系之一，取材广泛，调味多变，菜式多样，口味清鲜醇浓并重，以善用麻辣调味著称，并以其别具一格的烹调方法和浓郁的地方风味受到人们的喜爱。以下是在川菜推介会上对其进行的概述。

请先熟悉列出的词汇与短语再听录音，并在录音停顿时将下列篇章口译成英语。

词汇与短语

川菜	Sichuan Cuisine
八大菜系	eight regional cuisines
红辣椒	red chili
青椒	green chili
豆豉	fermented soybean
煨	to braise
腌制	to pickle
花椒	Sichuan pepper
火锅	hot pot

女士们、先生们：

晚上好！很高兴大家能来参加今晚的川菜推介会。首先，让我们用热烈的掌声欢迎美国代表团的到来。借此机会，我想为各位来宾简单介绍一下川菜。//

中国地域辽阔，民族众多，因此中国饮食口味多种多样，各具特色，令人垂涎。总体来讲，中国饮食可以分为八大地方菜系。川菜，即四川菜肴，就是这八大菜系之一。//

川菜菜式多样，口味清鲜醇厚并重，以善用麻辣调味著称，着重使用红辣椒，搭配使用青椒和花椒，产生出经典的刺激的味道。此外，大蒜、姜和豆豉也被应用于烹饪过程中。// 川菜取材广泛，野菜和野禽常被选用为原料。炒、爆、煸、炸、煮、煨等都是川菜基本的烹饪技术，尤以小炒、干煸、干烧为其独到之处。// 川菜的代表作品很多，比如：鱼香肉丝、宫保鸡丁、麻婆豆腐等等，可以说没有品尝过川菜的人不算来过中国。//

如果你吃川菜，发现它过于柔和，那么你可能吃的不是正宗的川菜。红绿辣椒被用在许多菜肴中，带来特别的辣味。花椒的运用常会在口中留下麻木的感觉，在中国文字里这叫作"麻"。// 然而，多数青椒是在18世纪从美国传入中国的，因此川菜的精妙在某种程度上要感谢全球贸易。四川火锅也许是世界上最出名的火锅，尤其是半辣半清的鸳鸯火锅最受欢迎。//

话不多言。现在请大家品尝美味的川菜。//

Text F Hermes Scarf

主题导入

爱马仕是一家忠于传统手工艺、不断追求创新的国际化企业，拥有箱包、丝巾、领带、男女装和生活艺术品等系列产品。爱马仕的总店位于法国巴黎，分店遍布世界各地。爱马仕一直秉承着超凡卓越、极致绚烂的设计理念，造就优雅之极的传统典范。以下是著名艺术家杉本博司为爱马仕设计的围巾的简介。

请先熟悉列出的词汇与短语再听录音，并在录音停顿时将下列篇章口译成汉语。

词汇与短语

limited edition	限量版
coveted	梦寐以求的
accessory	装饰物（如手袋、皮带、珠宝等）
Metropolitan Museum of Art	大都会艺术博物馆
Tate Gallery	泰特美术馆
artistic director	艺术总监
Hiroshi Sugimoto	杉本博司（人名）
Pierre-Alexis Dumas	迪马（人名）
Isaac Newton	牛顿（人名）

第 6 单元　口译笔记 1/ 商务陈述

Ladies and gentlemen,

Good morning! Today I would like to introduce a limited-edition Hermes scarf by Hiroshi Sugimoto, which is definitely one of the art world's most coveted accessories this summer. //

As we know, Mr. Sugimoto is a famous Japanese artist, whose work is included in the collections of the Metropolitan Museum of Art in New York and Tate Gallery in London. // He agreed to the project after Hermes heir and artistic director Pierre-Alexis Dumas visited him in Tokyo a few years ago. Mr. Sugimoto believed that art can be wearable, who based his line on a long-running project of his called "Colors of Shadow", which was inspired by Isaac Newton's studies of color. //

Mr. Sugimoto created 20 multicolored designs for Hermes, which offers seven of each. Since mid-June, Hermes unveiled the 140-centimeter-square scarfs and sold them online for 8,800 USD. Two of the styles have already been sold out. //

This collaboration is the 3rd and the most successful of a series of initiatives with Hermes and artists. Mr. Sugimoto and Mr. Dumas selected 20 images to turn into scarfs. Hermes technicians spent months working with Mr. Sugimoto to interpret the color that he really appreciated. // Mr. Sugimoto held the idea that the world is filled with countless colors, so he hoped that the customers could get a truer sense of the world from those disregarded intra-colors. //

Now, please appreciate the sample of these fabulous scarfs. //

情景口译

提示：
学生三人或四人一组，根据下面的主题提示进行模拟口译，注意使用本单元介绍的技能和句型。

主题一　最新款跑步鞋推介

参与人： 1. 赵阳先生，某著名鞋业集团设计总监

2. 参加新品发布会的中外嘉宾

3. 译员

地　点： 某酒店多功能厅

内　容： 1. 赵先生简单地介绍跑步鞋产生的背景

2. 赵先生指出老款跑步鞋的弊病

3. 赵先生利用实物介绍新款跑步鞋的材质和设计亮点等

4. 赵先生邀请现场嘉宾试穿新款跑步鞋，并谈及体验感受

主题二　某著名品牌平板电脑推介

参与人：　1. 泰勒女士，某国际著名科技公司技术总监

　　　　　2. 参加新品发布会的中外嘉宾

　　　　　3. 译员

内　容：　1. 泰勒女士介绍该平板电脑的产生背景

　　　　　2. 泰勒女士通过幻灯片演示该平板电脑的产品特点和技术支持

　　　　　3. 泰勒女士介绍可以与该平板电脑配套使用的键盘及蓝牙笔

　　　　　4. 泰勒女士利用实物进行现场演示、讲解

✽ 句式扩展

1. We're very honored to have the opportunity to talk to you about the changes in four areas and how your company can benefit from these changes.

   我们很荣幸有机会向您介绍四个领域的变化，以及贵公司如何能从这些变化中受益。

2. If you have any questions, please feel free to interrupt at any time.

   如果您有任何疑问，随时可以打断我。

3. Last year we acquired Dutch TMNS, which provides an important guarantee for increasing the competitiveness of the product.

   去年，我们收购了荷兰的 TMNS 公司，为提升产品竞争力提供了重要的保证。

4. It has two core processors inside so that the CPU performance gets twice as fast as it used to be.

   它内部拥有双核处理器，因此中央处理器的运行速度比原来快了一倍。

5. What I want to talk about is that all companies must be ready for continuous change, and prepared to meet those challenges.

   我想说的是所有的公司都必须准备好不断变化，应对挑战。

6. The slide shows four major sales areas: industrial machinery, robots, computers and at the bottom home appliances.

   幻灯片显示出四个主要的销售领域：工业机械、机器人、计算机，以及最基本的家用电器。

7. In our company, we train our employees worldwide by giving them practical experience in solving real-life problems and we also give them international working exposure.

   在我们公司，我们为世界各地而来的员工提供培训，和他们分享解决真实问题的实际经验，并让他们身处国际工作环境。

8. Over the years, the sales of new products have grown steadily.

   在过去的几年，新产品的销售量稳步增长。

9. I firmly believe that our company can play a leading role in international trade and continue to be a winner against the backdrop of globalization.

   我坚信我们公司会在国际贸易中处于领先地位，会继续在全球化背景下成为赢家。

10. We think our employees are our best assets and we mean it.

    我们认为员工是最宝贵的财富，我们真是这么想的。

11. 我们坚信，2017年我们的品牌必将走向辉煌。

    We firmly believe that our brand will achieve great success in 2017.

12. 接下来，我想要谈一谈我市就业市场的情况，为下面的讨论提供背景信息。

    Next, I would like to talk about the job market in our city in order to provide background information to future discussions.

13. 我们的雇员不仅关心自己的各种福利，他们也期望过着平衡的生活。

    Our employees not only care about their various welfares, but also expect to lead a balanced life.

14. 我们公司致力于为广大消费者提供最满意的售后服务，产品终身保修。

    Our company is committed to providing the best after-sale service to consumers and our products enjoy a life-long warranty.

15. 这家保险公司拥有优秀的销售队伍，杰出的管理体制，雄厚的资本实力。

    This insurance company boasts outstanding sales team, excellent managerial system and abundant capital resources.

16. 我们是敢于创新的企业，我们的产品一直走在时代的前沿，在全球市场上处于领军者的地位。

   We are a company that dares to innovate, so that our products are always at the frontline of the era, playing a leading role in the global market.

17. 从当前的情况看，我们面临着国内外竞争对手的双重压力，如果不及时采取措施，将会有严重的后果。

   Judging from the current circumstances, we are faced with dual pressure from competitors from both home and abroad. If we don't adopt immediate measures, we will be subject to serious consequences.

18. 公司必须以人为本，才能留住最核心的员工。

   A company must put its people first so that they can retain the core employees.

19. 如果您对我们的产品感兴趣，请在我的陈述后与我联系。

   If you are interested in our products, please contact me after my presentation.

20. 感谢大家参加本次年会，我们已取得既定目标，希望我们的公司在明年再创辉煌！

   Thank you for attending this annual conference. We have achieved our planned goals; I hope we can have a bright future next year!

❋ 口译小贴士

林超伦博士（英国外交部首席中文译员）对口译笔记本的建议

建议你使用带有活页圈的笔记本，见下列照片。有活页圈才能来回翻倒方便。笔记本的大小以自己感觉舒服为准。我喜欢用英国制的A5开。躺在我的巴掌上不大不小，刚刚好。只是英国这些为速记设计的本子印有横杠。空白页更为理想。

持笔记本的手势见下列照片。记完一页，翻过去一页。发言人讲完后，一把抓地全部翻回来，落眼处正是这个段子的开头。然后，译一页，翻过去一页。这段译完后，把翻过去的几页一把压在手掌中。这等于是用手掌把已经翻完的和下一段的笔记清楚分开。这点很重要。否则，很容易出现发言人讲完后，你来回翻找本段首页的难堪局面。

第 6 单元　口译笔记 1/ 商务陈述

如果是坐在桌前，笔记本放在桌面上，也是记完一页，翻过去一页。也千万不要忘记在发言人开口说下一段之前，把已经翻完的笔记页压到笔记本下。

笔，我建议用按压式的。这样，一手持本，另一手随时都可以掏出笔来，一按就开始记。如果是旋转开盖的笔，则需要两只手操作。笔套不紧的，还时不时要掉，很分心。我长年惯带两支笔，多次免遭墨水用尽之难。

口译笔记 2/商业展览

第 7 单元

口译主题：商业展览

　　商业展览是指众多企业利用展览会、博览会、展销会、供货会、商品洽谈会等交易会形式聚集在一起，向参观者展示各自的商品，边展边销，以展促销，借交易会之机把涉及商品的宣传、销售、市场调研、公关等活动有机结合在一起的一种促销方式。

　　近年来，商业展览越来越受到企业的重视，国内外各种商业展览发展异常迅猛，会展业已经成为经济增长的动力之一。

✻ 学习目标

- 了解口译笔记中常用的符号
- 完善自己的笔记系统
- 了解商业展览相关文体的特点和常用口译句式

第 7 单元 口译笔记 2/ 商业展览

✱ 技巧讲解

口译中可以充分利用字母、缩写、数学符号、标点符号、表情符号等来记录信息，节省记录的时间。口译笔记符号完全没有必要建立一一对应的关系，恰恰相反，能够做到一个符号代表多个相似或相近的意思最为可取。以下就对口译笔记中可以用到的各类符号举例说明。

字母符号：口译笔记中，可以充分利用英文中的 26 个字母来表示相关的意思。例如：

y: 年	w: 周	h: 小时	m: 分钟
s: 秒钟	d: 日子，今天	B: 但是	f: 金融
R: 改革	v: 胜利，成功		

图像符号：笔记时采用一些形象的图形符号，直观性强，寓意形象清楚，便于辨认分析。例如：

O：国家、民族、领土	⊙：会议、开会
Θ：国际的、世界的、全球的	@：在
&：和	w/：with
w/o：without	↑：上升，增加，提高
↓：减少，下降，恶化	→：导致，出口，相当于 to
←：由于，进口，相当于 from	$：资金，钱，投资
✱：重点，重视，主要的	[ ]：在……内，在……之中
⌒：关系，联系	⊥：压力
⊕：医院、诊所、红十字会	
°：字词的右上角加圆圈表示人，如：中°（中国人）	

数字符号：数字符号既简单又容易记忆，是口译笔记理想的标志。

√：正确的，对的	×：错误，不行，没有，反对
>：大于，多于，好于，超过	<：小于，少于，差于
+：加上，以及	—：减去，除去
=：等于，相当于，就是	≠：不等于，不相当
≈：大约	∵：因为，由于
∴：所以，结果	

"·"点的位置不同，表示的概念也不一样，如："·d"表示昨天，"·y"表示去年，"·2m"表示两个月前，"2y·"表示两年后。

标点符号：标点符号也是口译笔记中非常有效的符号。

: : 说	！: 奇迹，惊叹，需要注意
? : 问题，疑问	// : 结束
__ : 下划线加在词下强调程度，严重，很	

缩写符号：英语中常用的缩略语也可以在口译笔记中得到充分的利用，如：

SOE: 国有企业	Co.: 公司
gov: 政府	edu: 教育
eg: 例子	info: 信息，消息
demo: 示范，表演	EU: 欧盟
APEC：亚太经合组织	R&D：研发

自创符号：口译符号的创造绝没有固定的模式，译员可以利用自己的记录方式创造属于自己的符号系统。如：

⊖: 发展中国家	○: 发达国家
⊙: 最不发达国家	儿: 小孩, 小朋友, 儿童

笔记符号系统一旦建立，各种符号所代表的意思要相对固定。口译初学者最容易出现的问题是：习惯性地每听到一个单词就立即以该单词的首字母或头几个字母作为笔记符号，比如：听到"science"以"s"记录，听到"society"还以"s"记录；再或者，听到"regular"以"re"记录，听到"regulation"以"re"记录，听到"recruit"还是以"re"记录。这样口译笔记恐怕留下的只是不能识别的意思，想译也译不出来了。

✳ 技巧练习

🎧 **请根据录音将下列段落口译成英语或汉语，尝试以口译笔记作为辅助。**

1. 世博会不同于贸易展览会，后者主要是由政府和国际组织参加。相反，世博会展示的是经济、文化和技术领域的成就和前景，它是全世界人民聚在一起交流经验、互相学习的大事。// 世博会长期以来一直被誉为"经济、技术和文化的奥运会"，每隔五年举办一次，自 1851 年首次在伦敦举行以来一直在发达国家举行。//

上海申办的 2010 年世博会使得中国成为主办这一盛事的第一个发展中国家，对中国产生积极的影响。因为中国不仅学习别国的经验来推进改革开放，而且增进与他国之间的友谊。此外，这促进了全球范围内经济、文化和技术的发展。//

2. The 14th China High-Tech Fair opened in Shenzhen, with the number of foreign participants surging compared with last year. The number of overseas companies attending the event grew 37.5%, while the number of pre-registered overseas buyers has doubled, a growth that was "unexpected" for the organizers. // About 3,000 exhibitors from China and abroad are attending the fair, according to

the organizers. Companies from the United States, Japan and South Korea are showcasing their latest technology. // Cloud computing, the "Internet of things", and 4th generation mobile Internet devices are some of the highlights of the event. The fair is expected to be an excellent opportunity to promote technological communication among countries and regions.//

主题口译

Text A 预订展位

主题导入

在广交会筹备过程中，来自澳大利亚小野人皮具公司的格林女士致电广交会预订部，想预订展位。以下是她与预订部职员之间的对话。

请先熟悉列出的词汇与短语再听录音，并在录音停顿时将下列篇章口译成英语或汉语。

词汇与短语

广交会	Canton Fair
中国进出口商品交易会	China Import and Export Fair
招展	to solicit
标准展台	row booth
角落展台	corner booth
半岛型展台	end booth
岛型展台	island booth
光地	raw space
围板	boarding
射灯	spotlight
插座	socket
公司楣板	company signage
预付款	down payment
预订确认信	reservation confirm letter
Crumpler	小野人
beauty cases	化妆袋
briefcases	公文袋
travel bags	旅行包
trolleys	拉杆箱
trolley backpacks	拉杆背包

A: 早上好,广交会服务中心,有什么可以为您效劳? //

B: Yes, Please. This is Christine Green. I'm with Crumpler in the Australia. We are interested in attending the Canton Fair. Could you please give me some information? //

A: 当然,我非常乐意。中国进出口商品交易会,简称为"广交会",每年春秋两季举行,从1957年创办至今已有59年历史,是中国目前历史最长、层次最高、规模最大、商品种类最全、到会客商最多、成交效果最好的综合性国际贸易盛会。//

B: It sounds good. What types of booths are available? //

A: 您的运气不错,因为我们刚招展不久,因此所有类型的展台都有,有标准展台、角落站台、半岛形展台和岛形展台。//

B: Well, we plan to exhibit some beauty cases, briefcases, travel bags, trolleys, trolley backpacks, and handbags, so I think maybe end booth will be the best. How much is it? //

A: 9平方米的半岛形展台,每个起价是2.3万元人民币。//

B: Wow, it's expensive! Is it negotiable? //

A: 因为你们是新顾客,我们第一次合作可以给您打个九折。//

B: Sounds acceptable. What does the price include? //

A: 每个展台的配置包括光地、地毯、围板、一个柜子、两把皮椅、一个废纸篓以及三盏射灯、一个插座、一个公司楣板。//

B: OK. One nine-square meter-end booth, please. //

A: 您希望摊位的位置是怎样的呢?//

B: Can I reserve a space in the center? //

A: 当然可以。中心区刚好还有一个A-234号展位。//

B: Good! I'll take it. //

A: 谢谢您,格林女士。您预订了中心区的一个9平方米的半岛形展台。展台的编号是A-234。//

B: How do I pay for that? //

A: 参展商需在签订展位预订合同后即付35%的预付款,余额需在一个月内全部付清。请问您的信用卡号码是多少?//

B: The number is 8453-1940-0327. //

A: 谢谢。我很快会发一份预订确认信给您。还有什么我能为您效劳的吗?//

B: No, thank you very much. Goodbye! //

A: 谢谢您的来电,再见。//

第 7 单元 口译笔记 2/ 商业展览

Text B 建立业务往来

主题导入

在展会上，中国纺织品进出口公司的代表周小姐正在接待来自美国的史密斯女士。史密斯女士很喜欢展出的中国丝绸产品，想做进口。以下是她们的对话。

请先熟悉列出的词汇与短语再听录音，并在录音停顿时将下列篇章口译成英语或汉语。

词汇与短语

中国纺织进出口公司
　　　　China Textile Import & Export Corporation
光泽　　luster
纯度　　purity
密度　　density

A: 早上好！欢迎来到我们的展位。请问有什么可以帮您的？//

B: Good morning! I'd like to know some about your products. //

A: 请问您怎么称呼？//

B: My name is Hannah Smith. I'm from America. //

A: 很高兴认识您，史密斯女士。我叫周洋，是中国纺织进出口公司的代表。//

B: Nice to meet you, too. Could I have your latest catalogues or something that tells me about your company? //

A: 当然可以。您请看。//

B: Thank you. OK, I've read about it, but I'd like to know more about your company. What products are you specialized in? //

A: 我公司是国家大型专业进出口总公司之一，拥有资产近 20 亿，主要经营丝绸及其制品，纺织品及其制品，企业职工超过 500 人。我们的产品在市场上表现出了巨大的潜力。您对哪方面的产品比较感兴趣呢？//

B: I'd like to buy some silks with high quality. //

A: 好的，我想您来对地方了。我们的丝绸不仅质量精美，而且品种繁多，光泽优雅柔和，纯度高，密度大。您可以看看我们这一款样品，您觉得怎么样？//

B: It's very elegant! //

A: 我强烈推荐这款丝绸，这是我们最新的设计。//

B: I'm satisfied with the quality of your samples, and could you give me an idea of your prices? //

A: 这是我们的价格表。//

B: Oh! I think it's a little bit expensive. //

A: 您知道，我们的产品质量很高。同国际市场上的其他产品相比，我公司的价格是很低的。我们一直保持着较低的利润。//

B: Is there a good market for these silk products? //

A: 很好，这些丝绸产品在国外市场很受欢迎，需求量大。我相信在贵国市场也会表现出巨大的销售潜力。//

B: Then what about delivery? //

A: 我们会在您订货后一周内发货，并通知您。//

B: OK, thanks for your detailed and patient explanation. I will consider about it. //

Text C 艺术展览

主题导入

艺术展览也是一种展览形式，它既是艺术品爱好者获取信息和娱乐的综合体现，也是一种营销媒介。以下是艺术展览的一个简要介绍。

请先熟悉列出的词汇与短语再听录音，并在录音停顿时将下列篇章口译成英语。

词汇与短语

艺术画廊	art gallery
补充	to supplement
回顾展	retrospective
相对湿度	relative humidity
强度	intensity
恶化	deterioration
保护	preservation
破坏行为	vandalism
巡逻	patrol

传统说来，艺术展览是艺术品与观众接触的空间。艺术品可能展示在博物馆、艺术俱乐部、私人艺术画廊中，或者在一些主营业务并非是展示或售卖艺术品的地方，比如咖啡馆。//

艺术展览有不同类型，如商业展览和非商业展览。商业展览通常指展示艺术家或艺术品经销商作品的艺术展会，参观者通常需要缴纳一些费用。// 临时博物馆展览通常展示博物馆某个特定时期自有的藏品，带有一定的主题或题目，以从其他博物馆借来的藏品作为补充。展品通常不可出售。这类展览与博物馆的永久展览是有区别的，大部分大型博物馆都会专门留出一个区域用于此类临时性展览。//

商业展览馆中的展览通常是由可以出售的艺术品构成，但也可能有不可出售的作品作为补充。一般来说,参观者需要缴费才能进入博物馆观展,但是艺术画廊中的商业展览则不需要。// 回顾展是用以回顾某个艺术家作品的展览,其他常见的类型还有个人展览、团体展览以及关于某个具体主题或题目的展览。//

艺术展览环境的主要考虑因素包括光线、相对湿度以及温度。展区的可见光强度要低以避免损伤展品,但又要足够明亮以供参观。展区的相对湿度值要设定在35%~50%。为了保护藏品,通常建议保持较低的温度,展区温度不得超过 22 摄氏度。//

因为艺术展览中的展品通常具有特殊价值,这就需要高级别的安保来减少偷盗或破坏行为带来损失的风险。展示柜需要安全锁定。无论何时,展区都要有人巡逻;当有珍贵展品展出时,要提供 24 小时的安保。//

Text D Hong Kong Houseware Fair 2016

主题导入

由香港贸发局主办的香港家庭用品展是亚洲地区规模最大的家庭用品展览会,在全球排名第四位。展会汇聚亚洲精品,尽显东方魅力,吸引了世界各地买家前来参观。该展会和广交会客户资源共享,是亚洲厂商拓展业务和接单的绝佳良机。以下是对 2016 年第 31 届展会基本情况的介绍。

请先熟悉列出的词汇与短语再听录音,并在录音停顿时将下列篇章口译成汉语。

词汇与短语

Hong Kong Houseware Fair	香港家庭用品展
Hong Kong Convention and Exhibition Center	香港会议展览中心
Hall of Elegance	精萃廊
Creative Arts & Cultural Crafts	文化创意工艺品
sanitiser	消毒杀菌剂
convivial	欢乐的;活跃的

As Asia's trade fair capital, Hong Kong is an ideal place to host Asia's leading houseware event—Hong Kong Houseware Fair. Featuring more than 2,100 exhibitors from around 30 countries and regions, the 31st fair was held at the Hong Kong Convention and Exhibition Center in April 2016. //

To meet buyer's specific sourcing needs, the fair was again divided into different themed zones focusing on key categories in houseware, such as Interior Decor, Hall of Elegance, Creative Arts & Cultural Crafts, Green Living, and World of Pet Supplies. //

To meet the growing demand for baby products in Asian markets, the Baby Products zone was expanded to showcase products that meet all the needs of parents with babies and kids. Exhibits covered baby care products, baby and children's furniture, children's tableware, baby toys, nursery products and sanitisers. //

The fair was much more than just a market. Seminars presented by industry insiders provided insights into such topical issues as R&D and upcoming trends. Networking events enabled buyers, exhibitors, industry officials and international media to exchange ideas and strengthen relationships in a convivial atmosphere. And with the Product Demo and Launch Pad, buyers could interact directly with exhibitors and get a close-up view of the latest products. //

Text E 香港美食博览会

主题导入

香港美食博览会为来自世界各地的美食制造商提供了积极结交买家，扩大人脉的机会，同时综览全球市场概况及美食发展趋势。以下是第27届香港美食博览会的概述。

请先熟悉列出的词汇与短语再听录音，并在录音停顿时将下列篇章口译成英语。

词汇与短语

香港美食博览会	Food Expo
贸易馆	Trade Hall
尊贵美食区	Gourmet Zone
公众馆	Public Hall
中医药展区	Chinese Medicine Zone
清真食品区	Halal Food Zone
亚洲·料理	Asian Cuisine
摩登·煮意	Chic & More
甜艺·风情	Sweet Delight
欧美·恋馔	Western Delicacy
绿色·味力	Green Palate
日本和牛	Wagyu beef
幸运抽奖	lucky draws

香港美食博览会是香港一年一度的美食盛会，吸引着国际买家及美食爱好者前来参观选购。本次美食博览会汇聚了来自20个国家及地区的超过1 300家供应商，为贸易买家及大众带来了林林总总的美食。//

美食博览会共划分为三个不同展区，包括"贸易馆""尊贵美食区"及"公众馆"。本次"贸易馆"新增"中医药展区"，展示中药及保健等相关产品。// 上届博览会首次设立的"清真食品区"及"食品及农业科技区"则载誉重来，继续提供相关的食材、服务及技术。//

"尊贵美食区"汇集超过70家参展商，以五大主题呈献环球顶级美食，包括："亚洲·料理""摩登·煮意""甜艺·风情""欧美·恋馔"以及本届新增以有机及绿色食品为主

打的"绿色·味力",让参观者品尝日本和牛、海产、新鲜水果、精品咖啡、高级餐酒等佳肴美食。//

"公众馆"的参展商带来了一系列美食,并在展会期间举办了多项有趣活动。//

大会还为贸易买家及参观者安排了一连串精彩活动,其中包括探讨食品业最近发展及市场机会的研讨会,为贸易买家提供了宝贵咨询。// 此外,大会还安排星级名厨烹饪示范、互动游戏、营养咨询讲座及幸运抽奖,为参观者带来了无限欢乐。//

Text F Speech by the Head of German Publishers and Booksellers Association from the Opening Ceremony of Frankfurt Book Fair 2016（excerpt）

主题导入

法兰克福书展是德国举办的国际性图书展览,是全世界规模最大的书展,被称为出版业的"奥运会",对全球下一年度图书出版产生重要的影响。以下节选自德国书商协会主席在2016年法兰克福书展开幕式上的讲话。

🎧 请先熟悉列出的词汇与短语再听录音,并在录音停顿时将下列篇章口译成汉语。

Ⓦ 词汇与短语

German Publishers and Booksellers Association	德国书商协会
Frankfurt Book Fair	法兰克福书展
to foster	培养

Dear friends and colleagues from all over the world,

Ladies and gentlemen,

On behalf of all the German Publishers and Booksellers Association, I would like to welcome you to the 68th Annual Frankfurt Book Fair. For the next five days, books and ideas will once again take center stage here at the largest book fair in the world. //

"This is what we share." This motto is the focus of attention at the 2016 Frankfurt Book Fair. The act of sharing—it represents the things that connect us to one another, that is, what binds us to one another as human beings. // People share values, attitudes and goals—hopes, fears, desires. To share means to give someone a part of our own thoughts and possessions. By definition, those who share enter into contact with others. The act of sharing stands for dialogue, exchange and understanding. //

And all of us—authors, publishers, booksellers, translators and everyone who helps to shape the cultural and creative sector—share something very important: we hold in our hands the ability to foster understanding and dialogue. // We create and provide platforms for opinions and ideas. We shape the ways in which opinions are formed in society. Never before have people working in the book and cultural sector been as important as they are today. //

Let us become more aware of what we share. Together we can create a strong market for books. We can call for tolerance and help to shape a free society. Let us use these strengths as much as possible!

Thank you very much! //

情景口译

提示：

学生三人或四人一组，根据下面的主题提示进行模拟口译，注意使用本单元介绍的技能和句型。

主题一　某国际会议中心展馆情况介绍

参与人： 1. 孙凯先生，某国际会议中心的负责人

2. 三位来自挪威的海产品生产厂商

3. 译员

地　点： 某国际会议中心

内　容： 1. 孙先生介绍该国际会议中心的面积及展台数量

2. 孙先生介绍该国际会议中心曾成功举办的大型展会的规模及影响力

3. 孙先生欢迎各参展商踊跃参与最近在该国际会议中心举办的渔博会

主题二　某高新技术展介绍

参与人： 1. 伯奈特女士，英国某科技公司营销部经理

2. 朱涵先生，某会展中心负责人

3. 译员

第7单元 口译笔记2/商业展览

地　点：某会展中心

内　容：1. 伯奈特女士简单地介绍了该科技公司的运营情况和主要产品

2. 伯奈特女士询问该高新技术展的规模及影响

3. 双方讨论展台的大小、位置、交通食宿等安排

4. 双方互留电话和邮箱以便再次联系

❋ 句式扩展

1. This fair will give us an excellent opportunity to meet friends from overseas and introduce to them our technological development and various problems encountered.

   这次展会给我们一个极好的机会和海外的朋友见面，向他们介绍我们的技术进步和遇到的各种问题。

2. I hope that all who visit this exhibition will make a careful study of everything that is on view.

   我希望所有参观展会的人仔细研究所有展品。

3. China's exhibition industry has been booming in the past two decades with the sustained and rapid growth of national economy.

   随着国民经济的持续快速增长，中国展览行业在过去的20年里一直蓬勃发展。

4. Exhibition industry has been playing an important role in introducing advanced technology and equipment to China and in promoting trade and economic cooperation between China and the world.

   展览行业在中国引进先进技术和设备、促进中国和全世界各国的经贸合作方面发挥着重要的作用。

5. During the last fall fair, we had several rounds of discussions about the deal.

   去年秋季交易会期间，我们举行了几轮关于协议的讨论。

6. The five-day exhibition is a most exclusive opportunity to meet potential clients from around the world.

   五天的展览是不可多得的机会，让你遇到来自世界各地的潜在客户。

7. For buyers seeking top branded products and designs, this hall is the zone to visit.

   寻求顶级品牌产品和设计的买家请到这个区域参观。

8. Innovation is the soul of our forum and cultural interaction is an important mission of the World Expo.

创新是我们论坛的灵魂，文化互动是世博会的一个重要的使命。

9. We have made a great effort on security guard and food quality that during the fair, no infectious disease has been reported.

   我们在安保和食品质量上已经做出了很大努力，展会期间没有出现传染病现象。

10. Central air conditioner, automatic fire alarm, closed circuit TV watching system, communication network, public broadcasting and cable TV are all available in the exhibition hall.

    展览大厅配有中央空调、自动火警、闭路电视、通信网络、广播和有线电视。

11. 参展商不仅有来自中国大陆和港澳台地区的，还有来自美国、加拿大以及欧洲的，大大促进了中国同世界各国的贸易发展。

    Exhibitors are not only from the Chinese Mainland, Hong Kong, Macao and Taiwan, but also from the United States, Canada and Europe, which has greatly promoted the trade development between China and all countries in the world.

12. 展区根据主题划分，在收到参展商填写的报名表和参展费用后，我们就会安排展台。

    The exhibition zone is divided according to different themes. After receiving the filled application forms and the booth fees, we will arrange the booths.

13. 高层次、大规模的展会能吸引媒体的关注，有利于改善举办城市的形象。

    High-level, large-scale exhibitions can attract media's attention and improve the image of the host city.

14. 大连政府十分重视会展业的发展，建立服务体系以支持大型会展的举办。

    Dalian government attaches great importance to the development of exhibition industry and establishes a service system to support the large-scale exhibitions held here.

15. 本次会展旨在为中外合作交流搭建平台，通过五次会议讨论行业发展经验和成果。

    The fair is aimed at building a platform for cooperation and exchange between Chinese and foreign enterprises. We will discuss the experience of this industry's development and fruitful results through five meetings.

16. 中国政府鼓励企业对外投资，推动在东盟国家建立经济贸易合作区。

    The Chinese government encourages enterprises to invest abroad and promote the establishment of economic and trade cooperation zones in ASEAN countries.

17. 大连把会展业看作是现在服务业的重要组成部分，是城市营销的重要载体。

Dalian regards the convention and exhibition industry as an important part of the service sector and an important carrier of urban marketing.

18. 几年来，我市承办展会数量大幅地增加，展会的质量不断提升，拉动了我市经济的增长。

    Over the years, the number of exhibitions held in our city has soared, and the quality of exhibitions has been improved, thus promoting the economic growth in our city.

19. 上海世博会为中国会展业吸引了大量外国资金、技术和人才。

    The Shanghai World Expo has attracted a large amount of foreign capital, technology and talents for China's exhibition industry.

20. 中国会展业起步较晚，国内会展商的素质难以令人满意，会展业的发展还有很长的路要走。

    China's exhibition industry started relatively late, and the quality of domestic exhibitors is not satisfying, thus the exhibition industry still has a long way to go.

✳ 口译小贴士

口译笔记训练中的常见问题和解决策略（上）

问题1：刚涉猎口译笔记时，听与记无法同步协调进行，经常听时忘了记，记时忽略了听。最终，笔记不完整，遗漏了很多重要的信息；短期记忆也没起作用。在口译的表达阶段，完全回想不起所听的内容。

对策：口译过程中，协调好各阶段精力的分配非常重要。在进行口译笔记时，要根据材料的难度合理分配在听与记两个环节的精力。如果材料难度大，或听到难点及主要信息点需要分析时，可以适度放慢记录的节奏，把更多的精力投入到听辨上；当听辨内容相对简单时，在笔记方面就可以适度多投入精力，加快书写的节奏。总之，要根据口译材料的难度做好精力的适度调配。

问题2：讲话开始后，立即动笔，一刻不停，总希望把所有的信息尽可能全面地记下来，不分主次。最终笔记呈现的状态是，内容记得不少，但信息杂乱无章，根本无法读出笔记。

对策：针对上述问题，首先，初学者要克服心理上的障碍，改变过度依赖笔记的思想，要时刻提醒自己笔记只是脑记的补充。其次，要培养自己抓关键词和逻辑线索的听辨思维能力。这种能力的培养要循序渐进：从单句入手，识别关键词；再扩展到段落，识别主干意群或中心句；最后拓展到篇章，概括中心思想。再次，口译笔记时，要明确记录的应该是关键信息、逻辑线索及难以记忆的信息，如数字、专有名词等。

问题3：口译笔记中记录的信息不少，但是缺少逻辑线索的相关纪录，导致笔记的层次性和结构性欠缺。因此，信息输出时，译语的逻辑性差，信息表达杂乱无章，无整体性。

对策：逻辑的分析和理解是口译听辨和笔记的重要基础。初学者可以在训练听辨中逻辑思维的同时，强化口译笔记中逻辑线索的记录。建议初学者在建立自己的笔记系统时，在页面的最左侧留出些许空白，专门记录逻辑关系词，这样在阅读笔记时，逻辑关系一目了然。也可以有针对性地进行逻辑线索的专项训练，其方法是听难度适中的音频或视频资料，在笔记中只记录逻辑关系词，其他信息依靠脑记。音频或视频结束后，根据逻辑关系词复述所听内容。

口译笔记 3/ 市场营销

第 8 单元

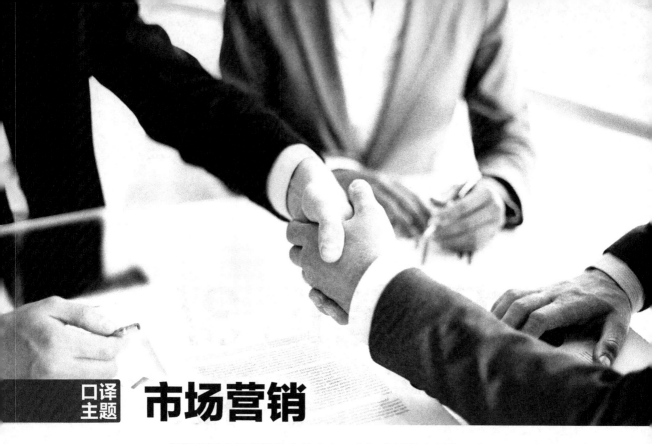

市场营销

_{口译主题}

根据美国市场营销协会的定义，市场营销是在创造、沟通、传播和交换产品中，为顾客、客户、合作伙伴以及整个社会带来价值的一系列活动、过程和体系。

"市场营销"这个词本身既可以做动词理解，也可以做名词理解。作为动词，它指的是企业/公司的具体活动或行为，此时也可以称为市场经营；作为名词，它指的是研究企业/公司市场营销活动或行为的学科，此时将它称为市场营销学更为恰当。本单元练习的内容主要涉及前者。

✱ 学习目标

　　　　了解口译笔记练习的基本步骤

　　　　继续完善自己的口译笔记系统

　　　　掌握市场营销主题的常用口译句式

✼ 技巧讲解

口译初学者通常在口译笔记训练阶段陷入几种困境：一是听得懂却记不下来，讲话结束后，根本无法回忆起所讲内容；二是一开始记笔记就无法集中精力进行听辨，不知该记，还是该听；三是讲话开始就不停地写，听到什么写什么。讲话结束后，除了笔记上记下的只言片语，完全回忆不起讲话内容。

造成这些困境的主要原因是：听辨能力不够强，不能很好地分辨意群和主次信息；没有调控好精力在听辨、脑记、笔记三方面的分配，缺少同时完成多任务模式的能力；笔记技巧不熟练，完全没有形成自己的笔记系统。

在了解了口译笔记的基本结构和口译符号的基本形式之后，初学者可以结合自己的思维方式和理解习惯，遵循以下训练步骤，循序渐进地建立自己的笔记系统。

一、无限时视记练习。视记练习，顾名思义，就是边读文本边进行逻辑分析，边记口译笔记。在没有时间限制的条件下，初学者可以认真地分析原文结构，找出关键信息和逻辑线索，再进行笔记。记录完毕后，不看原文，用中文或英文读出笔记所记录的内容。针对同一个段落篇章可以如此反复练习三四次，直到产生最简洁有效的笔记为止。视记练习的目的在于在没有听辨困扰、没有时间压力的情况下，初学者可以充分熟悉口译笔记结构，设计自己的笔记符号系统。该练习应该从中文材料入手，再过渡到英文材料，逐渐体会中英文语言差异对笔记的影响，完善笔记符号体系。

二、限时视记练习。练习者以正常语速朗读练习材料，记录下所需要的时间。然后以略长于朗读时间的时间为限，看该练习材料，记口译笔记。比如：如果朗读完原文的时间为2分钟，则限定时间为2分30秒。在2分30秒内要完成笔记，然后用中文或英文读出笔记。

如果在2分30秒内完成笔记，则将限定时间缩短为2分15秒，然后再进行"笔记—阅读"练习。达到目标后，再将限定时间缩短为原文正常的朗读时间，再进行练习。该练习的目的在于模拟听记的时间压力，培养训练者有意识地区分主次信息、选择关键信息点的能力。

三、中文听记练习。大多数中国学生对母语的听力输入是不成问题的。因此，在完成视记训练之后，可以进行中文的听记练习。练习者在中文材料听辨上的精力要远远小于听辨英文材料时所需的精力，因此从中文材料入手可以帮助练习者逐渐将听辨与笔记结合起来，协调在听辨和笔记之间的精力分配，找到听与记的平衡点。具体的操作方法是：边听中文原文，边记笔记，然后用英文进行口译。同一个段落篇章可以反复练习两次，并将两次的笔记进行对比，分析出问题所在，进行总结改进。

四、慢速英文听记练习。中文听记练习熟练后，可以过渡到慢速英语的听记练习。练习的方法是：以慢速的英文音频或视频为练习材料，主题应该是练习者所熟悉的，边听英文原文，边记笔记，然后用中文进行口译。同一段落篇章可以反复练习两次，再将两次笔记进行对比分析，找出问题所在，体会中英两种语言差异对笔记的影响。这种练习的目的在于：尽管语速较慢，但对英语的听辨能力要求提高，需要练习者更好地在听与记之间协调精力分配。

五、标准语速英文听记练习。练习方法同上。只是在材料的选择上，以标准语速的英文材料入手，目的就是要充分消化听辨的压力。材料的选择应该从易到难，从熟悉的主题入手，难度逐渐加大。作为过渡，也可以充分利用慢速英文材料，采用音频变速软件（如喜马拉雅、枫叶音频器等），将慢速英文材料的语速逐渐提高，最终达到与标准语速一致。这样做的目的在于利用熟悉的材料逐步调整听辨与笔记的协调平衡分配。

练习材料内容和体裁的选择要丰富多样，可以从逻辑结构清晰的演讲或者新闻入手，逐渐过渡到访谈、报道、大会发言等需要较高逻辑分析的材料。在反复练习中最终实现手耳并行，有条不紊。

值得注意的是：在上述口译笔记的练习中，反复研读自己每次练习的笔记，找出差距和有待改善之处，借鉴他人笔记，让其优势融入自己的笔记，也是非常必要的。缺少了这个过程，即使做了大量的笔记练习，口译笔记也很难有所提高。

✱ 技巧练习

> 🎧 请根据录音将下列段落口译成英语或汉语，请用口译笔记作为辅助。

1. 我们本次销售会议得出结论，我们应该让本公司的产品在海外市场销售。这是根据以下三点做出的决定。//

首先，我们的调查显示，到目前为止，此类产品在北美的市场上尚未出现激烈的竞争，因此有足够的空间让我们盈利。//

第二，我们的调查还表明，大多数美国消费者希望购买这类尚未在美国上市的低价产品，他们将会成为我们的潜在客户群。//

第三，我们已经确认本公司已经积累了足够的资金来投入海外市场。所以我们有较为雄厚的资金支持。我们可以先让本公司产品在美国销售，然后再进军到世界各地。//

2. At our company, our goal is quite simple: Customers always come first. We start with high quality to provide exceptional value. Then we add a special personal feature. It is this high quality that enables us to enhance everyday living, make life healthier and more comfortable by creating everything you want. //

We believe this is what "putting you first" really means. Our customer-first philosophy is the reason why our company can generate 12 billion USD a year with branches in over 120 countries. The future always brings change. But at our company, our goal to satisfy customers will remain unchanged. //

第 8 单元　口译笔记 3/ 市场营销

✱ 主题口译

Text A　跨界营销

主题导入

"跨界"代表一种新锐的生活态度与审美方式的融合。跨界合作对于品牌的最大益处是让原本毫不相干的元素相互渗透、相互融合，从而给品牌一种立体感和纵深感。在营销中，建立"跨界"关系的不同品牌一定是互补性而非竞争性品牌。这里所说的互补，并非功能上的互补，而是用户体验上的互补。以下是淘宝和优步在跨界营销方面的尝试。

请先熟悉列出的词汇与短语再听录音，并在录音停顿时将下列篇章口译成英语。

词汇与短语

跨界营销	crossover marketing
共有消费者	shared consumers
叠加效应	additive effect
日料	Japanese cuisine
试衣间	fitting room

跨界营销在营销界早已经不是什么新鲜名词，许多品牌之间针对同一档次的目标消费者，即"共有消费群"，联合举办一次营销活动。看似风马牛不相及的产品通过跨界营销，将各自已经确立的市场人气和品牌内蕴相互转移到对方品牌身上，实现双赢，产生品牌叠加效应。//

在跨界营销，优步和淘宝可以说是玩得最为风生水起的品牌，创意营销更是层出不穷，花样迭出。//

在年轻人越来越引领时尚、消费趋势的今年，淘宝为扩大在年轻群体尤其 90 后中的声量，让品牌更加年轻化，将上新活动升级为"淘宝新势力周"，在一周内淘宝集结了 10 万家店铺，发布 60 余万件新品，打造了一场互联网时装周。// 作为与天猫在品牌价值上有差异化的平台，此次战役以"新势力，独立上身"为活动口号，提出"每个年轻人都该有一张独立的面孔"，以此展现淘宝品牌独立、个性的态度。//

热衷于跨界营销的优步在今年暑假与"梦龙""Enjoy"等品牌合作推出过送雪糕、日料上门等服务。而在近期，优步则与淘宝合作打造移动试衣间。杭州、成都、广州三地优步用户可一键呼叫，体验神秘专业人士的一对一换装搭配指导和全新造型打造。//

119

商务英语口译

Text B Avon in the Chinese Market

主题导入

美国雅芳产品有限公司是全美500强企业之一，1886年创立于美国纽约。如今，雅芳已发展成为世界上最大的美容化妆品公司之一，也是世界领先的美容化妆品及相关产品的直销公司。以下是雅芳公司CEO对中国市场发展的简介。

请先熟悉列出的词汇与短语再听录音，并在录音停顿时将下列篇章口译成汉语。

词汇与短语

at an all-time high	达到历史新高
Fortune	财富
Business Week	商业周刊
direct selling company	直销公司
beauty boutiques	美容精品店
vision	愿景

With sales this year reaching 6.7 billion USD and a stock price at an all-time high, we've had some incredible results. Avon has been named one of *Fortune* magazine's most admired companies and we've made *Business Week*'s list of the world's most valuable brands for three years in a row. //

Of all the countries where Avon does business, China is, without doubt, our fastest growing market. Avon entered China in 1990, and we were the first international direct selling company to open doors here. Over the years, we have adapted our selling techniques to the unique needs of the Chinese consumer. // Today, we sell our products in a variety of different ways, with broad distribution through 5,000 independent beauty boutiques, owned and operated by entrepreneurs who are building successful Avon businesses. //

More than three quarters of these beauty boutique owners are women, in keeping with Avon's founding principles of providing business and financial support for women. This is really the core of our business vision and it is consistent from market to market all over the world. //

Text C 中国文化"走出去"的三大战略

主题导入

中国文化是中国56个民族文化的总称。随着中国国力的强盛，国际地位的提高，世界各国包括亚洲、欧洲在内的一些国家都对中华文化给予了高度的认同和重视。中国文化"走出去"变得尤为重要。以下是对中国文化"走出去"战略的简述。

第 8 单元　口译笔记 3/ 市场营销

> 请先熟悉列出的词汇与短语再听录音，并在录音停顿时将下列篇章口译成英语。
>
> **词汇与短语**
>
> | 站稳脚跟 | to gain a foothold |
> | 销售渠道 | sales channel |
> | 海外营销机构 | overseas marketing agency |
> | 奠定良好基础 | to lay a solid foundation for |

中国文化产品的出口仍然落后于西方发达国家。这对于中国的文化企业来说，既是机遇，又是挑战。//

首先，我们要提高文化产品的质量，必须打造一定数量的品牌，使其在国际市场上站稳脚跟。这是一项系统的工程，既要有对中国文化的深入了解，又要有谦虚的态度来学习其他文化。这时，企业的责任就是不断推出具有市场竞争力的品牌产品。//

其次，我们要增强产品销售渠道。缺少海外营销机构严重制约了中国文化产业的发展。所以，可以在美洲、欧洲等重点城市建立海外营销机构，针对目标市场进行开发和产品推广，建立中国文化产品可靠的营销渠道。//

再次，政府应该对重点文化产业进行扶持，提供个性化的政策引领，为文化产品发展奠定良好的基础。//

Text D McDonald's Market Performance

主题导入

麦当劳是全球大型跨国连锁餐厅，1955 年创立于美国，在很多国家代表着一种美式生活方式，受到人们的喜爱。以下是对其销售市场的分析。

> 请先熟悉列出的词汇与短语再听录音，并在录音停顿时将下列篇章口译成汉语。
>
> **词汇与短语**
>
> | slump | 衰退 |
> | gloss | （表面的）光泽 |
> | to contract | 收缩 |
> | to set a high bar to beat | 设置一个很难逾越的较高标准 |
> | Big Mac | 巨无霸 |

McDonald's comparable sales for November showed weakness globally, even though the fast-food chain has generally succeeded in winning market share in the slump. //

U.S. sales unexpectedly fell, as rising unemployment hit breakfast sales in particular and the rivals increased the price of marketing campaigns. // Previously strong European sales managed only 2.5% growth, half what was expected. And despite their positive macroeconomic gloss, emerging market sales contracted. //

In Asia, last November's 13% growth set a high bar to beat. But there was poor month in China, which suggests consumer confidence is lagging improvements in output—particularly in the coastal regions where McDonald's has many of its restaurants. //

This softness means McDonald's will probably open only 140 stores in China this year, not the expected 175. But that should leave it with opportunities ready to go as the Chinese rediscover their taste for Big Macs. //

Text E 销售代表年会上的发言

主题导入

企业的销售代表主要职责是销售产品，一些企业会举行年会以总结年度销售业绩，表彰公司杰出的销售代表。以下是某公司销售代表年会上关于一位成功销售员经验的介绍。

请先熟悉列出的词汇与短语再听录音，并在录音停顿时将下列篇章口译成英语。

词汇与短语

归功于	to be attributed to
无人可比	incomparable
拓展人脉	to expand connections
双赢	win-win result

在准备今晚演讲时，我想起了我们最成功的销售员陈耕先生。他的成功主要归功于一些重要观念：首先，陈耕先生会努力全面了解买主的需求并提供他们最满意的商品。// 他对客户的特别关怀和照顾使客户们了解到他所关心的是客户的福利，而非仅仅是做买卖而已。他对公司产品的知识了解无人可比。他会花很多时间在市场调查上，阅读所有关于产品领域的资料。// 长时间以来，他对这个行业的了解比任何人都要多。而且，他还能针对新闻上的重大议题发表看法。他不是那种强记许多事实、到时候应用的人，而是一个热爱生活的人。//

我认为一个成功的推销员最重要的部分，就是把你客户的需要放在第一位，对你所从事的行业有深刻的了解，而且要待客户如朋友，再发展成生意伙伴。这样才能拓展人脉，达到双赢。//

第 8 单元 口译笔记 3/ 市场营销

Text F Management Principle of Starbucks

主题导入

星巴克是美国一家连锁咖啡公司的名称，1971年成立，为全球最大的咖啡连锁店，其总部坐落于美国华盛顿州西雅图市。以下是星巴克CEO对其经营理念的一个简短介绍。

请先熟悉列出的词汇与短语再听录音，并在录音停顿时将下列篇章口译成汉语。

词汇与短语

inspirational	鼓舞人心的
arrogance	傲慢

I think that the Starbucks' name was a magic and the people who were working for the company were so passionate about the coffee and the customer. And I believe that we could make history. //

I also believe that people, regardless of the differences, want to be part of something larger than themselves. They want to be a part of something that they can go home at night, share with their family and friends that they are proud to be a part of. // So we've created an environment both for our customers and people. That's inspirational. When you are managing a company and managing people, it's really important that everyone is treated equally and there is no arrogance. // At the end of the day, as a manager, I would say to future entrepreneurs and business people as well: You wanna demonstrate to your people not how much you know, but how much you care, and if you can do that in a genuinely authentic way, that is gonna cross all over the cultural differences because you want to build emotional connection with people. It's a common language. The CEO's job is to ensure that people are heard, valued and supported. //

✱ 情景口译

提示：

学生三人或四人一组，根据下面的主题提示进行模拟口译，注意使用本单元介绍的技能和句型。

主题一　在公司销售年会上的讲话

参与人： 1. 冯佳女士，某家具公司的销售部经理

　　　　2. 参加公司销售年会的中外嘉宾

　　　　3. 译员

内　容： 1. 冯女士介绍该公司的年度销售额和公司销售情况

　　　　2. 冯女士分析现在经济大背景和竞争对手情况

　　　　3. 冯女士对明年销售业绩进行预测，鼓励销售员工齐心协力再创佳绩

主题二　产品营销方案的介绍

参与人： 1. 施密特先生，瑞士某表业公司代表

　　　　2. 参加国际钟表展会的中外采购商

　　　　3. 译员

地　点： 某国际会展中心

内　容： 1. 施密特先生简单介绍该表业公司的历史和发展历程

　　　　2. 施密特先生分析该品牌钟表的特点和优势

　　　　3. 施密特先生介绍新系列产品特征及适合人群

　　　　4. 施密特先生提出四种产品营销方案

✲ 句式扩展

1. Competitive domestic markets have driven companies to look further in their search for competitive advantage.

   竞争的国内市场使得公司进一步寻找竞争优势。

2. A clothing company that only buys from Asian suppliers at low cost will find that labor costs increase over time, then it'll have to find new labor supplier.

只从亚洲供应商以低成本购买货物的服装公司会发现，随着时间的推移，劳动成本增加，将不得不寻找新的劳动供应商。

3. It's dangerous to deliver outstanding performance in one area such as cost or flexibility.
   只在一个领域表现出色是很危险的，比如在成本或灵活性上。

4. If it's going to be a long-term partnership, you need to discuss how much sharing of information and resources will be necessary to gain profits.
   如果是一个长期的伙伴关系，你需要讨论需要共享多少信息和资源来获得利润。

5. G company is currently doing 1 billion dollars of business on the Internet and plays a leading role in its field.
   G公司目前在互联网上的业务价值有十亿美元，并在此领域起着主导作用。

6. Since oil is a primary ingredient of many products, our company is very much affected by its price.
   由于石油是许多产品的主要成分，我们公司受石油价格的影响很大。

7. In the retail business, we have to consistently provide new ideas, new innovation and cater to the market.
   在零售业，我们必须不断地提供新的想法，进行新的创新来迎合市场。

8. Our company has more than 1,000 shopping malls across the country and aims at middle class in particular.
   我们公司在全国有1 000多个购物中心，主要针对中产阶级。

9. Retailers are offering special online deals as well as free delivery service to encourage spending through the holiday.
   零售商将推出网购特惠活动以及免费送货服务来鼓励假日消费。

10. Our New Year plan will be the launch of promotion campaigns to stimulate customers' spending.
    我们的新年计划将推出促销活动来刺激顾客消费。

11. 我们要加快发展连锁经营和电子商务以降低成本和销售价格。
    We will speed up the development of chain management and e-commerce in order to reduce costs and selling prices.

12. 国有企业要想发展壮大，必须在国际市场上具备核心竞争力。

    If state-owned enterprises want to develop, they must have the core competitiveness in the international market.

13. 上述产品是特意为贵方制造的，我公司是经营这些产品最大的公司之一。

    The product mentioned above is especially manufactured for you, and my company is one of the largest companies making these products.

14. 至于我们产品的质量，可以说是中国最好的、最信得过的。

    As for the quality of our products, I can say that they are the best and the most reliable in China.

15. 推出一个新产品，成功还是失败，就看对该产品的开发和市场开拓的工作做得如何。

    The success or failure, when a new product is launched, depends on its development and market exploration.

16. 在意大利已有生产，而且在国际市场上成功打开了销路的产品，可以在中国生产并出口。

    Products that have already been produced in Italy and achieved success in the international market can be manufactured in China and exported to other countries.

17. 我们必须开发满足市场需求的产品，而且要物美价廉。

    We must develop products that meet the market demand and also have high quality with comparatively low prices.

18. 政府举办多种形式的展销会，搭建平台，促进市场信息的流动，为人们提供前沿信息。

    The government should organize various forms of fairs and build a platform to promote the flow of market information, thus providing the latest information for people.

19. 今年我们零售企业销售额同比增长13%，表明经济已经复苏。

    The sales of retail enterprises increased by 13% this year, showing that the economy has recovered.

20. 我们通过细致的市场调查，使产品真正能够给消费者带来好处。

    Through careful market research, we make sure that the products can really bring benefits to consumers.

口译笔记训练中的常见问题和解决策略（下）

问题 4：口译笔记上多是听辨过程中听不懂或没听清的内容，所以在解读笔记时，无法读出笔记的含义，更不用说进行译语的表达了。

对策：出现这种情况的根本原因是没有树立正确的口译笔记观。口译笔记是在理解原文的基础上进行的，每个笔记符号都传达一定的信息。将听不懂或没听清的信息记录下来，在本质上是一种干扰。遇到听不懂的信息时，应该把精力集中到听辨上，以理解为主，而不是盲目地进行记录。要养成不理解，不动笔；没听懂，不记录的习惯。

问题 5：由于时间紧迫，口译笔记潦草，在表达阶段无法辨认，影响译语的表达流畅性。

对策：口译笔记的个性化特点说明口译笔记只要译员本人在工作的当时可以对笔记进行解读即可。迫于时间的压力，译员应该选用自己最熟悉、最简单的单词、符号等进行记录，使笔记上呈现的信息清楚明了，没有歧义，同时避免自己也无法解读的潦草字迹。

问题 6：由于时间有限，口译笔记中应该多用符号，少用单词或汉字。所以在建立笔记系统时，创造的符号越多越好，这样会提高记录的效率，可以在有限的时间内记录更多的内容。

对策：如果每一个词都创造一个符号，无疑就是创造了另外一种语言，对译员来说反而是一种负担。口译笔记符号在精不在多。一个符号可以表示一类词语及其同义词和近义词。以↑为例，它可以表示与"上升"相关的所有词语，如汉语中"增长""增加""升值"等，英语中"increase""grow""soar""rise""raise"等。此外，符号之间还可以自由组合，比如：E 表示"欧洲"，º 表示"人"，那么 Eº 就可以表示"欧洲人"。这样就在很大程度上减少了符号的数量，提高口译笔记的效率。

数字口译 1/ 商务谈判

第 9 单元

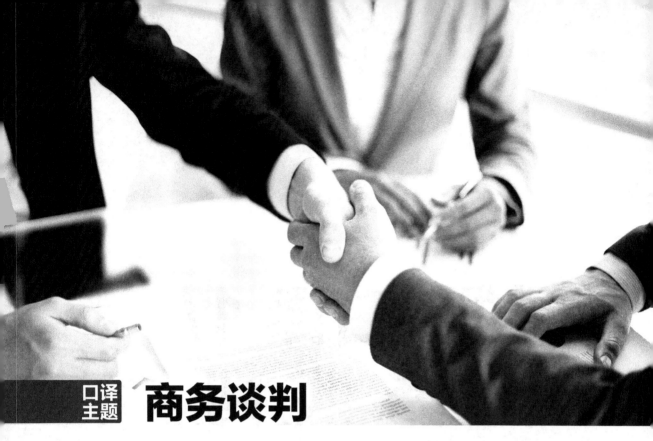

口译主题：商务谈判

　　商务谈判是商务活动的一个重要组成部分，是指买卖双方为了促成交易而进行的活动，或是为了解决买卖双方的争端，并取得各自的经济利益的一种方法和手段。通过商务谈判，各方陈述己方观点、听取对方意见，经过磋商，消除距离，彼此让步，最终取得一致，达成协议。商务谈判一般包括申明价值、创造价值和克服障碍三个步骤。

　　商务谈判一般有如下过程：初始阶段，双方相互寒暄、了解，先谈一些不相干的话题营造和谐的谈判气氛；谈判主体阶段，双方交流与工作相关的信息并进行磋商，力求说服对方；谈判尾声，双方表明底线，做出让步并最终达成协议。

✲ 学习目标

　　　　了解数字口译的特点

　　　　逐步掌握数字口译的方法并加强练习

　　　　了解商务谈判的文体特点

　　　　掌握商务谈判的常用口译句式

第 9 单元　数字口译 1/ 商务谈判

✽ 技巧讲解

数字口译是口译训练中的重点和难点，即使是资深译员在遇到数字时也不敢马虎，因为发言人提出数字，必然是想通过数字具体客观地反映重要的事实，一旦漏译或误译，势必影响口译效果，甚至在商业活动中，会导致谈判中断、合作破裂。但是，数字的出现往往是独立的，与上下文不含任何的逻辑关系，一旦漏掉，不可能再推测出来，因此数字一直是口译中的一个难点。在处理数字口译时，需要重点注意以下几个方面：

数字

数字分为基数词和序数词。基数词表示数量多少，序数词表示顺序。由于数字通常用来表示精准的数量或次序，因此一就是一，二就是二，不容混淆。此外，数词在日常交际中也被赋予了特殊的文化意义，在一定语境中也能表达情感，例如："三百六十行，行行出状元""知己知彼，百战百胜"都是在利用数词的模糊义传递信息。这一点会在下一单元具体讲述，本单元着重讲述精确性的数字口译。

由于口译的即时性，即使是复杂的一长串数字，译员也只有一次听的机会，况且数字排列毫无逻辑可言，译员单凭耳听是不够的。一般情况下，口译中，不论是交替传译还是同声传译，译员遇到数字都会记录下来，一方面是为了准确记录数字，另一方面，落到纸面上后，译员在口译时进行转换也会方便。由于汉英数字分段方式不一样，汉语是四位一段（"个""十""百""千"，每四位为一段），英语是三位一段（"个""十""百"，每三位为一段），汉语中的"万""十万""千万""亿"在英语中找不到与之直接对应的词，因此，汉英互译中需要经过转换。而数字的转换，即使是已经落在纸面上，也需要译员对于数位分段非常熟悉，才能做出迅速反应，这是需要长期练习的。以下简单介绍几种记录数字的方法。

1. 记缩写

有时候出现的数字非常整齐，这时就可以听到什么记什么，不做任何转换。例如：

10,000,000 记作：10m，million 缩写为 m

1,300,000,000 记作：1.3b，billion 缩写为 b

五万七千九百八 记作：5.798 万

九百六十三万 记作：963 万或 9.63m

一亿两千三百四十五万六千七百八十九 记作：1.23456789 亿或 123.456789m

2. 填空法

译员事先预料到会出现数字时，可以根据汉英数字的分位制作如下表格，听到数字时对号入座填进去即可。

trillion			billion			million			thousand		
万亿	千亿	百亿	十亿	亿	千万	百万	十万	万	千	百	十	个

例如：听到英文数字 twenty-three billion forty-nine million three hundrend and fifty-six thousand seven hundred and ten 时，可以利用上述表格把数字按照相应的数位填进去，再根据下方汉语的提示，顺次译出汉语即可。所以，上述数字填入表格为：

trillion		2	3	billion	4	9	million	3	5	6	thousand	7	1	0
万亿	千亿	百亿	十亿	亿	千万	百万	十万	万	千	百	十	个

顺次读出，就得到了"二百三十亿四千九百三十五万六千七百一十"。同样的方法也适用于汉英数字的口译。

量词

量词是表示单位的词。汉语量词分为两类：表人或物的量词叫物量词，如"里""吨""个""头"；表示动作或行为的量词叫动量词，如"次""遍""顿"。汉语的量词非常发达，几乎一个名词就有一个与之对应的量词，使用起来非常复杂，如"一辆车""一头牛"等。

而英语中没有量词，仅把表示量的词划入名词范畴，叫作"单位名词"。英语中表示数量概念时，要么数词或不定冠词直接放在名词之前，如"three boys""a Chinese book"；要么用"量词+of+名词"的形式，如"a pair of shoes""a dozen of eggs"。

通过对比可以发现，汉英量词在口译时需要视情况而定进行转换。例如：由于度量单位不同，"里""英里""英尺"等需要经过计算换算。由于汉语中有许多英语没有的度量单位，汉译英时，越来越多的度量单位音译了过去，也逐渐被英语国家所接受，如"chi"（尺）、"jin"（斤）。不过，大多数情况下，汉译英可以简单地忽略掉汉语的量词，转换为英语中"数字 + 名词单复数"的形式。而英译汉时则需要根据汉语的习惯加上量词。如：

原文 1 We plan to buy 3,000 machines if the price is reasonable.
译文 1 如果价格合理的话，我们打算购买 3 000 台机器。

以下列出常用的度量衡单位供大家参考：

计量单位	中文	英文	缩写	计量单位	中文	英文	缩写
重量单位	克	gram	g.	体积单位	立方米	cubic meter	m³
	千克	kilogram	kg.		立方厘米	cubic centimeter	cm³
	公吨	metric ton	m.t.	容积单位	升	liter	l.
	长吨	long ton	l.t.		毫升	mililiter	ml.
	短吨	short ton	sh.t.		加仑	gallon	gal.
	磅	pound	lb.		蒲式耳	bushel	bu.

计量单位	中文	英文	缩写	计量单位	中文	英文	缩写
长度单位	千米	kilometer	km.	数量单位	只	piece	pc.
	米	meter	m.		双	pair	
	厘米	centimeter	cm.		打	dozen	doz.
	毫米	millimeter	mm.		卷	roll/coil	
	码	yard	yd.		桶	barrel	
	英尺	foot	ft.		件	package	pkg.
	英寸	inch	in.		套	set	
面积单位	平方米	square meter	m^2		罗	gross	gr.
	平方千米	square kilometer	km^2		箱	carton	
	平方英尺	square foot	ft^2		袋	bag	

所指

在准确记录数字、数字的单位后,译员也必须清楚数字的所指,即数字代表的意义,否则即使费心费力记录了数字,也是无用功。如:

原文 2 Last year, the total volume of contracted foreign capital was 238.6 billion USD, with an increase of 15.6%, and actually utilized foreign capital is 78.4 billion USD, with an increase of 15.2%.

译文 2 去年,合同外资总额达 2 386 亿美元,增长 15.6%;实际利用外资 784 亿美元,增长 15.2%。

例句中出现了多个数字,而每个数字所指的意义也是口译中的关键要素。所以,在口译中,不仅要把数字记准翻对,数字所代表的意义也要译得准确。

✳ 技巧练习

🎧 请根据录音将下列对话口译成汉语或英语。

A: I'd like to know your quotation.//

B: 太阳镜的标签价是 50 美元一副,我给您 45 美元,怎么样?//

A: That's much more than I expected.//

B: 40 美元如何?//

A: I offer 30 USD a pair.//

B: 这样吧,我们双方各让一步,每副 35 美元,一分钱都不能少了,这样可以吗?//

A: OK, it's agreed. What about discounts?//

B: 您打算预订多少副?//

A: What discount would you offer on an order of, say, 2,000 pairs? //

B: 八五折。//

A: What about 3,000 pairs? //

B: 八折。//

A: I'm ordering in large quantities and I'm looking for a much larger discount. //

B: 如果您想要更低的折扣，您订的数量还得再大些才行。//

A: Isn't an order of 3,000 pairs large enough? Unless you make a concession we're getting nowhere. //

B: 那我们双方都做出让步，你订 3 000 副，我给你 7.5 折，可以吗？//

A: Fair enough. Thank you. //

主题口译

Text A 技术引进

主题导入

技术引进是指一个国家或地区的企业、研究单位、机构通过一定方式从本国或其他国家、地区的企业、研究单位、机构获得先进适用的技术的一种跨国行为。企业为获得或使用技术需缴纳一定费用，包括入门费和提成。支付入门费既作为使用对方技术的预先经济补偿，又起到定金的作用。转让方的提成收入则是指双方分享额外利润、按照一定比例计算出的部分。以下是关于技术引进的谈判。

请先熟悉列出的词汇与短语再听录音，并在录音停顿时将下列对话口译成英语或汉语。

词汇与短语

技术引进	to import advanced technology
工业产权	industrial property
入门费	initial down payment
提成	royalty
know-how	专有技术；诀窍
joint venture	合资企业
licensed item	许可产品

A: 我们要引进的技术不仅是世界先进的,而且也是适合中国需要的。//

B: Well, then could you be more specific about the term "technology" that you are referring to? //

A: 我们所说的"技术"主要包括两个方面:工业产权和专有技术。//

B: All right. We agree with that. As for the know-how we promise to transfer to the joint venture is what we are adopting in our production currently. As the leading producer in the world, our know-how is always considered cutting-edge, and this one is especially fit to the customers' demands in China. // And you've already known that you'll pay for it in the form of royalties apart from a certain initial down payment, right? //

A: 这个我已经知道了。由于是第一次做技术引进,我们对技术提成率不是很清楚。大概是多少呢？//

B: Well, the minimum generally accepted royalty rate of the technology is 7% of the sales price of all licensed items made and sold during the term of the agreement, in addition to an initial down payment of 150,000 USD. //

A: 入门费和提成率恐怕都太高了！起步阶段,公司的产量低、产品质量不稳定,恐怕会经历一段困难时期。而且,得到消费者的认可也需要时间。//

B: We understand that, but the initial down payment cannot be reduced. We may consider lowering the royalty rate. //

A: 好吧。如果贵公司可以免去前两个生产年度的提成费,再将提成率降到净销售价的4%,我们还是可以接受的。//

B: Well, that depends. Could you tell us how long the term of agreement generally lasts? //

A: 一般不超过十年。//

B: All right. If we enter into a 10-year-long agreement, we will accept your proposal to begin royalty payments in the third production year and cut the royalty rate to 4%. //

Text B 冰箱报盘

主题导入

报盘,也叫报价,是卖方主动向买方提供商品信息或者是对询盘的答复,是卖方根据买方的来信,向买方报盘,其内容可包括商品名称、规格、数量、包装条件、价格、付款方式和交货期限等。以下是一家德国代理商与某集团代表就 H 牌冰箱的报盘进行的谈判。

商务英语口译

> 请先熟悉列出的词汇与短语再听录音，并在录音停顿时将下列对话口译成英语或汉语。
>
> **词汇与短语**
> 报盘　　　　offer
> 到岸价　　　CIF

A: 我们开始谈正事吧。//

B: Yes, fine. I've come about your offer for H refrigerators. //

A: 我们的报盘已经准备好了，报价是这样的：10 000 台 H 牌冰箱，单价 500 欧元，这是德国主要港口到岸价，2017 年 1 月启运。目前市场价格上涨，相信我们的报价是最好的。//

B: 500 EUR! That's 10% higher than last year. //

A: 没错。因为我们利用了最新的科技，改善了产品性能，提高了产品效率，更加环保。此外，全球原材料价格在上升，相信您也是知道的。//

B: I understand. But we have such a large order and we can make it even bigger, say 15,000. Any discount? //

A: 鉴于我们良好的合作关系，10 000 台我给您九五折，15 000 台给您九折。//

B: Great. I'll take 15,000 this time. Last year, your refrigerators were rapidly sold out in less than five months. I'm sure we can do better this year. I am considering to put an order of 20,000. Could you please offer a larger discount? //

A: 由于国外需求量都很大，目前我们至多供应您 15 000 台。九折也是最大的折扣了。//

B: If you can't supply our need to the full, our customers will turn to other suppliers. Can you supply me another 3,000 refrigerators and a little bit more discount? //

A: 我们将尽最大的努力满足您的需求，再给您 3 000 台。如果您订购 18 000 台的话，就给您打个八八折吧。//

B: All right, I'll take 18,000 refrigerators this time. But I hope you could supply the other 2,000 when the next supply comes in. //

A: 一旦供货情况有所改善，我们会与您联系。//

第 9 单元　数字口译 1/ 商务谈判

Text C　独家代理

主题导入

独家代理是指在指定地区和一定的期限内，由该独家代理人单独代表委托人从事有关的商业活动。在进出口业务中，采用独家代理方式时，作为委托人的出口商即给予国外的代理人在规定的地区和期限内推销指定商品的专营权。委托人在代理区域内达成的交易，凡属独家代理人专营的商品，委托人要向他支付约定比例的佣金。以下是关于独家代理的谈判内容。

请先熟悉列出的词汇与短语再听录音，并在录音停顿时将下列对话口译成英语或汉语。

词汇与短语

独家代理	sole agent
佣金	commission
目录单	catalog
推销材料	promotional material
平摊	on 50-50 basis

A: 既然你要做我们的独家代理，我们想知道你推销我们产品的计划。你知道代理人会在打入新市场方面给我们很大帮助。//

B: Well, we'll do a lot of advertising in newspapers as well as on TV programs. Also we'll send our salesmen around the United States to promote the sales of your goods. We propose the guaranteed annual sale may amount to 265,000 USD for a start. //

A: 代理地区包括哪些地方？//

B: The territory to be covered is the whole of the United States. //

A: 你收取多少佣金？//

B: Our commission is quite reasonable. We usually get a 12% commission of the amount on every deal. //

A: 但是我们这类产品的所有代理商都只拿 9% 的佣金。//

B: Our customers are not familiar with your goods, so we'll have to spend a lot of money in advertising to gain the recognition for your products. As you indicated just now, a lot of initial work has to be done to draw business away from other manufacturers. I think you should take

137

advertising expense into consideration. Besides, the training for the salesmen adds to the expense, too. So what I have in mind is 12%. //

A: 我们产品的价格是要按照成本计算的。12% 的佣金意味着要提高价格。不过，为了帮助你们推销，我们这次可以破例，给你们 10% 的佣金，试销一年。//

B: For every 1,000 sets sold in excess of the quota, we will get 1% more in commission, is that all right? //

A: 好吧。对于你们的努力，超过定额每多销 1 000 台，我们便多给佣金 1%。我们免费给你们提供目录单和其他推销材料，广告费用我们平摊。如果合作愉快，我们再讨论下一年的佣金。//

B: Quite reasonable. We look forward to happy and successful cooperation between us. //

Text D　订购汽车

主题导入

车展是由政府机构、专业协会或主流媒体等组织，在专业展馆或会场中心进行的汽车产品展示展销会或汽车行业经贸交易会、博览会等。在某国际汽车展览会上，南非汽车经销商欲向百瑞汽车公司订购瑞格 SUV。以下是他们的对话。

请先熟悉列出的词汇与短语再听录音，并在录音停顿时将下列对话口译成英语或汉语。

词汇与短语

销售代表	sales rep
气囊	air bag
排气量	exhaust
信用证	L/C（letter of credit）
auto distributor	汽车经销商
Riggo	瑞格
oil consumption	耗油量

A: 早上好，先生。我是王萌，百瑞汽车公司的销售代表。有什么可以帮您的？//

B: I'm Alex Sanders, an auto distributor from South Africa. I've looked around the exhibition for a couple of days and found your range of Riggo SUVs particularly interesting. //

A: 这就有一款。这款车型的排气量为每分钟 1.5 升。车上装有司机和前排乘客的安全气囊，两侧和后面车窗镶有经过特殊热处理的玻璃。这款汽车才上市不到两个月就大受欢迎。//

B: What's the oil consumption? //

A: 每百公里 8.5 升。//

B: How many colors do you have for the SUVs? //

A: 6 种，黑、白、棕、红、蓝、黄。//

B: How much is it? //

A: 瑞格 7 系列标配每辆南非口岸的 CIF 价为 24 700 美元，瑞格 5 系列标配每辆 21 860 美元。//

B: Marvelous! I'd like to place an order for these two types. //

A: 好的，您打算订购多少呢？ //

B: I'd like to order 180 Riggo 7 SUVs equally in 6 colors and 300 Riggo 5 SUVs also equally in 6 colors. 480 SUVs in total. What's the total price? //

A: 180 辆瑞格 7 共计 444.6 万美元，300 辆瑞格 5 共计 655.8 万美元。总计 1 100.4 万美元。//

B: Could you please offer me a good quantity discount for so large an order? //

A: 是的，这样的订单我们给 12% 的折扣。//

B: How much shall I pay then? //

A: 总价 1 100.4 万美元，扣掉 12% 折扣，即 132.048 万美元，总计 968.352 万美元。您就付 968 万美元吧！ //

B: That's nice! How should I pay? //

A: 鉴于这是我们之间的第一笔订单，按照惯例，需要您以信用证的方式付款。//

B: No problem. //

Text E 议价

主题导入

议价，又称协商价格，是指买卖双方通过协商确定的一个双方均愿接受的价格。在一般情况下，议价往往以市价为上限，以变动成本为下限，在此范围内确定协商价格。以下是买卖双方就丝绸产品议价的对话。

请先熟悉列出的词汇与短语再听录音，并在录音停顿时将下列对话口译成汉语或英语。

词汇与短语

报价价格　　　　quotation

A: I have come to hear about your offer for your silk dress. //

B: 好的，已经准备好了。3 000条裙子，每条45美元，洛杉矶到岸价，2017年4月至5月运送，其他条件照旧，报价5天内均有效。//

A: Oh, your price has gone up sharply. It's 15% higher than that of last year! //

B: 的确，我们涨价幅度较大。不过你知道的，对此品质的绸缎原料需求猛增，涨价就不可避免了。即使如此，我们的报价在同类竞争者中也是打着灯笼难找的。//

A: I don't think so. Some of the quotations we have received are much lower than yours. Your price is already over the market price. We can't accept your offer unless your price is reduced by 10%. //

B: 10%？那太多了。我们互相迁就下吧，5%怎么样？如果咱俩不是老朋友，才不会给你砍掉5%呢。这已经是我能做的最大让步了。//

A: Thank you. I'll accept it. //

Text F 开具信用证付款

主题导入

信用证是目前国际贸易中最主要、最常用的一种结算（付款）方式，是一种由银行依照客户的要求和指示开立的有条件的承诺付款的书面文件。信用证是开给卖方的，以卖方为受益人，卖家按照合约要求把货物付运出去，然后取得一套单证，其中包括最重要的已装船提单，而且其中的数量、日期及表面状况与买卖合约是一致的，即可前往信用证指定的银行（议付行）申请结汇。以下是以信用证为付款方式的对话。

请先熟悉列出的词汇与短语再听录音，并在录音停顿时将下列对话口译成英语或汉语。

词汇与短语

采购订单	purchase order
律师	attorney
machine tool	机床
Shenyang Machine Tool Co., Ltd.	沈阳机床厂

第 9 单元 数字口译 1/ 商务谈判

A: 我们来讨论下采购订单的要点，好吗？之后可以让我们的律师检查一下，再签协议。//

B: Fine. We would like to buy a total of 40 units of machine tools from Shenyang Machine Tool Co., Ltd. But I should mention that we want to buy only a few sample machines first. I believe you mentioned the unit price for one order of more than 30 units was 58,000 RMB. //

A: 没错。//

B: Could we make an initial purchase of five units at the 40-unit price of 58,000 RMB? We would then follow that later with another order for the remaining 35 units. //

A: 由于您的第一笔订单只要 5 台，恐怕单价要按 63 000 元计算。//

B: Would it be possible to receive a L/C of 58,000 RMB for each of the five units purchased in our initial order if we follow up within three months with a second order for the remaining 35 units? //

A: 可以接受。一旦接到你方已开具信用证的银行通知，我们立即正式向沈阳机床厂下订单。//

B: Great! //

❋ 情景口译

提示：
学生三人或四人一组，根据下面的主题提示进行模拟口译，注意使用本单元介绍的技能和句型。

主题一 中国某知名电器公司海外代理

参与人： 1. 史密斯先生，英国某贸易公司中国业务部经理

2. 李锐先生，中国某知名电器公司海外业务部销售代表

3. 译员

内　容： 1. 史密斯先生介绍该公司的基本情况和销售范围

2. 史密斯先生询问代理该中国知名电器产品的相关问题

3. 双方就代理模式、推销模式、佣金、运输等问题进行谈判

 **主题二** 橄榄油进口交易

参与人： 1. 王林先生，东北地区食用油进口商

2. 格林先生，希腊橄榄油出口商

3. 译员

地　点： 某市进出口产品洽谈会

内　容： 1. 格林先生介绍旗下橄榄油品质

2. 王先生介绍东北地区橄榄油需求量

3. 双方就交易数量、价格、支付方式、运输、保险等问题进行磋商

❋ 句式扩展

1. I have here our price sheet on an FOB basis.

   这是我们以船上交货价为基础的价目单。

2. But first, you will have to give me an idea of the quantity you wish to order from us so that we can adjust our prices accordingly.

   不过要请你说明大概要订购多少，以便我们对价格做相应调整。

3. I will give you all the facts so that you can judge for yourself.

   我会给你所有信息以便你可以自己判断。

4. You made it a point to abide by the contract and especially you were always prompt and equitable in settling claims.

   你们很注意遵守合同、恪守信用，尤其是在理赔方面，反应迅速、公平合理。

5. When your last shipment arrived at our port last week, we had then weighed and the result proved that the goods were underweight.

   上一批货物上周到达我们港口后，我方过了磅，结果发现货物短重。

6. As the goods were sold on CIF terms, you must be held responsible for the shortage.

   鉴于货物是按到岸价条款成交，你方要为短重负责。

第9单元　数字口译1/商务谈判

7. In view of our friendly relationship, we are prepared to meet your claim for the 1.5 metric tons short weight.

   鉴于我们的友好关系，我们准备满足你方1.5公吨短重索赔。

8. We guarantee that the know-how transferred to us will be kept confidential and not let out or be passed on to a third party.

   我们保证转让给我们的专有技术将得到严格保密，绝不会泄露或转让给第三方。

9. To ensure proper work on the construction site, the installation and operation of the equipment you supply, it is necessary that some specialists should be sent here.

   为保证建筑工地工程以及由你方所提供的设备的安装和运转顺利进行，你方派遣几位专家是有必要的。

10. We know that you have rich experience in this field and that you offer technical assistance on favorable terms. I think you may win the tender.

    我们知道在这个领域你方经验丰富，你方还将以优惠条件提供技术援助，我认为你方可能会中标。

11. 谢谢您的询价。为了方便我方报价，能否请您谈谈你方的需求数量？

    Thank you for your inquiry. Would you tell us what quantity you require so that we work out the offer?

12. 请给我一个有效期为90天的CIF报价，目的港为旧金山，报价含10%的佣金。

    I'd like to hear your quotation on a CIF San Francisco basis valid for 90 days, with 10% of commission included in your quotation.

13. 我方无法满足你方的要求，因为你方的价格没有竞争优势。

    We are afraid that we can't comply with your request, because your price is not so competitive.

14. 这是我们最后的价格，如果你们再坚持的话，我们就没有必要再谈下去了，这生意没法做了。

    This is our bottom price. If you stand firm, there is no point in further discussions. We will call the whole deal off.

15. 谈到付款方式，能否告诉我，你们在这方面通常怎么做吗？

    Speaking of terms of payment, can you advise me of your general practice in this respect?

16. 如果今天下订单,什么时候可以收货?您可以确定发货日期吗?产品怎样包装、运输?

    When could I expect to get the supply if I gave you an order today? Could you confirm the dispatch date? How are the products packaged and shipped?

17. 我们已经查看过所有的文件,并意外发现每个文件或多或少地存在些可疑的问题。

    We have already checked all the documents available and unexpectedly find each of them has doubtful points more or less.

18. 我们会严格遵照形式发票和销售合同来支付押金和余额。

    We will obey all the payment terms strictly according to the P/I (proforma invoice) and sales contract.

19. 为了进一步扩大业务往来,也为了表示我们的诚意,我方准备破例降价5%。这样可以吗?

    In order to encourage future business and as a gesture of friendship, we are prepared to make this an exception by reducing our price by 5%, is that okay?

20. 如果用信用证,银行费用就会使我们的成本增加。由于我们的价格非常低,所以我们使用电汇方式付款,既便捷又能降低成本。

    If we open L/C, the bank charge will increase our cost. As our price is very low, we use T/T which is faster and costs less.

※ 口译小贴士

商务谈判口译

商务谈判涉及谈判各方的切身利益,译员在接到口译任务时必须认真做好准备工作,不容马虎。

首先,译员要通过各种可利用的渠道,了解所谈项目的内容、进度、双方立场及需要解决的难题。同时尽量了解自己服务的客户和对方成员的个人基本情况、他们的姓名和职位。有时客户可能不了解译员的工作性质,或受到时间等未知情况的限制,未提前与译员沟通工作内容,译员要主动沟通,并尽力做好准备工作。有时,有的客户会认为提前索要相关材料是译员不自信的表现,请不要在意这种看法,只有顺利完成口译工作才是对自己口译能力的最好证明。

第 9 单元　数字口译 1/ 商务谈判

其次，译员需要查阅资料，补充商务谈判方面的知识，如译员需掌握价格事项、付款方式、合同细节条款、双方权利义务、争端解决等专业术语的表述方法，做到用词准确、专业。同时，商业谈判中的数字既敏感又重要，一字之差，谬以千里，译员千万不能出错，实在没听清楚可以请发言人重复一遍。此外，译员对谈判双方的文化背景也要有所了解，以便做到准确传译，使谈判圆满完成。

再次，在商务会谈过程中，译员要牢记自己的身份，即便是简单的问题，也不要自作主张替本方或对方来回答或解释。在商务会谈中，双方常常需要斗智斗勇、声东击西或话藏玄机。译员要忠于职守，忠实全面地进行翻译，在不确定的地方，视情况询问后再翻译。在商务谈判中，不可避免会出现分歧，万一出现争执，译员要保持冷静，随机应变，利用委婉含蓄的表达方式从中调解，力求不着痕迹地避免、化解矛盾和冲突。但是，虽然译员需要起到调和剂的作用，但并不意味着译员可以随意篡改发言人的原意。谈判中，译员还是需要保持立场中立，忠实原意，不妄加篡改，有听不清、听不懂的内容要及时提问，不要不懂装懂而去胡说。

最后，译员要在商务会谈前后及过程中做好保密工作。不可把会谈内容泄露给第三方。有的公司很注重信息的保密工作，会要求译员把谈判时做的笔记留下来。在这种情况下，译员要积极配合。

第10单元

数字口译 2/商业投资

口译主题 商业投资

投资指的是特定经济主体为了在未来可预见的时期内获得收益或是资金增值,在一定时期内向一定领域投放足够数额的资金或实物的货币等价物的经济行为。投资要素包括投资主体、投资客体、投资目的、投资环境、投资方式、投资过程以及投资结果等。

改革开放后,中国鼓励"引进来、走出去",加快利用外资,巩固和发展外资企业,也鼓励中国企业走出国门开展对外投资。通过引进投资,不仅可以获得商业运营必要的资本,还能够引进外国先进的科学技术和管理经验,加快了中国经济的发展。

✻ 学习目标

    逐步掌握口译中数字的处理技巧

    了解商业投资文体的特点

    掌握商业投资的常用口译句式

第 10 单元　数字口译 2/ 商业投资

✳ 技巧讲解

对于数字口译有了基本了解后，我们来详细探讨不同类型的数字如何处理。

趋势

发言人常常会利用数据说明事物的变化趋势，即增加或减少。因此，译员应掌握一些表示变化趋势的表达，以便准确表达讲话的确切含义。

例如：通常表示"增加"的动词有：

增长 to increase/rise/grow/go up

暴涨 / 猛增 to jump/hike/shoot up/skyrocket/soar/surge/zoom

缓增 to climb/pick up

通常表示"减少"的动词有：

下降 to decrease/fall/decline/drop/go down/reduce

暴跌 / 猛降 to plummet/plunge/slash/tumble

稍降 to dip/slip/trim

掌握了这些表示趋势的动词可以使译文更加准确、生动，这都要依靠平时的积累获得。但是，如果只会用"increase"或者"decrease"表示"涨"或"跌"的趋势，遇到上述表达中的"暴涨""猛降"这样的字眼，又该如何处理呢？

在这种情况下，充分利用副词对"increase"或者"decrease"进行修饰也可以比较准确的表达趋势中的具体含义。下面的这些副词就体现了由极强至极弱的程度变化：

dramatically → sharp → substantially → considerably → far → much → a little → slightly → somewhat → marginally

此外，译员也要做好表示其他意义的词汇的储备，如表示"平衡"或"波动"的动词有：达到平衡 to level off/out；保持平衡 to remain stable；波动 to fluctuate；保持在 to stand/remain at；达到高峰 to reach a peak；等等。

倍数

倍数的增加和减少也是数字口译中的难点。倍数的增加通常有以下几种表达方式：

1. "to increase/rise/grow/exceed/expand/go up/multiply 等 +by+ 倍数"表示"增加 N 倍"。其中，需要注意的是"increase by"表示的是包括基数在内的增长，按原句中的倍数译，不减一，译为"增长了"；"increase to"表示的是不含基数的增长，是增长后的结果，译为"增长到"。如：

> **原文 1**　The sales volume of this company has increased by 6 times compared with that of ten years ago.

译文 1 该公司的销售额与十年前相比已经增加了六倍。

原文 2 The sales volume of this company has increased to 6 times compared with that of ten years ago.

译文 2 该公司的销售额已经增长到了十年前的六倍（即增加了五倍）。

2. "倍数 +as+ 形容词 / 副词 +as"包括基数在内，按英语原句中的倍数译，不减一。如：

原文 3 He is twice as high as his little son.

译文 3 他的身高是他小儿子的两倍。

3. "倍数 +more than"包括基数在内，按英语原句中的倍数译，不减一。如：

原文 4 The number of staff of this company has increased 6 times more than that 10 years ago.

译文 4 该公司员工数量比十年前增加了六倍以上。

4. "倍数 +the size/length/amount 等名词 +of+ 名词"包含基数在内，按英语原句中的倍数译，不减一。如：

原文 5 The earth is 49 times the size of the moon.

译文 5 地球是月球的 49 倍大。

此外，英语中还有用于表示倍数的词，例如："double""triple""quadruple"，这些词用起来事半功倍，译员应注意掌握。

倍数的减少通常是这样表达的：

1. 利用动词 "to decrease/reduce/drop/cut 等 +by times/folds/a factor of"表示。其中，"to decrease by"表示的是包括基数在内的减少，译为"减少了"；"to decrease to"表示的是不含基数的减少，是减少后的结果，译为"减少到"。

2. 英语中的"times"既可表示增加，又可表示减少，但汉语中一般不说"减少了几倍"，而是说减少了"几分之几"或"百分之几"。因此，在表达减少倍数的转换时应该符合汉语习惯，将"倍"转换为分数或百分数。如：

原文 6 The price of this car is twice cheaper than the average.

译文 6 这辆车的价格只有一般轿车价格的一半。

3. "as small/light/slow as"表示"和……一样小 / 轻 / 慢"，暗含减少之意。

4. "there is an N-fold decrease/reduction"则表示"减少至 1/N 或减少了（N-1/N）"。

每逢、每隔

在叙述一定数量间隔或次序时，常用"every 加基数词或序数词"表示，如：every three

days=every third day 的意思是"每逢三天 = 每隔两天"。

虚实

数词既有实指又有虚指。所谓"实指"表示数字有确定的意义，而"虚指"表示数字并不具有它的实际指称意义。数字的虚指往往需要从文化角度来考量，大多具有比喻、强调、夸张、委婉等含义，起到渲染的效果。由于汉英文化存在差异，处理虚指的数字时，需要考虑到汉英文化背景。如果有些文化意义可以对等，则可以直译，例如："a drop in the ocean"对应汉语中的"沧海一粟"，数字对等、文化意义对等。不过，如果一种数字虚指表达在另一种文化中并不存在、找不到对应，就依照目的语的语言习惯来翻译，例如："Two minds are better than one"一般译为"三个臭皮匠胜过一个诸葛亮"，译文中的数字无法对应，文化含义也有所不同，但却形象地传达了意思。

惯用语

在汉英两种语言中，含有数字的惯用语很多，遇到的时候往往不能简单地按照字面意思简单对译，而需要加强积累，产出符合汉英语言表达习惯的地道说法。以下简单列举一些英语中常用的数字惯用语：

a thousand and one ways to help	千方百计
The third time is the charm.	第三次准灵。
to have one thousand and one things to do	日理万机
to be six feet under	死亡、入土
a nine days' wonder	轰动一时、过后即忘的事情
A stitch in time saves nine.	及时处理，事半功倍。
to the nine	十全十美
One cannot be in two places at once.	一心不可二用。
Better master one than engage with ten.	会十事不如精一事。
An inch of time is an inch of gold.	一寸光阴一寸金。
a catch-22 situation	进退两难的境况
six of one and half a dozen of the other	半斤八两
a two-edged sword	双刃剑
to have nine lives	大难不死
to feel like a million dollars	感觉非常好
never in a million years	绝对未有
talk nineteen to the dozen	滔滔不绝

✷ 技巧练习

🎧 **请根据录音将下列段落口译成英语或汉语，注意数字的口译。**

1. 中国与葡语国家关系友好，经济互补性强，双方开展经贸合作的潜力很大。特别是近年来，中国与葡语国家的经济都呈现出良好的增长势头。// 2014年，中国经济增长7.4%，外贸总额突破4万亿美元大关，达到43 030.4亿美元，同比增长3.4%，实际吸收外商直接投资1 196亿美元。// 双方投资环境的改善为企业间扩大互利合作奠定了良好的合作基础。//

2. Li Ning announced in November that it would pay 41 million USD to buy 58% of Shanghai Double Happiness Co., a leading maker of ping-pong tables and equipment and a sponsor of the Olympics. Given ping-pong's popularity in China, analysts think the acquisition will strengthen Li Ning.

✷ 主题口译

Text A 中国与东盟的经贸合作

主题导入

中国–东盟商务与投资峰会从2004年起在广西南宁举办，是中国–东盟工商界最高级别的盛会，是中国和东盟各国之间交流与对话的深入和发展，也是中国与东盟各国共同谋求发展大计的一次盛会。以下节选自张高丽副总理在第十二届中国–东盟商务与投资峰会开幕式上的讲话。

🎧 **请先熟悉列出的词汇与短语再听录音，并在录音停顿时将下列篇章口译成英语。**

词汇与短语

东盟	Association of Southeast Asian Nations（ASEAN）
多极化	multi-polarization
社会信息化	social informationization
中国–东盟自贸区	China–ASEAN Free Trade Area（CAFTA）

中国与东盟国家是陆海相连的友好邻邦，互为天然的合作伙伴。今天，世界多极化、经济全球化、文化多样化、社会信息化深入发展。中国和东盟顺应时代潮流，不断推动友好合作关系向前发展，成为维护地区和平稳定的重要支柱和促进地区发展繁荣的中坚力量。//

中国是东盟第一大贸易伙伴，东盟是中国第三大贸易伙伴、第四大出口市场和第二大进口来源地。去年双方贸易额超过4 800亿美元，增长8.3%，比中国整体对外贸易增速高出4.9

个百分点。目前，双方相互投资累计超过 1 300 亿美元。//

中国与东盟要进一步深化经贸合作，共同打造中国 – 东盟自贸区升级版。挖掘贸易新增长点，扩大贸易和相互投资规模，努力实现 2020 年双边贸易额 1 万亿美元、至 2020 年中国对东盟新增投资额超过 1 000 亿美元目标，促进区域经济一体化发展。//

Text B　China's Outbound Investment

主题导入

在改革开放的进程中，中国不仅积极地吸引外资，而且逐渐增加海外投资。在"一带一路"政策的指引下，海外投资发展呈现良好的态势。以下是有关中国海外投资的情况介绍。

请先熟悉列出的词汇与短语再听录音，并在录音停顿时将下列篇章口译成汉语。

词汇与短语

outbound investment	海外投资
inward foreign direct investment	外来直接投资
the Belt and Road Initiative	一带一路

China's outbound investments will soon outgrow inward foreign direct investment. Nonfinancial outward direct investment reached 102.9 billion USD, up 14.1% from 2013, the first time it topped the 100 billion USD mark, maintaining China's position as the third-largest global outbound investor. //

On current trends, China's outward investment is set to continue to grow faster than its utilization of foreign investment, which will make China a net investor. In 2014, China's actual use of foreign investment stood at 119.6 billion USD, an increase of 1.7% over the previous year, growing faster than other major economies, including the United States, the European Union, Russia and Brazil. // This marked the 23rd consecutive year that China was the leading developing country in attracting foreign investment. //

Investment in developed countries from China also saw rapid growth. China's investment in the United States rose by 23.9%, and in the EU by 1.7 fold, both much faster than overall outward investment growth. //

China spent 64.6% of its total investments in the service sector, with investment in the sector up 27.1% than that of 2013, while investment in mining dropped by 4.1%, representing a declined share of 18.8%. //

China will focus on implementing the Belt and Road Initiative as it further steps up outbound investment and encourages the relocation of advantageous industries and excess capacity of countries along the Belt and Road route. //

Text C　金砖国家投资机会

主题导入

厦门国际投资贸易洽谈会，又称中国国际投资贸易洽谈会，于每年9月8—11日在厦门举办，是中国目前唯一以促进双向投资为目的的国际投资促进活动，也是通过国际展览业协会（UFI）认证的全球规模最大的投资性展览会。以下节选自中国厦门投资贸易洽谈会"金砖国家投资机会"专题论坛。

请先熟悉列出的词汇与短语再听录音，并在录音停顿时将下列篇章口译成英语。

词汇与短语

金砖国家	BRICS nations
消费市场	consumer market

根据国际货币基金组织的最新报告，在过去十年间，金砖国家对世界经济增长的贡献超过50%，预计在2030年之前，金砖国家经济增速仍然普遍高于发达国家和其他的发展中国家。// 金砖国家的人口占世界总人口的43%，经济总量占世界经济总量的23%。金砖五国的中产阶级群体达到6亿人，是美国和欧盟人口的总和，因此，金砖国家是全世界最大的消费市场。// 研究表明，到2020年，金砖国家的消费占全球的份额将从现在的23%增加到62%。这足以体现出金砖国家的经济分量和在世界上的影响力。//

金砖国家的经济互补性强，但是目前的合作还不够理想。2014年，金砖国家的贸易仅达到3 500亿美元，而且以中国和其他四国间的贸易为主，中国仅占总投资的2.32%。所以，金砖国家的合作面临着巨大空间和良好机遇。//

Text D　U.S.-China Two-Way Direct Investment

主题导入

中国和美国是世界上最主要的两大经济体，二者互有投资。但是近年来，美国与中国的相互投资及海外投资等呈现出新的形势。以下是两国投资情况的介绍。

第 10 单元　数字口译 2/ 商业投资

> 🎧 请先熟悉列出的词汇与短语再听录音，并在录音停顿时将下列篇章口译成汉语。
>
> 📝 **词汇与短语**
>
> | | |
> |---|---|
> | cross investment | 交叉投资 |
> | stock | 存量 |
> | direct investment | 直接投资 |
> | flow | 流量 |
> | foreign direct investment (FDI) | 外商直接投资 |
> | outward direct investment | 对外直接投资 |

There is surprisingly little cross investment between the United States and China, the two largest economies in the world. Only 1% of the stock of U.S. direct investment abroad is in China, and in recent years the flow of direct investment from the United States to China has been close to zero. // The stock of Chinese direct investment in the United States is also lower than would be expected given that the United States is the world's largest recipient of foreign direct investment (FDI). // In recent years, however, the flow of direct investment from China to the United States has accelerated rapidly. If current trends persist within a short time, there will be a larger stock of Chinese investment in the United States than of U. S. investment in China. //

The United States and China have been the two largest recipients of FDI in recent decades. At the end of 2011 the total stock of FDI in the world was around 19 trillion USD. Of this, 19% was in the United States and 10% was in China. // These two biggest economies in the world are also major providers of direct investment. At the end of 2012, the United States had a stock of outward direct investment of 4.5 trillion USD, about one quarter of all the FDI in the world. // China is a relative newcomer to outward investment, but its stock of outward direct investment has been growing rapidly. By the end of 2013, the outward stock had increased to 660 billion USD. //

Text E　外商投资在中国

> 🎯 **主题导入**
>
> 改革开放以来，中国各地方政府为了加快本区的经济发展，纷纷设立开发区和工业园区，通过税收优惠、基础设施配套和公共服务等举措进行全面的招商引资，创造了许多"经济奇迹"和"财富神话"。以下是中国招商引资的部分情况介绍。

商务英语口译

> 🎧 请先熟悉列出的词汇与短语再听录音,并在录音停顿时将下列篇章口译成英语。

> **词汇与短语**
>
> | | |
> |---|---|
> | 招商引资 | to attract foreign investment |
> | 引资 | to introduce financial resources |
> | 引智 | to introduce intellectual resources |
> | 外商投资企业 | foreign-invested enterprises |
> | 实际使用外资 / 实收资本 | paid-in capital |
> | 工业增加值 | added industrial value |
> | 母公司 | parent company |

坚持对外开放基本国策,坚定不移地发展开放型经济、奉行互利共赢的开放战略,是改革开放近 40 年来中国经济持续健康发展的一条成功经验。// 招商引资、择优选资,促进"引资"和"引智"相结合,是中国对外开放的重要内容。截至 2015 年 12 月底,中国累计设立外商投资企业 83.64 万家,实际使用外资 16 423 亿美元。// 目前,中国 22% 的税收、28% 的工业增加值、55% 的进出口、50% 的技术引进、约 5 200 万人的就业,都来自外商投资企业的贡献。// 对外开放、吸引外资是互利共赢的。对中国来说,通过持续吸引外资为国家现代化建设提供了必要的资金、先进的技术和宝贵的管理经验以及众多国际化人才。// 对外商投资企业来说,则赢得了可观的投资回报,不少在华外商投资企业成为其母公司全球业务的增长亮点和利润中心。//

Text F China's Service Outsourcing Grows in 2015

> **主题导入**
>
> 外包,于 20 世纪 80 年代流行起来的商业用语,是商业活动决策之一,指将非核心业务下放给专门营运该项运作的外间第三者,原因是为了节省成本、集中精神于核心业者、善用资源、获得独立及专业人士服务等。以下是中国外包业的情况介绍。

> 🎧 请先熟悉列出的词汇与短语再听录音,并在录音停顿时将下列篇章口译成汉语。

> **词汇与短语**
>
> | | |
> |---|---|
> | outsourcing | 外包 |
> | subdued | 减弱的 |
> | to ink | 签署 |
> | offshore service outsourcing | 离岸服务外包 |
> | tertiary industry | 第三产业 |
> | boon | 裨益;有用之物 |

China's service outsourcing industry continued to grow in 2015 despite subdued economic growth. //

Chinese companies inked service outsourcing contracts worth 130.9 billion USD, up 22.1% year on year. Of the total, offshore service outsourcing contracts reached 87.29 billion USD, rising 21.5% from a year earlier. //

Contracts fulfilled with businesses in the United States and European Union, two major trade partners, jumped 17.5% and 17.6% respectively in their value, while those with Japanese businesses fell 9.8%. //

Outsourcing deals signed with countries along the Belt and Road route stood at 17.83 billion USD, up 42.6% from a year earlier. //

China is the world's second-largest service outsourcing provider after India. The State Council described the sector as a "green industry" that will be a new engine for tertiary industry and a boon to employment. //

情景口译

提示：
学生三人或四人一组，根据下面的主题提示进行模拟口译，注意使用本单元介绍的技能和句型。

主题一　在华投资

参与人： 1. 琼斯女士，英国某电信公司代表

2. 刘辉先生，深圳某科技公司业务部经理

3. 译员

内　容： 1. 刘先生介绍中国投资环境

2. 琼斯女士与刘先生探讨在华投资前景

3. 刘先生给予琼斯女士在深圳投资的建议

主题二　新加坡某港务集团投资大连某物流园

参与人：1. 费舍尔先生，新加坡某港务集团总裁代表
　　　　　2. 张艺歌女士，大连某物流园项目负责人
　　　　　3. 译员

内　容：1. 张女士介绍该物流园项目
　　　　　2. 张女士介绍大连当地投资政策
　　　　　3. 费舍尔先生谈及投资设想和计划
　　　　　4. 双方探讨合作可能和发展前景

✱ 句式扩展

1. I think that the company is ready for a takeover. They have great market share, but they are in poor financial condition.

   我觉得是时候接管那家公司了。虽然他们占有很高的市场份额，但他们的财务状况太糟糕。

2. That company lives by mergers and acquisitions. They just keep growing and growing.

   那家公司靠合并和收购为生，不断扩张。

3. Actual foreign investment rose by 27.5% to 6.76 billion USD in the first quarter of this year while contracted FDI shot up by 70.3% in the same period.

   今年第一季度实际外商投资净增 27.5%，增至 67.6 亿美元，同期的合同外商直接投资飙升了 70.3%。

4. The New York Stock Exchange started in 1792 with just two equities and three government bonds. By last year, the NYSE's average daily turnover had reached 999 billion USD.

   纽约证券交易所于 1792 年成立时只有两种股票和三种国债。而到去年，纽交所的日成交额已经达到 9 990 亿美元。

5. Officials from 10 global banks and securities firms announced a 70 billion USD loan program that the companies could use to help ease a potential credit shortage.

   10 家全球性银行和证券公司的官员宣布了一项 700 亿美元的贷款项目供这些公司使用，

以便帮助缓解潜在的信用短缺。

6. Small high technology companies have several good business reasons why foreign opportunities might be considered in spite of the difficulties inherent in capitalizing on them.

   高科技小公司有充足的理由考虑在国外发展的机会,尽管从这些机会中获利存在着固有的困难。

7. Panicked investors are worried that giant financial bail-outs by governments around the world have failed to halt a downward spiral in global market.

   投资者们担心世界各国政府大规模的救市计划也无法阻止全球金融市场的螺旋式下跌,因而陷入恐慌。

8. Since 1990, the global stock of financial assets (shares, bonds, bank deposits and cash) has increased more than twice as fast as the GDP of rich countries, from 12 trillion USD in 1990 to almost 93 trillion USD today.

   自1990年以来,全球金融资产(股票、债券、银行存款、现金)总额增速比富裕国家GDP增速快两倍还多,从1990年的12万亿美元增长到了今天的93万亿美元。

9. The 20th century witnessed an unprecedented boom in mergers and acquisitions. In 2001 alone, the worldwide value of deals exceeded 2.3 trillion USD, or nearly 30% of the EU's economic output in this year. Yet studies showed that more than half of the takeovers failed to yield benefits to acquirers.

   20世纪并购空前繁荣。仅在2001年,全球交易额就超过2.3万亿美元,约是欧盟当年经济总额的30%。但研究表明,一半以上收购没能为收购方创造利益。

10. Angel investors currently put in more than 50 billion USD annually and are involved in 30 to 40 more deals each year than traditional venture capital firms.

    如今,天使投资人每年投资超过500亿美元,其涉及的交易比传统风投公司的多30~40个。

11. 外商投资规模进一步扩大,投资方式更为多元。

    Foreign investment scale is enlarging with more investment modes.

12. 中国吸收外商投资之所以能够取得如此巨大的成就,根本原因在于为全世界的投资者提供了适宜其投资、生产、经营的优良环境。

    The basic reason that the introduction of foreign investment by China obtained great success lies in that China provides all the investors in the world with excellent environment for investment, production and operation.

159

13. 业界消息称贵公司正在考虑加入通信业的投资。

    We heard from trade that your company is considering diversifying into telecommunication business.

14. 我今天想跟您谈谈合作投资建立一条新生产线的问题，不知道您是否感兴趣。

    I intend to discuss with you the possibility of an investment in a new manufacturing line. I wonder if you are interested in it.

15. 我们之间的投资份额可以对半开，在经营管理责权和利润分配上也可对半开。

    My suggestion for the investment share in the partnership is in the vicinity of 50 to 50, and the same applies to business management and profits share.

16. 我们的合作期定为10年，只要双方愿意，期满后我们还可以续签合同。

    We can begin with a 10-year term of a renewable partnership; we can extend our contract for another term before it expires, if both parties intend to.

17. 吸收外商直接投资是中国对外开放基本国策的重要组成部分。30多年来，随着改革开放逐步深化，中国吸收外资的规模和质量不断提高。

    FDI absorption constitutes an important component of China's basic state policy of reform and opening-up. With the reform and opening-up going into depth over the past three decades and more, China has been constantly improving its FDI utilization in terms of scale and quality.

18. 过去几年的增长主要来自于外商投资，中国也已经成为最大的外商投资目的国。政府大力投资基础设施建设，为未来生产力的提升奠定基础。

    Growth in the past several years has been driven by investment from other countries and China has typically been the largest magnet for FDI. The government has also been an enormous investor into infrastructure and these projects then pave the way for future increases in productivity.

19. 为了扩大国际经济合作和技术交流，中国允许外国公司或个人按照平等互利的原则与中国的企业建立合资企业。

    With a view to expand international economic cooperation and technical exchange, China permits foreign companies or individuals to join with Chinese companies in establishing joint ventures in China in accordance with the principles of equality and mutual benefits.

20. 为了进一步扩大西部地区吸收外商投资的领域，我们鼓励外商投资农业、林业、水利、交通、能源、市政公用、环保等基础设施及基础设施建设，以及矿产、旅游等资源开发。

To further expand areas for foreign investment in the west, we encourage foreign investment in agriculture, forestry, water conservancy, transportation, energy, municipal utility, environmental protection and other basic fields as well as infrastructure construction and mineral resources and tourism.

口译小贴士

译员的语言学习习惯

口译是"说"的艺术,更是语言的艺术。在口译学习的过程中,不少译员会遇到这样的难题——听懂了,记下了,却说不出来了!明明觉得译文就在嘴边,却偏偏找不到恰当的方式表达。信息的传达是口译的最后一步,也是最能直接体现译员职业水准的关键环节。"说不出来",究其根本,就是"脑子空",即语言的输入不够,没有足够的语言储备进行译语的输出。因此,要做一名合格的译员就要培养良好的语言学习习惯。

培养良好的语言学习习惯要从加强自己的母语——汉语学习入手。母语是学习外语的重要基础之一。何况在口译中,母语和外语就好比译员的双腿,要想走得远、走得快,双语要齐头并进。不少译员为了强化自己的外语水平,每天把自己"泡在"外语的环境中:听的是外语广播,看的是外语小说,练的是外语口语,却忽视了母语的学习。且不说在口译过程中可能随时会遇到汉语的古文精华、熟语、习语,就是单单利用好汉语中的四字成语就可以让译文简洁达意。因此,译员要培养良好的母语阅读习惯,不光要读现代汉语,更要读古文,全面提升自己的语言素养。

其次,要改变字字对应的记忆方式和表达思维。在短期记忆中运用好逻辑分析,从信息层面记录内容,而不是以词为中心。否则,一旦忘词,内容也就回想不出来了。在表达过程中,遇到不会翻译的字词应该灵活转换,在语境中找到替换的表达方式。而在学习中遇到生词则要多查字典,把意思吃透。要养成举一反三、刨根问底、灵活转换的习惯。词汇储备越多,用起来自然越轻松。

再次,进行一句多译训练。一句多译是培养译员灵活表达的最佳方式,一般可以通过更换词语、语法、句式等方式进行。例如:中国与东盟山水相连、文化相通,友好交往历史悠久。译文可以是:

1. China and ASEAN countries share the same mountains and rivers and the similar cultural backgrounds. Our friendship can be traced back to ancient times.

2. China and ASEAN countries are linked with common mountains and rivers, and have interlinked cultures and a long history of friendly contacts.

3. China and ASEAN countries are bridged by mountains and rivers, which leads to resemblance in cultural backgrounds and enduring friendship since ancient times.

不一样的说法,一样的意思,殊途同归。平时将一句多译作为常规性训练的一部分,就会培养灵活转换的表达意识,在口译工作中也就不难做到从容不迫了。

此外,语言学习,既要日积月累,又要与时俱进,要时刻关注一些新词和热点词汇的用法。译员应该每天关注社会热点和国际动态,每天问自己是否能列举出当天最热点的三条新闻,能否用双语将这些热点讲述出来,能否用逻辑性的双语语言表述自己对这些热点的看法。长此以往,既可以提高自己的双语表达能力,又可以跟进热点,积累信息,更可以锻炼自己的逻辑思维能力。

信息重组 / 全球采购

第 11 单元

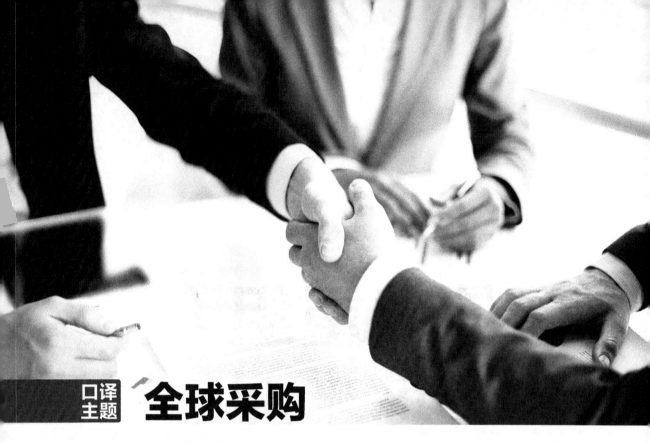

口译主题

全球采购

全球采购是指利用全球的资源,在全世界范围内寻找供应商,寻找质量最好、价格合理的产品的行为。跨国公司在全球采购已有数年经验。

全球采购也用来指不包括企业行为的"官方采购",如联合国、各种国际组织、各国政府等机构和组织为履行公共职能,使用公共性资金所进行的货物、工程和服务的采购。采购的对象包罗万象,既有产品、设备等各种各样的物品,也有房屋、构筑物、市政及环境改造等工程,还有种种服务。

降低成本是全球采购的重要原因,而低成本国家的供应商在全球采购中变得非常有竞争力,中国是这一趋势中的最大受益者。

✱ 学习目标

  了解信息重组的原因和技巧

  了解全球采购的优势和不足

  掌握全球采购的常用口译句式

✽ 技巧讲解

在口译过程中，由于时间和记忆容量等方面的压力，译员通常按照源语的顺序对句子进行逐一翻译。这样做能够减轻记忆负担，便于及时处理信息。然而，在英汉互译时不可避免地会出现译文听起来生硬、不通顺，甚至词不达意、不知所云的现象。因此，在口译活动中译员需要脱离源语的框架束缚，重意义、轻结构，用符合目的语的表达习惯的方式对信息进行重组。

信息重组常用的技巧主要有转换、释义、增补、省略等。

转换

转换主要体现在对源语的词性和句型进行转换，例如：英语中的名词和介词常常翻译为动词，如名词词组"a great actor"可译为"他演技精湛"，介词词组"with its headquarters in..."译为"总部设在……"。

释义

就英汉互译来讲，英汉词汇在不同语境中对应的译文也常常不同。由于英语通常需要避免重复，同样的意思，在汉译英时会尽量使用不同的英语词汇表达相同内容，如"留学生"可以用"international students"，也可用"global students"。serve as 表示"担任、充当、起……作用"，根据具体语境"it serves as a global forum for..."可以灵活译为"它是……的全球论坛"。对译员来说，对一词多译或一句多译的练习和掌握对提高口译质量显得尤为重要。

增补和省略

在对源语信息的重组过程中，需要根据目的语的表达习惯对源语隐含之意进行补充或对重复的信息进行省略，更准确地传达发言人的意图，也帮助听众更好地理解信息。

当然，对信息取舍时需要做好平衡。完全按照目标语的表达习惯翻译，尽管会比较流畅，但在语气表达的轻重和含义上偏差就有可能会比较大。如：

原文 1 Our aim is to coordinate our efforts as much as possible and to integrate the activities of other donors.

译文 1 我们的目的是竭尽全力，并协调好其他捐赠者的活动。

译文 2 我们的目的是尽可能地协调我们的努力，并统合其他捐赠者的活动。

译文1中的"竭尽全力"是按照中文表达习惯翻译的，它的语气超过了按英文直译的"尽可能地协调我们的努力"。

总之，在信息重组的过程中，会不可避免地出现信息的选择、取舍和重组。译员需要根据多个方面对译文进行选择，如听众水平、发言人的预期以及翻译任务等。如果听众是普通观众，而演讲内容又非常专业，译员需要对一些专业词汇做恰当的解释。如果发言人的发言比较啰唆，译员可以省略啰唆的部分，并把发言人想表达却没能表达出来的意思适度地表达完整。同时，译员需要考虑翻译要完成的任务。如果为英美客户服务，翻译目的是忠实表达英美客户的观点，翻译时可偏向英文习惯。但如果是为了表示英美客户对中华文化的了解，则应该考虑侧重按照汉语习惯表达。

另外，英语和汉语都有不同的口音和不同的表达。中国内地人的中文、香港人的中文、新加坡中文、印尼华人的中文等。这些中文在用词上、甚至在语法上都有巨大差异。因此在做口译活动时需要充分考虑听众、说话者和译员身份等因素。适时适当地选择是按英文习惯表达或按中文习惯表达。

✲ 技巧练习

🎧 请根据录音将下列段落口译成英语或汉语，注意信息传达的准确性。

1. 随着中国企业在海外持续扩张，2015年，中国对美国直接投资创历史新高，达到了80亿美元。// 根据中国商务部、国家统计局及国家外汇管理局的数据显示，这一数额占中国对外直接投资流量总额的5.5%，其中制造业吸引的投资最多。// 去年美国制造业吸引了中国40亿美元的投资，占中国总投资的一半，同比增长122.2%。// 在此期间，中国企业共对美实施并购项目97个，实际交易金额131亿美元。而从中国对美直接投资存量行业分布情况看，制造业以107亿美元高居榜首，占对美投资存量的26.3%。//

2. Through three and a half decades of development and integration of China-EU economic cooperation and trade, the difference brought to our two peoples and business communities could be felt everywhere and every day. Jobs were created. // According to the Chinese statistics, in the EU, imports from China help create over 2 million jobs. As Chinese companies began to make investment in the EU, we also offered local people high number of employment opportunities. In China, tens of millions of people work in foreign invested companies, a considerable part of which are from the EU. //

✲ 主题口译

Text A 全球采购

🔊 主题导入

全球采购有很多优点，它可以使企业充分利用全球的资源，扩大供应商价格比较范围，提高采购效率，降低采购成本，抵抗外汇风险等。当然全球采购也会面临很多风险，如：不确定性高、手续复杂，同时因运输、关税等方面的原因也会抬高采购成本。以下是有关全球采购的对话。

第 11 单元　信息重组 / 全球采购

> 请先熟悉列出的词汇与短语再听录音，并在录音停顿时将下列访谈口译成英语或汉语。

词汇与短语

供应链	supply chain
outlook	眼光；观点
hypercompetitive	极为激烈的
catalyst	催化剂
incentive	刺激；激励；吸引力
negative publicity	负面形象
island hop	转移；跳岛战略

A: 最近总是听到人们在谈起市场、供应链等的全球化问题，为什么全球采购一下子变得这样广泛？//

B: Well, I think there are several factors, really. I mean, as companies expand internationally, their outlook becomes increasingly global. What's more, hyper-competitive domestic markets have driven companies to look further afield in their search for competitive advantage. // Although I think the process has really been accelerated by rapid advances in IT and telecoms, that's been the real catalyst for change. //

A: 主要的诱惑是什么？为什么企业如此热衷于进行海外采购呢？//

B: It depends on the circumstances of the company in question. It could be anything from better access to overseas markets, lower taxes, lower labour costs, quicker delivery or a combination of all of these.//

A: 能否很公正地说，真正吸引他们的是利润上的回报呢？//

B: Yes, in most of the circumstances. Otherwise, I think few of the companies will be interested in it. Anyway, you know there is risk in it. //

A: 可以举个例子吗？//

B: Well, the most common mistakes companies make is that they only see the savings and don't bother to think about the effect on other key criteria like quality and delivery. A clothing company that only buys from Asian suppliers at low cost, for instance, will find that as labour rates increase over time, it'll have to island hop to find new low cost sites. // And this, of course, introduces uncertainty about quality — and that's critical for a clothing company. There are other possible risks as well. //

A: 例如？

B: Well, such as negative publicity as a result of poor working conditions in the supplier's country.

And, of course, there's always currency exchange risk. //

A: 您是怎样权衡这些因素选择供应商的呢?

B: It's crucial that companies know precisely what they're after from a supplier and that they fully understand their key selection criteria. They need to be careful to define them and make sure they're measurable and then rank them. // It's dangerous selecting a particular supplier just because they happen to deliver outstanding performance in one objective, such as cost or flexibility. //

Text B 中国制造

主题导入

中国制造既可以译为"Made in China",也可以译为"Manufactured in China"。前者是指原产地在中国,即原料是中国的,整个制造过程也是在中国完成的;而后者则多指原材料由国外提供,只是在中国完成加工装配的过程。以下是关于中国制造(Manufactured in China)的对话。

请先熟悉列出的词汇与短语再听录音,并在录音停顿时将下列篇章口译成英语或汉语。

词汇与短语

贸易逆差	trade deficit
全部价值	full value
资金流动	money flow

A: 美国很久以前从日本和其他亚洲国家进口的产品现在都来自中国,原因在于亚洲公司已经把他们的出口制造基地转移到了中国。随着中国在美国贸易逆差中所占份额的增加,亚洲其他国家的份额却在缩小。// 我们可以这样想:十年前我们买一台索尼电视,它的商标可能写着"日本制造",是进口产品。现在商标上写着"中国制造",它仍然是进口产品。//

B: Very interesting! I think we are both aware that a lot of what China exports is manufactured in China, but a significant amount is just assembled there with materials and components shipped into China from elsewhere, including the United States. The trade figures say the full value was imported from China, but the money flow says otherwise. //

A: 是的,有很多例子。比如说:你知道苹果的iPod吗?它在中国组装,但是组装仅仅占产品价值的一小部分。iPod大部分价值在于构成它的部件,它们在美国和亚洲其他地方制造,运到中国。一个研究显示，它一半的价值由美国的苹果设计者和销售者获得。// 我们还可以回到刚才说到的索尼电视那个例子。虽然是"中国制造"，工厂却是索尼公司的，这样从中国进口电视的利润实际上大部分由日本所有。//

Text C　重庆全球采购会

主题导入

中国（重庆）国际投资暨全球采购会（简称渝洽会），是由商务部、国务院三峡办、中国贸促会、重庆市人民政府联合主办的一项重要的贸易投资促进活动。随着重庆在全国乃至世界的影响和辐射作用不断提升，"渝洽会"平台作用越来越突出。以下是第 19 届重庆全球采购会的介绍。

请先熟悉列出的词汇与短语再听录音，并在录音停顿时将下列篇章口译成英语。

词汇与短语

重庆国际博览中心	Chongqing International Expo Center
专题活动	thematic activities
对接会	matchmaking
保税区	bonded area
战略交汇点	strategic intersection

女士们、先生们：

上午好！

第十九届"渝洽会"定于 2016 年 5 月 19—22 日在重庆国际博览中心举行。// 期间，将重点推介"一带一路"沿线和亚太国家的投资机遇，集中展示先进制造业、现代服务业和居民消费等领域的新产品、新技术，举办多场国际投资贸易高层次论坛及系列专题活动、专场投资采购对接会和区域合作等活动。届时，数千家国内外知名企业将齐聚重庆，共谋合作与发展。//

作为长江经济带和丝绸之路经济带的战略交汇点，重庆大力实施五大功能区域发展战略，全力构建大通道、大通关、大平台新格局，形成了水陆空三个交通枢纽、三个国家一类口岸、三个保税区"三个三合一"的开放特征。// 2015 年，全市进出口总额 750 亿美元，位列中西部第 1 位。实际利用外资 107.7 亿美元，实际对外投资 14.3 亿美元。实现地区生产总值 15 719.72 亿元，同比增长 11%，居全国第一。// 世界 500 强企业落户超过 260 余家，在中西部名列前茅，内陆开放的广度和深度不断拓展。//

Text D A Secret to Inditex's Success

主题导入

Inditex 作为世界最大的时装零售公司之一，在欧洲、美洲、亚洲和非洲的 73 个国家拥有 4 280 多个门店。公司除了最成功的品牌 ZARA 以外，还拥有另外七个品牌。以下是其卓越的商业模式的介绍。

请先熟悉列出的词汇与短语再听录音，并在录音停顿时将下列篇章口译成汉语。

词汇与短语

geriatric haddock	明日黄花
hemline	衣长；裙长
to quadruple	四倍于；翻两番
public offering	上市
stagnant	不景气

Ladies and gentlemen,

Good morning!

Flogging fashion is like selling fish. Fresh fish, like a freshly cut jacket in the latest color, sells quickly and at a high price. Yesterday's catch must be discounted and may not sell at all. //

This simple insight has made Inditex one of the world's two biggest clothes makers. From our base near the Spanish fishing port of La Coruña, our main brand, ZARA, has conquered Europe. //

Other fashion firms have their clothes made in China. This is cheap, but managing a long supply chain is hard. By the time a boat has sailed halfway round the world, hemlines may have risen an inch and its cargo will be as popular as geriatric haddock. //

Inditex, by contrast, sources just over half of its products from Spain, Portugal and Morocco. This costs more. But because its supply chain is short, Inditex can react quickly to new trends. Instead of betting on tomorrow's hot look, ZARA can wait to see what customers are actually buying — and make that. While others are stuck with unwanted stock, Inditex sells at full prices. //

Sales have quadrupled to 13.8 billion EUR since the firm's initial public offering in 2001. Inditex's operating profits are high and have been more stable over time than its peers'. The firm now faces two challenges. Can it go global? And will its "fast-fashion" model be copied, or bettered, by others? //

For now, Inditex is dependent on Europe: 70% of its sales in 2011 were there. Sales in Spain, which accounted for 25% of revenue, have stalled. Europe is stagnant and ageing. Inditex needs new markets. //

第 11 单元　信息重组／全球采购

Text E　海尔的采购战略

主题导入

对一个企业来说，科学合理的采购可以降低采购成本，节约采购费用，提高采购效率，为企业提供符合品质要求的原材料，保证企业的正常生产和经营。海尔集团的采购策略对其发展起到了重要的推动作用。以下是海尔采购战略的简介。

请先熟悉列出的词汇与短语再听录音，并在录音停顿时将下列篇章口译成英语。

词汇与短语

集中购买	centralized purchase
规模优势	advantage of scale
叉车	forklift
结算业务	settlement service
战略合作伙伴关系	strategic partnership
双赢战略	win-win strategy

海尔采取的采购策略是利用全球化网络集中购买，以规模优势降低采购成本，同时精简供应商队伍。据统计，海尔的全球供应商数量由原先的 2 336 家降至 840 家，其中国际化供应商的比例达到了 71%，目前世界前 500 强中有 44 家是海尔的供应商。//

对于供应商关系的管理方面，海尔采用的是 SBD 模式：共同发展供应业务。海尔有很多产品的设计方案直接交给厂商来做，很多零部件是由供应商提供今后两个月市场的产品预测并将待开发产品形成图纸，这样一来，供应商就真正成为海尔的设计部和工厂，加快开发速度。//

许多供应商的厂房和海尔的仓库之间甚至不需要汽车运输，工厂的叉车直接开到海尔的仓库，大大节约运输成本。海尔本身则侧重于核心的买卖和结算业务。这与传统的企业与供应商关系的不同在于，它从供需双方简单的买卖关系，成功转型为战略合作伙伴关系，是一种共同发展的双赢战略。//

Text F　Six Core Purchasing Strategies

主题导入

采购策略旨在确定物资采购及操作执行的管理原则，以提高采购效率、采购操作规范性及采购总成本的控制水平。以下是六种核心采购策略的简介。

> 请先熟悉列出的词汇与短语再听录音,并在录音停顿时将下列篇章口译成汉语。

词汇与短语

cost effective	有成本效益的
vendor	供应商
procurement	采购
predominent	占主导地位的
ad hoc	临时的
auction	拍卖
optimization	最优化
optimum	最适宜的
to discard	丢弃
six sigma	六西格玛(一项以数据为基础,追求几乎完美的质量管理方法)
to negate	使无效
to champion	支持

Companies implement purchasing strategies in order to make cost effective purchasing decisions from a group of efficient vendors who will deliver quality goods on time and at mutually agreeable terms. //

These purchasing strategies may include such choices as making procurement savings by using centralized purchasing which is concentrating the entire procurement activities within one principal location. //

Some companies may decide to undertake a single source procurement strategy that involves obtaining excellent dedicated service from a single vendor. These strategies are predominant when sourcing for IT or indirect purchasing, such as office supplies and cleaning. // Other companies may use a procurement strategy of using a core purchasing cycle. This is where they order from a group of regular vendors and use outsourcing procurement for their larger and ad hoc purchases. Still others, particularly when they are seeking labor for short-term projects will use procurement auctions in order to obtain the best pricing levels. //

Regardless of the size of the company, there is a core group of purchasing strategies that most of them implement. These are: //

Supplier optimization. The company chooses an optimum mix of vendors who can provide the best prices and terms. This process usually means that the less able suppliers who cannot provide a quality service at the terms and prices required are discarded. This is by far the most common of the various purchasing strategies. //

Total quality methods, or TQM, which requires the vendors to provide an ever increasing quality service with zero errors. The supplier ensures purchasing best practices using a number of tools, such as six sigma. //

第 11 单元　信息重组 / 全球采购

Risk management. As more companies obtain their supplies from some developing countries, they are more concerned with the risk management of this supply chain. Whilst these countries can supply products at very advantageous prices, these advantages can be soon negated by a natural or human disaster. //

Global sourcing. Large multinational companies see the world as one large market and source from many vendors, regardless of their country of origin. //

Vendor development. Some companies believe that they are working hand-in-hand with their vendors. They, therefore, spend some time in developing processes that assist these vendors. // There may also be the situation where a company is dependent upon just one supplier for their products. If this supplier is unable to perform to the required standards, the purchaser may assist the vendor in improving their service or implement processes to improve their procurement cycle. //

Green purchasing. This is one of the more common purchasing strategies for governments and local governments. This strategy champions the need for recycling and purchasing products that have a negative impact on the environment. //

A company will choose purchasing strategies that promote their procurement best practices of minimizing costs, maximizing quality and ensuring that quality products are delivered on time. //

情景口译

提示：
学生三人或四人一组，根据下面的主题提示进行模拟口译，注意使用本单元介绍的技能和句型。

主题一　有机食品采购洽谈

参与人： 1. 张兴蕾女士，大连某有机食品生产基地负责人
2. 汉密尔顿先生，某国际连锁超市全球采购部代表
3. 译员

地　点： 大连某有机食品生产基地

内　容： 1. 张女士介绍该有机食品生产基地的规模
2. 汉密尔顿先生询问生产基地的生产流程和质量控制流程
3. 张女士请汉密尔顿先生品尝有机食品

 **主题二** 电子产品全球采购展会

参与人： 1. 韦博先生，某国际知名科技公司销售代表

2. 孙岩女士，大连某贸易公司负责人

3. 译员

地　点： 德国柏林国际会展中心

内　容： 1. 韦博先生介绍该公司的最新鼠标及键盘产品的种类和特性

2. 孙女士询问批量订购鼠标及键盘产品的价钱、发货等情况

3. 双方建立联系

✱ 句式扩展

1. Marketing experts keep track of consumers by surveys, sales figures, databases, and the census.

   营销专家们利用问卷调查、销售数据、数据库和人口普查的方式来掌握消费者的动向。

2. Global sourcing cuts down on the role of intermediaries, and can reduce costs and increase profits to the producer.

   全球采购削弱了中间商的作用，降低了成本，增加了生产商的利润。

3. "Economic globalization" is now being used with increasing frequency in newspapers, magazines, seminars and international conferences.

   "经济全球化"一词越来越频繁地出现在报纸杂志、研讨会以及国际会议上。

4. With the basic feature of free flow of commodity, capital, technology, service and information in the global context for optimized allocation, economic globalization is giving new impetus and providing opportunities to world economic development.

   经济全球化的基本特征是商品、资本、技术、劳务和信息在全球范围更自由地流动以求最优化配置，为世界经济发展提供新的动力和机会。

5. The best policy is to follow the trend closely, availing the opportunities to develop ourselves and avoiding its possible impacts.

最好的办法就是紧跟这个趋势，利用时机发展自己，同时规避可能带来的冲击。

6. Maybe we can say few topics are as controversial as globalization. But like it or not, it has become an objective trend in world economic development.

   或许可以说很少有什么话题像全球化这样引发争议。然而不管人们喜欢与否，全球化已经成为世界经济发展的客观趋势。

7. Global sourcing is the practice of sourcing from the global market for goods and services across geopolitical boundaries.

   全球采购指的是跨越地理限制在全球市场采购商品和服务的行为。

8. Global efficiencies include low-cost skilled labor, low-cost raw material and other economic factors like tax breaks and low trade tariffs.

   全球效率包括低成本的熟练工人，低成本的原材料以及其它经济相关要素，如税收优惠和低贸易关税。

9. A large number of information technology projects and services are outsourced globally to countries like Pakistan and India for more economical pricing.

   由于价格低廉，大量全球范围内的信息技术项目和服务外包给了巴基斯坦和印度这样的国家。

10. One common example of globally sourced products or services is labor-intensive manufactured products produced by low-cost Chinese labor.

    全球采购产品和服务的常见实例之一就是采购中国的廉价劳动力生产的劳动密集型产品。

11. 全球采购也包括雇用菲律宾、巴基斯坦和印度国内廉价的讲英语员工的呼叫中心。

    Global sourcing also includes call centers staffed with low-cost English speaking workers in the Philippines, Pakistan and India.

12. 许多例子说的都是从低成本国家采购，然而全球采购并不仅局限于低成本国家。

    While some examples are about low-cost country sourcing, global sourcing is not limited to low-cost countries.

13. 如今，大多数公司都致力于利用全球采购来降低成本。

    Majority of companies today strive to harness the potential of global sourcing in reducing cost.

14. 产品和服务的全球采购既有优势也有劣势，不仅仅是个低成本的问题了。

    The global sourcing of goods and services has advantages and disadvantages that can go beyond low cost.

15. 全球采购的优势，除了低成本以外，还可以学习如何在潜在市场开展业务。

    The advantage of global sourcing, beyond low cost, includes learning how to do business in a potential market.

16. 全球采购的一个主要的劣势可能就是在不同的文化背景下以及不同的时区产生的隐性成本。

    One key disadvantage of global sourcing can include hidden costs associated with different cultures and time zones.

17. 对商品制造而言，一些主要的劣势包括交货时间长，中断供应风险以及产品质量控制的难度。

    For manufactured goods, some key disadvantages include long lead time, the risk of interrupting supply, and the difficulty of monitoring product quality.

18. 全球采购的目的通常都是在生产和服务中利用全球性效率。

    Global sourcing often aims to exploit global efficiencies in the delivery of a product or service.

19. 对一家公司而言，国际采购组织（IPO）可能是全球采购战略的一个要素。

    International procurement organizations (IPOs) may be an element of the global sourcing strategy for a firm.

20. 全球采购也经常和跨国集中采购策略相关联。

    Global sourcing is often associated with a multinational centralized procurement strategy.

译文的长度

大家一般都有这样一个感觉：若会议或交谈使用的是交替传译，会议或交谈的信息量会明显下降，速度减慢。因此，大家都希望翻译能在最短时间内简明扼要地把信息快速地传递过去。通常情况下，口译的译文长度不应超过原文长度的3/4。译员可以省去发言人思考下文或选择词语的停顿，或去掉说话人无意中的重复。

第 11 单元　信息重组／全球采购

另外，由于时间关系，在某些场合中，活动主办方会要求译员按原讲话的 2/3 的时间译出发言人主要的信息，甚至按 1/2、1/4、1/10 的时间概括译出全文。译员需要有思想准备，按主办方要求进行翻译。其实压缩译文已经成为国际会议的惯例。译员要按照限定的时间、比例整合讲话，使之成为一篇压缩但信息完整的讲话。

想要在口译中简洁明了地将意思和语气准确地传达过去，并不是说不负责任地盲目偷工减料，而是在理解的基础上，在保证译文完整、准确的前提下，对原文再加工，以便更好地传递信息。做到简洁，可以从以下几个方面着手：

1. 简化词和短语。词是翻译中最小的单位，要做到简洁，应该首先从词入手。一般来讲，汉语多重复，语言较累赘，而英语多用代词，简明易懂。因此，在汉英口译时，可以多用指代词，多用短小词。

2. 省略冗余。翻译过程中，常常会有重复累赘的部分翻来覆去地出现，这个时候就需要译员自己加工，删去冗余部分，力求简洁。

例如：在表达感谢时，中文会使用很多程度副词，如："衷心感谢你们的盛情邀请"。而字对字的翻译在英文中显得啰唆，也不符合英语的表达习惯，而用"Thank you for your invitation"则简洁、清楚地将说话人要表达的信息和情感都自然地表达出来了，也不会给人感谢过头或言不由衷的感觉。此外，汉译英时应省略重复或语气强调词，只译出关键词即可。如："不断扩大"译为"expanding"；"更新更高的要求"译为"higher demand"；"坚决、彻底、全面的改善"译为"thorough improvement"。

3. 多用简称、缩写来指代。很多专有名词全称冗长，但简称或缩写往往更简明、上口。口译中，为求节省时间，提高译文质量，保证简明，专有名词第一次出现全称之后，再次出现时，可以以简称或缩写指代。如："中小型企业"在第一次出现时译为"small and medium sized enterprises or SMEs"，再次出现时就可以直接用"SMEs"进行指代。

4. 简化句子。翻译中，很多时候需要译员跳出源语，根据自己的理解加工，运用解构、拆分、省略、压缩、解释、总结等方法重新组合信息，产出译文。

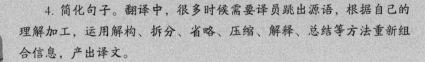

模糊用语 / 商务访谈

第 12 单元

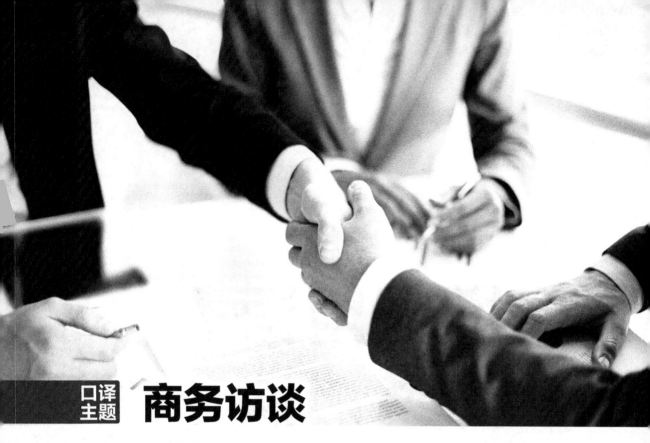

口译主题:商务访谈

随着资讯行业的迅速发展,商务访谈越来越常见。媒体针对影响国际、国内的重大事件,对经济行业的领军人物进行采访,既使普通老百姓对经济事务增加了了解,同时也提高了相关企业、个人的知名度。

商务访谈的基本形式是由主持人或采访人、特邀嘉宾(来自商界或与商界有关的一位或几位权威人物)组成,就某一经济政策或人民群众普遍关心或感兴趣的事件或话题进行介绍或展开讨论。所以,访谈一般形式较为正式。

访谈开始前,采访人或主持人会对特邀嘉宾加以介绍,使观众对访谈有基本的了解并拥有合理预期。访谈开始后,一般围绕某一特定主题或事件,由采访人或主持人提问,受邀嘉宾阐明观点看法。

商务访谈语言一般较正式、主题一般较明确。通过面对面的互动,受访嘉宾的观点能够原汁原味地呈现给听众。

✻ 学习目标

了解模糊用语

逐步掌握口译中模糊用语的处理

了解商务访谈文体的特点

掌握商务访谈的常用口译句式

第 12 单元　模糊用语 / 商务访谈

❋ 技巧讲解

精确性和模糊性都是语言的客观属性。所谓模糊性，指的是词语所指范围边界的不确定性。时间词、颜色词、年龄词、象声词、可分等级的词、数词以及模糊限制语都是具有模糊性的表达。语言具有模糊性的主要原因在于人的认知具有局限性和主观性。在日常口语交际中，模糊表达使用频繁，在商务交流中，人们甚至有意使用模糊表达以达到交际目的。

模糊语的种类

通常来说，语言的模糊性可以分为：语音模糊、词汇模糊、语义模糊、跨文化模糊。

1. 语音模糊

口语表达中，由于发言人有口音、吐字不清、设备问题或是发言人为某种交际目的使用谐音、双关的手法特意为之等问题，常常会出现语音模糊的现象。通常来说，个别语音的模糊，对译员理解发言人的整体意思不会造成太大困扰，但往往也会影响交际效果。

2. 词汇模糊

精确性和模糊性都是相对的概念，没有绝对的界限和划分标准。词汇层面上的模糊性也是如此。例如：表示频率的"有时""常常"，形容人的年龄大小、个子高矮、样貌美丑，这些概念都是相对而言的。只要将模糊的词汇放在特定的语境中，一般不会造成太大的误解。

3. 语义模糊

由于语言自身的灵活性，按照一定的语言规律，词汇可以相互叠加使用。但在搭配、叠加的过程中，往往会造成语言上的歧义、语义上的模糊。例如："a student's book"可以理解为"一位学生的书"，也可以理解为"一本学生用书"。

4. 跨文化模糊

东西方文化的巨大差异，往往可以体现在语言中。例如：龙在东方文化中是祥瑞的象征，而在西方文化中则是凶残的象征。中国人自称的"龙的传人"，译员直译为"descendants of dragon"显然是不合适的。

模糊语的功能

1. 委婉礼貌

交际中，人们往往喜欢使用委婉、模糊的表达使交流含蓄些、礼貌些，尤其是在谈论某些敏感性、有分歧的话题时。商务交流中也是如此，利益冲突和分歧难以避免，通过使用模糊语能够避免局面紧张，维护友好氛围，使商务活动顺利进行。举例来说，当谈判双方就价格产生分歧，买家不愿接受卖家的高价时，可以说：

We have received many other offers from plenty of sellers and hope to make a deal at a satisfactory level.

此句中，"many other offers""plenty of sellers""at a satisfactory level"都是模糊表达，委婉地阐明了买家不愿让价的立场。

2. 简洁凝练

使用模糊语可以起到笼统概括的作用，从而提高语言效率。例如：

That bookish man loves literature and thus has a large collection of books, novels, poetry and so on.

此句中，"so on"一个简单的表达，概括了除小说和诗歌以外的所有文学作品。

3. 提升语言灵活性

在日常交际中，人们往往乐于使用模糊语，避免太过绝对、精确地表达，以便留出余地，达到交际目的。例如：

Our products are low in price and fine in quality and therefore, enjoy great popularity in the market.

此句中，"low""fine""great"都是范围模糊的形容词，很难界定，利用这些修饰词，既正面夸耀了自家产品，又不显得夸大其词。

口译中模糊信息的翻译

模糊语在日常交际中十分常见，在商务交流中也是频繁地出现。口译中如何处理模糊信息呢？以下简单介绍几种处理方法。

1. 显化

模糊与精确是相对的。根据语境，处理模糊信息时，可以用明晰清楚的语言传递出原本模糊的意思，化隐为显，化模糊为精确。例如：

原文1 For over three decades, China has been growing fantastically and kept increasing its international presence.

译文1 30多年来，中国以惊人的速度发展壮大，国际影响力不断增强。

"fantastically"和"presence"都是抽象模糊的表达，直译为"神奇地""存在感"，并不符合汉语习惯。此时就可以化抽象为具体，化虚为实，显化地处理模糊信息。

2. 隐化

与显化相对应，隐化就是故意忽略原语中的模糊信息或删去不译原语中的模糊信息，即发言人"和稀泥"，译员也"和稀泥"。在译员无法确定发言人使用模糊语意图的情况下，隐化能够避免译员犯错，毕竟误译不如不译。例如：

原文2 We, as the seller, reserve the right to lodge a claim for direct losses sustained, if any.

译文2 译文2：作为买方，我们有权对遭受的直接损失提出索赔。

遭受损失提出索赔，这是双方都心知肚明的问题，如果译出来摆在明面上说得太直白，一来太啰唆，不符合汉语习惯，二来损害彼此的友好关系，伤感情。因此，此处"if any"最好选择隐化不译。

3. 直译

在处理模糊语时，所谓直译，指的就是对等保留模糊信息，用目的语的模糊语翻译源语中的模糊语，即发言人怎么说译员怎么译，完全遵守忠实原则。直译是最常见的处理模糊语的方法。例如：

原文 3 Thanks to the soft feel, bright colors, fine quality and novel designs, our dresses have gained great popularity among customers at home and abroad.

译文 3 由于手感舒适、色泽艳丽、质地优良、设计新颖，我们的连衣裙受国内外顾客的喜爱。

4. 意译

由于汉英语言本身的差异，在翻译模糊语时也必须考虑到语言本身的特点和习惯，不拘于形式，以达到交际目的为宗旨。这时，就需要采用意译的方法，或增补或删减，以目的语听众能够接受的方式传达信息。例如：

原文 4 我方相信贵方会按时发货，因为延迟势必会给我们造成很大不便和经济损失。

译文 4 We trust you will see to it that the order is shipped within the stipulated time, as any delay would cause us no little convenience and financial losses.

❋ 技巧练习

🎧 **请根据录音将下列访谈口译成英语或汉语，注意模糊语的处理。**

A: 突然间变得这样乐观了吗？你曾经将金融行业的一些工具称作是"大规模杀伤性武器"。// 听起来很像德国总统豪斯特·科勒对于金融市场的描述，他说的是"怪物"。//

B: I don't condemn the entire industry. When I mentioned weapons of mass destruction, I was merely referring to the out-of-control trading in derivatives. // It doesn't make sense that hundreds of jobs are being eliminated, that entire branches of industry in the real economy are going under because of such financial gambles, even though they are in fact completely healthy. // Besides, these types of constructs are so complicated that hardly anyone understands them anymore. //

A: 即使是银行家都不知道现在是什么情况了。//

B: They concocted a poisonous brew, and in the end they had to drink it themselves. This is something bankers are normally extremely loath to do. They'd rather sell it to someone else. //

商务英语口译

主题口译

Text A 索罗斯访谈

主题导入

乔治·索罗斯，匈牙利出生的美国籍犹太裔商人，著名的慈善家，货币投机家，股票投资者。他曾在2013年接受专访，回顾1992年狙击英镑，迫使英国退出欧洲汇率体系的事件。以下是访谈的部分内容。

请先熟悉列出的词汇与短语再听录音，并在录音停顿时将下列访谈口译成英语或汉语。

词汇与短语

英镑	pound sterling
预言家	prophet
jugular	要害
speculator	投机者

A: 1992年你成功狙击英镑，这是人们经常提到的一个案例。你也被称为"打垮了英格兰银行的人"。一边是你在抛售英镑，一边是英国政府为阻止英镑贬值，被迫大量购入。在这个猫鼠游戏中，你是否觉得乐在其中呢？//

B: Well, of course it was a very exciting adventure. And that is exactly what captured me, and that's why I didn't stop the money making. //

A: 那一战里最刺激的是什么？//

B: When British government decided to raise interest rates in order to stop the pressure on sterling, I said to my partner, "Now this is the wrong policy for the British government in a long term. They cannot sustain this. Therefore, you can sell any amount of sterling, because it cannot be maintained." So I said, "Go for the jugular! Go for the kill!" //

A: 你听起来像是个预言家。//

B: That's right. It's like in the fight, you know, when you finally found the weak point in your opponent, then you push your advantage. I was only one of many market participants that were selling sterling, so I did not really break the Bank of England. Because if there weren't so many other people doing it, it wouldn't have happened. // I just became identified as the embodiment of the financial markets, you see. But I can't really change the direction of the market by myself. Because the markets are, of course, much much larger than any single participant. I can only succeed in making money if I guess the direction of the market right. And it's difficult to guess that when there's a change in the trend. So that's the skill of finding the right moment when the market is turning. //

A: 但是你在这一战中获得了超过十亿美元的利润，所以你也不能怪大家把你当作英镑狙击战的领导人之一。//

B: The authorities like to blame the speculators. But actually it was their mistake that the speculators recognize; that's why the speculator, I, was successful, because I discover the mistake of the authorities. But it is the authorities that were making the mistake. Of course they don't like to admit it. //

Text B 经济学家罗伯特·希勒的访谈

主题导入

罗伯特·希勒，著名经济学家，现就职于耶鲁大学 Cowles 经济学研究基地。2014 年夏季达沃斯期间，在接受中国记者采访时，希勒教授谈及了他对中国房市及收入差距的看法。以下是部分采访内容。

🎧 **请听录音，并在录音停顿时将下列段落口译成英语或汉语。**

A: 您的一些文章认为，就房地产价格和人们的年收入来看，如果两者的比例超过八倍或十倍，就意味着市场处于泡沫之中。在北京和上海，这个数字甚至超过了一百倍。那是否意味着您相信中国的房地产市场已经处于泡沫之中了呢？//

B: Well, let me say this. I would not invest in Beijing or Shanghai real estate. Not personally. They seem, um, as I understand it, to be extremely pricy. But I think men want the prices to be low, so normally it's not an inspiring story. //

A: 但是您是否认为中国的房地产市场已经到了一个转折点？因为过去一年里我们已经看到它的增长在减速，甚至某些二线城市的房价在下降。您认为中国房地产市场总体上是否已经处于一个转折点呢？//

B: Well, I wouldn't venture to say that I know. At least in other countries that I've studied, when it starts to slow down, sometimes that's the beginning of price decline. So it does look like that. // Now another thing about the recent slowdown in Chinese real estate market is some bit of seasonal. At least I assume it is. Because in the United States, prices always tend to be weak in the winter and spring. So, it's not so obvious to me what's happening right now in China. // But on the other hand, maybe there's the beginning of a downturn in real estate prices, and I would worry about that. //

A: 过去人们喜欢将效率置于公平之前，两者似乎不可兼得。经济效率和公平，我们能够两者同时兼而有之吗？//

B: I think we can. I think that ultimately in economy or investment people feel good about it, and feel positive. So, the problem is, around much of the world that the rapid growth of economies, everywhere, has led to income inequality, and especially there's corruption involved. It causes real anger. //

Text C　瑞德勒的访谈

主题导入

斯科特·瑞德勒是 T3 唯实的首席策略执行官，也是 T3 交易集团有限责任公司的合伙人之一。2016 年，在接受媒体专访时，瑞德勒分析了中国金融市场现状，探讨中国未来经济走势。以下是专访的部分内容。

请先熟悉列出的词汇与短语再听录音，并在录音停顿时将下列访谈口译成英语或汉语。

词汇与短语

硬着陆	hard landing
MSCI (Morgan Stanley Capital International)	摩根士丹利资本国际公司
S&P 500	标准普尔 500 指数
parameter	参数，系数
phantom	幽灵，幻影
volatility	反复无常

A: 如果 MSCI 今年宣布纳入 A 股，是否能给国际投资者投资带来更大的信心呢？//

B: I do think that they do get at least a few things that are positive. One, there are inflows that have to go in, so that means there's an automatic input of volume. And, two, it would feel as if they are more regulated, because sometimes U.S. investors think that the overseas markets are a little bit of the wild west, which may not be the case, but you know, here we have the S&P 500. // If a company actually gets into the S&P 500, all of a sudden, it gives a credibility. Because an investment has to go in there, and it's also a parameter, and it's also regulation. So let's just say, the FXI or the HK share is getting to the MSCI. Maybe it would actually help out. //

A: 你如何看待美国股市和中国股市的相关性？//

B: For the past year, it's been very tight. Because the Shanghai Exchange has been in crushing mode, from the one 5,000, then the one below 4,000, and then the one below 3,500. // So every day you turn on TV, and you see on CNBC, FOX Business, on Bloomberg: if China is in a hard landing, it's gonna affect this year, because it's the second biggest economy. //

A: 上周，索罗斯也对亚洲市场做了评论。您认为中国经济硬着陆也是不可避免的吗？//

B: How do I know? I'm not so smart to know whether it's unavoidable. All I know is that the Chinese stock markets were getting beat up real bad and destabilized. So I want to say this trend of flows can continue. A lot of people talking about bad loans in China and the real estate market and the phantom cities, a lot of these are all hearsay. // So I know when a big name like Soros comes out and says it has a hard landing. You know what? This guy has been wrong in the past. And at this point, just to say, Shanghai market, I would see whether it holds 2,800. If it breaks below 2,800 on the Shanghai, you are gonna probably see volatility spike again; if it gets 3,000, maybe it starts to turn again the same thing with the FXI, because price to me is king. //

Text D 对特拉维斯·卡兰尼克的专访

主题导入

特拉维斯·卡兰尼克，Uber创始人。Uber全球与滴滴出行达成战略协议，双方将相互持股，共同占领中国的网约车市场。以下是特拉维斯·卡兰尼克在中国接受专访的部分内容。

🎧 **请听录音，并在录音停顿时将下列访谈口译成英语或汉语。**

A: 首先正式开始之前，我知道您仅去年就在中国待了70天，您觉得值得吗？//

B: I mean you know you cannot start a business and run a business in China without automatically becoming a Chinese. //

A: 你怎么证明你现在就是个中国人呢？//

B: Look, I'm not Chinese yet. But I'm trying very hard. And 70 days is a very good start. But it means that you must get good at listening how China works. It's been one of my highlights as entrepreneur because so many things are different here. // It requires me the business built in more than 68 countries, but when I come to China, I actually have to start all over again. And that's in technology. That's in product. That's in finance. That's in operations. That's in government relations. That's in public. That's in everything. It starts all over again. So it's entrepreneur. But that's what I love to do. So even though I might say Uber is my baby, is my child, Youbu is my second. //

A: 中国现在推行二孩政策呢。//

B: Yes, I heard that. That's right. //

A: 你也提到了，Uber 已经在超过 68 个国家的 400 个城市有自己的业务了，是吧？//

B: Yeah. //

A: 那么，你觉得为什么中国市场与其他国家有如此大的不同呢？//

B: I think maybe one of the most surprising things now that we've seen is how open China is to innovation and to the innovation that brings progress. We have actually in China seen more acceptance and bigger embrace of our kind of innovation and our kind of technology than what we've seen in any countries around the world. And at least the reasons are that the progress that we bring. // You know half of trips are Uber pool. So you push the button and car comes just like you did before. But you open the door, and someone else is in the car because two people are taking the same ride at the same time, going to similar places. So half of our rides in China now are pooled rides. // So now you're taking two cars and you are turning into one. You are taking conjunction off the streets. When you taking conjunction off the streets, of course, that does miracles for the air and taking pollution off air. So we are purposed to make city better. // So what we found is that government officials and city officials are very much in line with seeing progress in their cities. And they are very much used to, here in China, bold broad change that happens quickly. //

Text E 苹果公司总裁蒂姆·库克访谈

主题导入

蒂姆·库克，现任苹果公司首席执行官。在中国记者的专访中，他谈及了苹果公司的环保项目及其新产品计划。以下是专访的部分内容。

请先熟悉列出的词汇与短语再听录音，并在录音停顿时将下列访谈口译成英语或汉语。

词汇与短语

太阳能	solar energy
市值	market capitalization
特斯拉	Tesla
数码终端	digital hub
人工智能	artificial intelligence
HoloLens	微软发布的头戴式显示器
Titan	巨人（此处表示苹果公司的项目）

A: 库克先生，很荣幸能采访您，因为这是您首次接受中国电视媒体的专访。//

B: I'm happy to be here. //

A: 新闻说您这次来中国要种树，您的环保项目进展的如何了？//

B: Our whole objective is to get to a net zero impact, meaning that if we use a paper, we want it coming out of a managed forest. So you protect the natural forest that are protected. And this is something that is the largest project that we've ever done, and another one of our pillars of our environmental strategy. That is running our company in 100% renewable energy. And then net zero in terms of paper use. //

A: 这的确是社会责任的表现。但是我也看到一些和太阳能有关的项目，这是出于商业方面的考虑吗？//

B: The latest step in doing now is to put a 40 megawatts solar facility in China in Sichuan Province. And what this will do is that it will power all of our stores, all of our headquarters and all of our offices throughout the entire mainland China. //

A: 谈谈苹果公司吧，现在苹果公司是世界上市值最高的公司。但是现在微软最近推出了HoloLens，让世界眼前一亮，还有特斯拉的电池项目。人们想知道苹果何时能推出一款让世界眼前一亮的产品。//

B: You know I'm wearing it. It's here. We just shipped the watch two weeks ago. So we just launch the entire new category. //

A: 是的，但是苹果似乎仍然关注触屏的数码终端，人们何时才能看到全新的产品呢？是现在传言的苹果汽车项目泰坦吗？还是人工智能方向？或者是完全超乎我们想象的产品。苹果是否有5年或10年的计划呢？//

B: We're always very secretive about our 5-year, 10-year and 15-year plan. But you can always count on great things from us. We're always focusing on not doing a ton of projects but picking ones that we can make them most impact. And we stay very focused. So we have just a few products. But we've got very deep in them. //

Text F　领英总裁里德·霍夫曼访谈

主题导入

里德·霍夫曼，领英联合创始人，是硅谷最有名的天使投资者之一。在中国记者对霍夫曼的采访中，他谈及了领英的中国市场和与中国企业家的合作。以下是专访的部分内容。

🎧 **请听录音，并在录音停顿时将下列访谈口译成英语或汉语。**

A: 中国市场对于领英来说意味着什么呢？//

B: China is the world largest collection of professionals. LinkedIn's mission is to connect world professionals to make them more successful. So China is the essential part of our mission in terms of enabling Chinese professionals to connect among China to find kind of technology information and help them do their jobs, do their works, do their careers much better both within China and connecting China with rest of the world. //

A: 对于许多像谷歌和脸书这样的美国科技公司而言，进入中国是有难度的，甚至是没有可能的。领英却是第一个进入中国市场的。那么，您认为领英要在中国取得成功的关键因素是什么？//

B: I think LinkedIn very naturally aligns with what Chinese professionals need, which is how you get more knowledge, how you enhance your career competitiveness, how you connect with other people in order to be more successful. And those services are important to anyone in the world and also I think it's very welcome in China. //

A: 领英在中国的运营结构是怎样的？它与其他国际公司的不同是它更独立。为什么会这样呢？//

B: It's because we feel that China has unique culture and also has unique requirement to the market. So you need to build your product. So it actually meets local needs. It meets Chinese needs. //

A: 请跟我们透露一点您和沈博阳的合作。您对他过去一年所做的满意吗？//

B: Very much. Derick is excellent. I think we could not hope to find better partner for building LinkedIn in China because he is, on the one hand, an accomplished Chinese entrepreneur, but also is very interested in how you do professional development, how you help entrepreneurs, managers, employees be better and how you provide them with other kinds of experience which is very aligned with LinkedIn products. //

A: 我知道沈博阳想推出一款专为中国市场定制的应用。您刚听到他这个想法的时候，是不是觉得很疯狂呢？//

B: No, actually I think it's brilliant. As I mentioned, we are trying to figure out how we have a great local product connected to global network. //

❋ 情景口译

提示：

学生三人或四人一组，根据下面的主题提示进行模拟口译，注意使用本单元介绍的技能和句型。

第 12 单元　模糊用语 / 商务访谈

 **主题一**　**对大连名达科技公司总裁的专访**

参与人： 1. 张喜胜先生，大连名达科技公司总裁

2. 伯尔尼先生，某国际知名报刊记者

3. 译员

内　容： 1. 伯尔尼先生询问张喜胜先生目前人脸识别技术的发展现状

2. 张喜胜先生向伯尔尼先生介绍人脸识别技术在公司管理方面应用的几种形式

3. 伯尔尼先生与张喜胜先生探讨人脸识别技术的发展趋势

 **主题二**　**对麻省理工大学 4D 打印研发中心主任的专访**

参与人： 1. 保尔森先生，麻省理工大学 4D 打印研发中心主任

2. 刘雯女士，中国某财经报刊记者

3. 译员

内　容： 1. 刘雯女士向保尔森先生询问 4D 打印技术的研发现状

2. 保尔森先生介绍 4D 打印技术的优势和经济发展前景

3. 刘雯女士询问 4D 打印技术在中国的应用前景

✲ 句式扩展

1. Good to have you with us, Sir/Madam.
   非常高兴邀请到您。

2. What have you learned so far from the job?
   目前为止您从这份工作中有哪些收获呢？

3. What parts of your ordinary life have you had to give up for this job?
   为了这份工作，您牺牲了您生活中的哪些部分呢？

191

4. What did you learn from that experience?

   从这次经历中你有什么收获呢?

5. What do you think of the current economic situation?

   你怎样看待当前的经济形势?

6. Could you give us some comments on your new partner?

   您能评价下您的新合作伙伴吗?

7. Well, let's move on to the next point.

   好的,我们来谈谈下一个问题。

8. I'm not sure whether I'm getting this or not. Do you mean that you have planned to reduce the property price?

   我不确定我是否理解到位了。您是说已经计划削减房价了吗?

9. We really appreciate your joining us, and we appreciate your distinct insight into all of this. Thank you.

   非常感谢您来到这里,也感谢您跟我们分享了这么多真知灼见。谢谢!

10. I learned a lot from talking with you today, and I wish we could talk more. I'm really looking forward to the next time we meet.

    从今天的谈话中我获益良多,希望有机会再次与您交谈。期待下次见面。

11. 怎样处理供应商、生产商和经销商三者之间的关系?

    How do you think a balance can be stricken among suppliers, producers and dealers?

12. 你投身商界的第一步为什么选择了当时名不见经传的一家小公司呢?

    After you decided to do business, why did you choose a small company to start with?

13. 您认为"中国制造"最重要的是什么?

    What do you think is the most important part in "Made in China"?

14. 您的经营理念是怎样的呢?

    What is your business philosophy?

15. 在竞争日益激烈的市场中,怎样处理好品质、品牌、服务这三个问题,以求可持续的良性发展?

In this increasingly competitive market, how can your company maintain sound and sustainable development? Could you share with us your opinions from the perspective of quality, brand and service?

16. 是什么让您放弃了您当时如日中天的事业，毅然决然地开始自己创业？

    Why did you give up your flourishing career and decide to start up your own company?

17. 您的人生经历过这么多次成功转型，这肯定离不开对机遇的把握，但其期间有没有跌倒的经历呢？

    You have experienced so many times of successful transformation due to your keen eyes for opportunities. But during this whole process, have you met with any hardship?

18. 作为一个企业家，您觉得应该通过什么方式来回报社会？

    As an entrepreneur, what can you do to contribute to the society?

19. 通过努力，您取得了非凡的成就，是如何做到这点的？未来五年的战略目标是什么？

    Through relentless efforts, you've made enormous achievements. How did you do that? And what is your strategic goal for the next five years?

20. 机遇总是留给有准备的人。回顾您多年来的奋斗经历，能跟观众们分享一下您的宝贵经验吗？

    God helps those who help themselves. Is there anything you would like to share with the audience when you look back at your extraordinary experience?

✳ 口译小贴士

塑造良好的声音形象

　　声音是译员工作的必要条件。美好悦耳的嗓音会带给人舒服愉悦的感受。另外，在不同场合，译员要学会调整自己的音量、语速、语调，配合场合的需要，如领导致辞、宴会祝酒、招商引资就不能用一种声音，一个语调。译员同时要注意保护好自己的嗓子，如果可能，向专业人士请教发声的技巧，争取拥有悦耳动听的嗓音。

　　在音量方面，不同场合对译员音量的要求也不同，如近距离交流时，译员在语调上要有一定的亲和力，音量适中。在会场口译时，如果没有扩音设备，译员需要适当调高音量。如果译员的声音非常小，只能自己听清楚，而很多离得稍远的听众会听不清，影响口译效果，同时也容易显得不自信。另外，有的译员上台后声音就发颤，让听众听着非常不舒服，影响现场口译的效果。

商务英语口译

在语速方面，有的译员语速特别快，认为这样可以更快速地进行口译，信息量也更大。而有的译员语速过慢。这些做法的效果都不会太好。

在音质方面，在某些重大场合，大会组织者也会很在意译员的声音的音质。这时在无法改变声音效果时要积极与音响师联系，通过音响师的调音，也能使译员的嗓音得到美化，达到理想效果。

此外，译员的声音经常是通过麦克风传播出去的，因此适当注重麦克风礼仪也是十分必要的。比如：译员要调整好麦克风的位置，控制好自己的呼吸，不要让换气的声音时不时地传到听众的耳朵里。

文化因素的处理 / 企业文化

第 13 单元

口译主题 企业文化

  文化由社会中转变的行为、信仰、态度、人的思维及创造力的总和构成。它影响着人们处事的方式、行为以及反应的方式和人们表达情感的方式等生活中的方方面面。

  文化对商业经营和企业行为的影响也随处可见。有足够证据可以表明民族文化和价值观对人类的进步起着决定性的作用，并会影响经济的繁荣。尽管民族文化对国家发展有着全面的影响，但是每个国家内部也存在不同类型的企业文化。

  企业文化是指在特定条件下，企业及企业员工在生产和管理中逐步形成的，为全体员工普遍接受和共同奉行的思想观念、文化形式、价值体系和行为准则。企业文化指导员工的思想、行为和感受。它是动态的，不是一成不变的。开展企业文化建设可以提高企业的综合实力，提升企业的核心竞争力，保持企业的可持续发展。同时，企业文化又是实行现代企业制度，进行企业机制创新的思想基础。

✻ 学习目标

  了解口译文化因素处理的基本原则和基本要求

  了解口译中文化因素的处理方式

  了解企业文化的表达内容和语言特点

  掌握企业文化相关的常用口译句式

第 13 单元　文化因素的处理/企业文化

❋ 技巧讲解

口译一方面是语言层面上的沟通，而另一方面也是文化层面上的交流。在口译过程中，译员除了要精通不同的语言外，还需在不同的文化方面架起沟通的桥梁。因此，如何处理好两种文化之间的差异便成为译员在口译过程中遇到的最具挑战和最棘手的问题。

每个国家和民族都有其各自不同的历史传统、地理环境、宗教信仰、风俗习惯和表达方式等。这些因素直接影响着不同国家和民族的发言人。他们在交流活动中会表现出各自不同的思维方式和行事方式，或者在言语里很自然地使用一些带有文化印记的表达。在跨文化交际活动中，要想顺畅地与外国人交流，译员必须努力消除语言与文化双方面的障碍，不仅要传达语言所表述的表层含义，还要尽量把语言所蕴含的文化的深层含义体现出来。

如何将深层次的文化内涵在口译过程中传达出来，取决于译员的跨文化意识程度和处理文化因素的能力，同时这也是衡量一名译员是否优秀的一个重要标准。译员应尽力加强和增进不同文化在听众心目中的可理解性，使源语与目的语在各自文化里的含义相当，尽量缩短两种语言文化间的距离，消除由于缺乏理解甚至误解造成的沟通障碍，真正让译文成为传播文化的一种媒介。因此，译员在平时应多积累源语和目的语国家或地区的文化知识，了解不同国家或地区的历史传统和文化差异，提高跨文化交流意识和处理语言中文化因素的能力，从而保证交流活动的顺利进行。影响口译的文化差异主要体现在以下几个方面：

民族习俗的差异

民族习俗差异是指在历史发展过程中，不同民族、不同文化逐渐形成了包括礼仪、习惯、喜好和禁忌在内的各种特点。译员必须要根据具体情况做出适当的调整，否则就会造成不必要的误解甚至造成语用失误。

思维方式的差异

在跨文化交流活动中，来自不同文化和社会的人们不只是进行语言层面的交流，更是进行思想和文化等层面的交流。这一交流同时也反映了交际双方的思维过程。不同民族和文化的人们存在不同的思维方式。因此，译员除了要具备扎实的语言基本功及流利的语言表达能力之外，还要对源语和目的语文化及思维方式有所了解，不然口译只能是文字字面的翻译，很难将发言人想表达的意思有效传递。

习语表达的差异

各民族语言在长期使用过程中产生了大量的习语表达，它们具有鲜明的文化个性，是民族语言的精华。习语包括成语、谚语、格言、俚语、俗语、歇后语和历史典故等。它们蕴涵着丰富的文化内涵，带有浓厚的民族色彩。这些习语结构简单，但意义深远，通常不能单单从字面意义去理解和翻译。在口译过程中，译员需要注意两种语言之间习语表达的异同，运用正确的口译技巧，在准确传达原习语意义的同时，充分考虑原文所体现出的民族风格。

因此，在口译过程中要克服两种语言之间的文化差异，译员不仅要了解两种语言不同的表现形式，更要了解在不同语言背后的文化差异所构成的障碍。译员一定要充分重视语言中的文化因素，注意文化之间的异同。只有熟悉和了解两种语言中的文化差异，译员才能将两种语言所表达的思想内容、感情、风格等忠实而准确地表现出来。在口译实践活动中，译员要根据实际情况，运用各种翻译技巧对原文灵活地处理，争取最大限度地传递文化信息。下面几种方法可做参考：

对源语加以解释

发言人用源语讲一句话，为了使听众能明白，而且在时间允许的情况下，译员完全可以用几句，甚至十几句来较完整地传达这句话所蕴含的文化信息。这是口译相对于笔译的优势所在。比如：许多成语、典故蕴意很深，且涵义与字面意思相差甚远，译员如果处理不好，就有可能使听众不知发言人要表达何意而产生困惑和疑问，这样不仅达不到发言人所要表达的效果，而且有可能适得其反。

一般情况下，在不影响理解的前提下，对成语、典故的翻译只要把表达的主要意思译出即可。但是语境中需要听众完全了解其字面意与蕴含意，就得加以解释了。比如："塞翁失马"一般可以译成"Misfortune may prove a blessing in disguise"。但在必要时，则可以简单地讲一下这个典故："This is an allusion to a story popular for more than 2,000 years in China. It's about an old man at the frontier who lost his horse..."

当然，还有一种比较理想的情况，就是在目的语中可以找到与源语相对应的表达法，这时，只要将其替代即可。如："拆东墙补西墙"与"He robs Peter to pay Paul.""有情人终成眷属"与"All shall be well, Jack shall have Jill.""挂羊头，卖狗肉"与"cry up wine and sell vinegar"，等。

对源语略作改动

由于文化差异，来自不同文化背景的人有着不同的说话习惯和方式，译员就不能原样照搬，而应使其符合听众国家文化的习惯。

在中国文化中，中国人秉承谦虚谨慎的传统美德，面对他人的赞美通常是推辞。如："刚才的发言真精彩。"，"哪里，哪里，讲得不好。"如果译员直接按字面意思或中国人的语言习惯，将其译成"No, my speech was not good at all."无疑会让对方疑惑甚至感到尴尬。因此，译员应遵循英语的文化习惯，将其译为"Thank you"即可。拘泥于字面意思去翻译，反倒会产生不好的效果。

再如，中国人见面，习惯问"吃了吗？"，遇到这种情况，译员应将其译成一句英语中的问候语，如"Good morning"或"Hello"等等，这样才算真正达到了语际转换的目的。

但是，改动一定要慎重，译员应注意不要把文化差异抹得平平的，把英语中的"to meet one's Waterloo"非译成"走麦城"不可，认为只有这样才可以消除文化的差异。

对源语忽略不译

在有些情况下，发言人所使用的语言虽带有鲜明的文化色彩，但如果忽略不译，也不会影响理解和交流。比如：中国人做自我介绍时喜欢说："我姓孙，孙悟空的孙"或者"我

第 13 单元　文化因素的处理 / 企业文化

姓李，是木子李。"这两句话的后半句进行口译时皆可省略不译，一是译起来费劲，二是译出来也没什么意义。英语中也有类似这样的例子，如 "I'm as poor as Job" 不必译成 "我像约伯一样穷"，然后再解释一句 "约伯是《圣经》中以忍耐贫穷著称的圣徒"，而只要直接译成 "我一贫如洗" 即可。

在一些场合，比如：中国人送别人礼物，喜欢自谦为 "略备薄礼"，请人吃饭，则是 "粗茶淡饭"，而且 "招待不周"。若全部照译，西方人会以为受到了怠慢。在这类场合，到底翻译什么，忽略什么，就要由译员自己根据具体情境来决定了。

上述简要地介绍了译员在处理语言中的文化因素方面可以采取的几种主要方法和技巧。在实践中译员应恪守以下原则，即：一切以尽量正确地传达发言人的意思为取舍、改动的宗旨。只要是围绕这一宗旨进行的翻译再创作活动就是可取的。总之，口译过程也是一种跨文化交际的过程。译员应在平时尽可能多地了解和积累源语与目的语国家的人文历史、风俗习惯等文化知识，在口译过程中时刻保持跨文化意识，才能有效地清除发言人和听者之间因文化差异可能导致的交流障碍，协助双方顺利地进行交流。此以，译员一定要端正态度，对来自各文化背景的人都不抱偏见，一视同仁。

✱ 技巧练习

🎧 请根据录音将下列段落口译成英语或汉语，注意文化因素的处理方法。

1. 我想起两位伟人的诗，一首是毛泽东主席的 "雄关漫步真如铁，而今迈步从头越"，一首是爱国诗人屈原的 "路漫漫其修远兮，吾将上下而求索"。// 对今年的工作，我始终保持清醒的头脑，安不忘危，治不忘乱，要有忧患意识，看到前进中存在的困难和问题。// 中国的崛起不会妨碍任何人，也不会威胁任何人，也不会牺牲任何人！海不辞水，故能成其大。//

2. Today I'd like to address the topic of "The United States as a Multicultural Society" as much as I understand it, and in that connection, I'd like to say a few words about the implications of multiculturalism for cross-cultural communication. //

Some people say that the United States is "a melting pot", while others say it is "a salad platter." In my view, rather than a melting pot, the United States today may be more accurately described as a multicultural society in which acculturation is defined more in terms of "integration" than "assimilation." // In other words, people in the United States today can maintain some original cultural identity and values and participate meaningfully in the larger society. //

The melting pot myth is never true. The United States has always been a heterogeneous society with cohesion based partly on mutual respect and partly on one group's values dominating all others. // The salad platter analogy suggests that the elements of the salad maintain their own taste or identity but exist together to create the whole. //

主题口译

Text A 企业文化的意义

主题导入

企业文化是一个公司的核心价值观，是企业团结凝聚全体员工向心力的源泉。以下篇章解释了企业文化对于招聘及管理员工和运营公司所起到的作用，强调了企业文化存在的意义及其重要性。

请先熟悉列出的词汇与短语再听录音，并在录音停顿时将下列篇章口译成英语。

词汇与短语

提心吊胆	to dread
引发	to provoke
维持	to sustain
招聘	to recruit
格子间	cubicle
平庸的	mediocre
透明性	transparency
流动性	turnover

每个企业文化都有着不同的战略和其独特的品质。但是，普遍地，企业文化都是关于员工的，确保员工们有个轻松愉快和富有成效的工作环境。//

工作场所不应该是让人们每天都提心吊胆的地方。员工们应该期待着去上班。事实上，他们应该舍不得离开，因为他们喜欢挑战、身边的同事和工作环境。工作不应该引发员工的压力感。// 虽然工作可能有难度，但企业文化不应该增加工作压力。相反地，企业文化应该设计为减轻工作相关的压力。这就是企业文化的重要性。它维持着员工的热情。//

企业文化也是个招聘工具。如果你打算招贤纳才，那么把你的公司装满格子间，限制员工的自由是毫无意义的。这样的话，你的公司只能吸引来平庸的员工，你的公司也只能是一个普普通通的公司。// 相反，如果你的公司拥有着公开透明的工作环境和员工自由度，就会吸引到人才。从人们走进办公室开始，他们就应该知道这是一个有着独特企业文化的不凡之地。//

促进员工幸福的企业文化意味着更低的流动率和更好的公司业绩。员工忠诚，公司业绩更好。这是双赢的。//

如果你的公司有了更多的员工，企业文化将会成为雇员和应聘者的自我选择机制。那些适合企业文化的人将会被其所吸引，最终得到工作。//

第 13 单元　文化因素的处理 / 企业文化

Text B　Create a Culture with a Passion for Learning

主题导入

企业文化，或称组织文化，是一个组织由其价值观、信念、仪式、符号、处事方式等组成的其特有的文化形象。企业在经营活动中形成的经营理念、经营目的、经营方针、价值观念、经营行为、社会责任、经营形象等的总和，是企业个性化的根本体现，它是企业生存、竞争和发展的灵魂。以下是对企业文化概念及内涵进行的介绍。

请先熟悉列出的词汇与短语再听录音，并在录音停顿时将下列篇章口译成汉语。

词汇与短语

barrier	妨碍；障碍
to integrate	整合；纳入
to leverage	利用；影响
adaptability	适应性
collective innovation	集体创造力

Culture can be a barrier to integrating professional development into a company strategy, but it can also be the source of competitive advantage. // A culture of excellence leverages continuous learning to create an environment where preparation, adaptability, and ongoing support to do a job are ever present. This is where out-of-the-box contributions emerge. // Instead of just getting work done, the culture transforms a company into a place where employees feel motivated and empowered to develop new ideas, concepts, and recommendations that are actively advancing individual and collective innovation well beyond what's normally expected. // This allows companies to better monitor and evaluate employee progress and provides an opportunity for employees to be constantly aware of their performance while identifying areas where support exists to help master new skills. //

Text C　腾讯公司人才发展理念

主题导入

腾讯公司是目前中国领先的互联网增值服务提供商之一。其人才发展策略是公司文化的重要组成部分。以下是腾讯公司人才发展理念的简介。

🎧 请先熟悉列出的词汇与短语再听录音，并在录音停顿时将下列篇章口译成英语。

词汇与短语

管理理念	management philosophy
激励机制	incentive
腾讯学院	Tencent Academy
双通道	double paths

腾讯公司管理理念的中心思想就是关心员工成长。为此，腾讯公司为员工提供了良好的工作环境和激励机制；不断完善员工培养体系和职业发展通道，使员工与企业同步成长；充分尊重和信任员工，不断引导和鼓励，使其获得成就的喜悦。//

腾讯公司自成立以来，一直对员工的培训与发展非常重视。除了提供专业的学习平台外，还遵循着相对完善的培训机制。2007年8月，腾讯学院正式成立，这标志着腾讯员工培训发展工作进入新的里程碑。// 腾讯学院始终以成为互联网行业最受尊敬的企业大学为愿景，通过开展各类课程与培训，努力成为腾讯员工的成长顾问与业务团队的发展伙伴，为腾讯的现在培养人才，更为腾讯的明天培养人才。//

腾讯公司还不断完善员工发展机制，从制度上保证员工在公司内有多通道发展，建立了员工管理和专业"双通道"的职业发展体系。//

Text D Nurturing Cultural Values

主题导入

作为一位领导者，如果你只赞赏那些说话嗓门最大、挥手姿势最坚决的人，那你就会忽略种类多样的其他才能，从而难以发挥团队成员的协作和创新潜力，把企业文化转化为生产力。以下是有关企业领导者如何培养企业文化的介绍。

🎧 请先熟悉列出的词汇与短语再听录音，并在录音停顿时将下列篇章口译成汉语。

词汇与短语

to coin	创造；发明
to execute	执行
morale	士气
business transformation	企业转型
to hinge on	依赖于；取决于
underserved voices	被忽视的声音
attribute	品质；因素
authenticity	真实性；可靠性

第 13 单元　文化因素的处理 / 企业文化

Peter Drucker, founder of modern management, reportedly coined the phrase "culture eats strategy for lunch". Culture used to be viewed as the "touchy-feely" side of business, but that's no longer the case. If you don't have a defined culture behind you, then you aren't going to be effective at executing your strategy. // When a culture is broken, the cracks show—morale is weakened, so is profit and performance. That's why culture has to be at the core of any business transformation. //

We all want to build strong organizations and drive effective strategies, but success hinges on nurturing our cultural values. One way to get started is to look out for underserved voices on your teams and help make sure they're heard. // Take care to build teams that represent a variety of backgrounds, experiences, and leadership attributes. Then, make sure you are encouraging authenticity by creating an environment where people feel comfortable just being their true selves. //

Text E　中国药膳

主题导入

药膳发源于中国传统的饮食和中医食疗文化，是在中医学、烹饪学和营养学理论指导下，严格按药膳配方，将中药与某些具有药用价值的食物相配伍，采用中国独特的饮食烹调技术和现代科学方法制作而成的具有一定色、香、味、形的美味食品。它是中国传统的医学知识与烹调经验相结合的产物。以下是对中国药膳文化的简介。

请先熟悉列出的词汇与短语再听录音，并在录音停顿时将下列篇章口译成英语。

词汇与短语

中国药膳	Chinese medicated diet
配膳	diet preparation
调料	condiment
远古时代	remote antiquity
运用药膳	to prescribe medicated diet
食疗	dietetic therapy

中国药膳不是食物与中药的简单相加，而是在中医辨证配膳理论指导下，由药物、食物和调料三者精制而成的一种既有药物功效，又有食物美味，用以防病治病、强身益寿的特殊食品。// 中国药膳源远流长。古代关于"神农尝百草"的传说，反映了早在远古时代中华民族就开始探索食物和药物的功用，故有"医食同源"之说。// 中国药膳强调要"注重整体""辨证施食"，即在运用药膳时，首先要全面分析患者的体质、健康状况、患病性质、季节时令、地理环境等多方面情况，判断其基本症状类型；然后再确定相应的食疗原则，给予适当的药膳治疗。//

Text F A Lesson Learned from the Enron Case

主题导入

安然事件，是指2001年发生在美国的安然公司破产案以及相关丑闻。安然公司曾经是世界上最大的能源、商品和服务公司之一，名列《财富》杂志"美国500强"的第七名，自称全球领先企业。然而，2001年12月2日，安然公司突然向纽约破产法院申请破产保护，该案成为美国历史上企业第二大破产案，严重挫伤了美国经济恢复的元气，重创了投资者和社会公众的信心，引起美国政府和国会的高度重视。以下是对安然公司企业文化所导致该事件的简介。

请先熟悉列出的词汇与短语再听录音，并在录音停顿时将下列篇章口译成汉语。

词汇与短语

entrepreneurial culture	企业文化
nimble	聪明的；敏捷的
outfit	机构；小公司
an army of	大批
academics	学者
paragon	模范；典范
stodgy	平凡的；庸俗的
paramount	最重要的；主要的
to tumble down	倒下；绊倒
to distill	提取；蒸馏
alleged	所谓的；声称的
debacle	崩溃；灾害
acclaim	欢呼；喝彩
to minimize	减少到最小；最小化
leeway	余地

Ladies and gentlemen,

Good afternoon. Today I'll focus on the definition and the importance of entrepreneurial culture, drawing on the lessons from the Enron case. //

For most of the 1990s, CEOs of Old Economy companies struggled to turn slow-moving organizations into nimbler, more flexible outfits. The truth is, real transformations are the exception rather than the rule. Changing the core values, the attitudes, and the fundamental relationships of a vast organization is overwhelmingly difficult. // That's why an army of academics and consultants descended on Enron in the late 1990s and held it up as a paragon of management virtue. Enron seemed to have transformed itself from a stodgy regulated utility to a fast-moving enterprise where its performance was paramount. //

If only that were true. Enron tumbled down. Many of the same academics are now busy distilling the cultural and leadership lessons from the debacle. Their conclusion so far is like this: Enron didn't fail just because of improper accounting or alleged corruption at the top. It also failed because of its entrepreneurial culture—the very reason Enron attracted so much attention and acclaim. // Too much emphasis on earnings growth and individual initiative, coupled with a shocking absence of the usual corporate checks and balances, turned Enron's entrepreneurial culture from one that rewarded aggressive strategy to one that increasingly relied on unethical means. In the end, too much leeway was given to young, inexperienced managers without the necessary controls to minimize failures. //

❋ 情景口译

提示：
学生三人或四人一组，根据下面的主题提示进行模拟口译，注意使用本单元介绍的技能和句型。

主题一　某国际知名信息咨询公司企业文化的介绍

参与人： 1. 刘洋女士，某国际知名信息技术公司（大连）有限公司人力资源部经理

2. 前来参观的海内外人士

3. 译员

地　点： 某国际知名信息技术公司（大连）有限公司会议室

内　容： 1. 刘女士简单地回顾该公司的成立背景

2. 刘女士具体介绍（大连）公司企业文化的理念、价值和内容

3. 刘女士分享（大连）公司员工对公司企业文化的反馈

主题二　对惠普公司亚太区行政总监的专访

参与人： 1. 劳伦斯先生，惠普公司亚太区行政总监

2. 陈伟先生，某国际知名杂志记者

3. 译员

地　点： 惠普公司会议室

内　容：　1. 劳伦斯先生谈及惠普公司的发展历程

2. 陈先生向劳伦斯先生了解中美文化方面的异同以及给惠普公司的业务带来的影响

3. 劳伦斯先生详细地解析惠普公司的企业文化

✽ 句式扩展

1. It is just the designed products that bear the corporate culture to contact with customer.

   精心设计的产品承载了企业文化的内涵去和消费者交流。

2. Aggressive, moderate, strict and self-disciplined corporate governance culture can help improve corporate governance efficiency and enhance international competence.

   积极向上、相互协调合作、严格自律的公司治理文化有助于提高公司治理效率，增强公司的国际竞争力。

3. Culture refers to the total way of life of a people, that is, the customs, traditions, social habits, values, beliefs, languages, ways of thinking and daily activities of a people.

   文化是指一个民族的整个生活方式，即一个民族的风俗、传统、社会习俗、价值观、信仰、语言、思维方式以及日常活动。

4. Most Chinese try to find the meaning of life through working in their jobs, and view work as essential for having membership in a community. Put it in another way, they regard work as prerequisite to gain social acceptance in the community.

   大多数中国人想从工作中找到生活的意义，他们将工作视为能使自己成为团体一分子的必不可缺的条件。换言之，他们认为工作是使自己得到社会认可的先决条件。

5. Chinese businessmen tend to have business negotiations in a rather indirect manner, as opposed to the more direct style of American businessmen, who are said to work with the "get-down-to-business-first" mentality.

   中国人在商务谈判时倾向于使用一种迂回婉转的方式，而被认为在工作时具有一种"公务为先"的心态的美国人则往往表现出一种比较直截了当的作风。

6. IKEA, the Swedish furniture retailer, has just reported a turnover of 56 billion EUR from its 150 stores worldwide. It puts its success down to corporate culture.

   据瑞典家具零售商宜家的最新报道，其在全球150家分店的总营业额已经达到了560亿欧元。宜家把成功归于它的企业文化。

第13单元 文化因素的处理／企业文化

7. Recruitment at our company is an extensive process, based on judgments about the candidate's value systems and attributions. We can add retail skills, no problem, but it's tough to change one's mindset.

    我们公司的招聘建立在对求职者价值观和品行的判断基础之上，是一个广泛的过程。我们可以增加一个人的零售技巧，这没问题，但很难去改变一个人的心态。

8. A multicultural society faces the communication challenges presented by multiple language use, contrasting values, and cultural prejudice.

    一个多元文化社会面临着许多交际的问题，这些问题是由语言的差异、不同的价值观以及文化偏见等因素所造成的。

9. Innovation is an attitude. It does not stop at building a strong R&D, but extends through the whole organization.

    创新是一种态度。创新不能只停留在建立强大的研发部门上，而是要延伸到整个企业。

10. Increased competition and the ever-accelerating speed of innovation mean that we need to be able to shift and scale up and down quickly, i.e. maintaining our strategic agility.

    竞争日趋激烈，创新速度不断加快，这意味着我们必须拥有快速改变方向、自如调整企业规模的能力，即保持战略灵活性。

11. 企业文化包括：正直、激情、胜利、创新、双赢。

    Corporate culture includes integrity, passion, triumph, innovation, win-win situation.

12. 企业的健康发展既需要硬性的人力资源管理和软性的企业文化，还需要两者的相互补足和配合。

    The healthy development of the enterprise needs not only hard human resource management and soft enterprise culture, but also their mutual complement and cooperation.

13. 本公司"坚持创新、追求完美"的企业文化使我们与众不同。

    Our corporate culture, which is "stick to innovation, strive for perfection", makes us larruping.

14. 每个民族的文化有不同于其他民族文化的礼仪规范。

    The culture of a nation has a set of etiquette patterns that distinguishes it from those of other cultures.

15. 文化的差异会导致误解逐渐加深，产生故意不信任、导致冲突和关系破裂，因此，造成了合作失败。

    Cultural differences cause failure because they provide fuel to a downward spiral of misunderstanding, mistrust of intention, conflict and a broken relationship coil by coil.

16. 文化是一个国家的身份证，是一个国家根之所系，脉之所维，是精神和智慧的长期积累和凝聚。

    Culture is the identity and root of a nation and it is the long-term accumulation and condensation of spirits and wisdom.

17. 在公司里，我负责做总经理助理，还协助监督400名员工的工作，包括中方及外籍经理。

    Within my corporation, I'm responsible for supporting the general manager and helping to oversee 400 employees, including Chinese and foreign managers.

18. 企业文化的核心是企业价值观，是企业精神。现代企业应该具有什么样的价值观？应该具有什么样的企业精神？这是众多企业家和专家关注的课题。

    The core of corporate culture is corporate value or corporate spirit. What kind of corporate value or corporate spirit should modern enterprises have? This is the concern of many entrepreneurs and specialists.

19. 中华民族历来尊重人的尊严和价值。还在遥远的古代，我们的先人就已提出"民为贵"的思想，认为"天生万物，唯人为贵"。

    The Chinese nation has always respected human dignity and value. Even in ancient days, our ancestors came up with the idea of "people being the most important," believing that "man is the most valuable among all the things that heaven fosters."

20. 现代企业应该具有学习的精神。在处理企业与企业之间的关系时，现代企业强调互相学习，共同进步。学习是一种态度，更是一种文化，是一种方法，更是一种哲学。

    Modern enterprises should be armed with a learning spirit. When handling the business-to-business relationship, modern enterprises should emphasize mutual learning and make concerted progress. Learning is more than a kind of attitude—it's a kind of culture; it's more than a kind of method—it's a kind of philosophy.

口译小贴士

口译中的临场应变技巧

在口译前一定要做好充分的准备，包括语言准备、心理准备和相关主题知识的准备。一般来说，口译现场常见的问题主要有以下几类：

1. 没听清、听漏了或者没听懂

对待这些情况首先要分清这部分内容是否重要、是否影响对其他部分的理解，如果是次要内容，并不影响大局，可以省略不译或采取模糊处理的办法。如果是关乎全文的关键性内容，就必须认真对待。在相对宽松的环境下，如果方便得体，最好立刻询问发言人，或者请教现场的相关专家，不能硬着头皮往下译，造成误解，影响会谈和交流；如果是非常正式的场合或者大会发言，只能先用比较中性或模糊的话过渡，然后集中注意力，找机会调整补救。

2. 错译

最优秀的译员在现场口译中也难免出错。认识到自己译错了以后，不要惊慌，也不要马上承认错误。这样不仅会让听众产生理解混乱，还会损害译员和译文的可信度。此时可以重译，并且对正确的译文采取重音重复的办法，就像平时说话要强调某事一样。

3. 不会译

不会译是由于两种原因造成的，一是没听懂，此时可以按本文的第一种情况处理；二是听懂了，却一时找不到恰当的表达，此时可先直译，再按自己的理解进行解释，虽然译文难免生涩，原文韵味丧失殆尽，但不会造成误解，也不会影响交流的进程。口译中遇到习语、典故、诗词、幽默或专有名词时，如果没有充分的准备或事前不了解讲话的内容，一时就很难在目标语言中找到对应的表达。此时要力争译出原文的大意，传达出发言人的主旨，并且使交流顺利地进行下去，哪怕译文欠妥也无伤大雅。译专有名词时，如果拿不准，还可以在译文后重复原文，听众中的专业人士很可能立刻就清楚了。

4. 发言人说错

口译中也可能遇到发言人说错的情况，如果有违事实、史实或常识的错误，或者是发言人口误，译员意识到了这个错误，并且能改正，应该在译文中予以纠正。如果译员怀疑发言人说错，却又不能肯定，在方便的情况下，应向发言人确认；在大型会议场合中，应按原文翻译。

5. 发言人逻辑混乱

口译常常译的是即席讲话或发言，而人们在即席口头表达中，由于思维和语言水平的限制，经常会出现不必要的重复、拖沓、语言模糊，或者断句、层次不清、逻辑关系混乱等现象，这给译员造成了很大困难。译员要善于对原文进行梳理，分清逻辑层次，迅速抓住主干信息，对于啰唆重复的部分，应删繁就简、同义合并；对于逻辑不清的部分，要尽量理出层次和头绪，并在译文中体现出来；对于断句或语意不完整的部分，应首先进行句法转换，并加以补充，力求完整，另外，如果下文接着说相关内容，则应该在下文的翻译中，做到与此句相呼应，体现上下文的关联性和逻辑关系。

6. 发言人语言不得体

由于英汉两种语言的文化背景迥异，思维和表达方式上差异很大，双语交流时难免有文化的冲突，汉语中的一个问候译成英语可能就变成无理的冒犯；而英语的一句赞扬译成中文也许会令人尴尬。译员应掌握两种文化背景知识，提高敏感度，在发言人言语不得体的时候，要灵活处理，或者略去不译，或者淡化，或者变通，避免误解，使交流能顺利地进行。

译前准备 / 战略管理

第 14 单元

口译主题: 战略管理

战略管理是企业为了实现其长期目标而制订、执行和评估跨部门决策的艺术、科学和工艺，是一系列决定企业长期绩效的决策和措施。企业根据其外部环境和内部条件设定企业的战略目标，为保证目标的正确落实和实现进行谋划，并依靠企业内部的能力将这种谋划和决策付诸实施，以及在实施过程中进行控制的一个动态管理的过程。

战略管理可分为战略分析、战略规划和战略实施三部分，这三部分构成了战略管理的核心框架。战略管理的目的是有效协调和整合企业内各职能部门的活动，以实现企业的长期组织目标。战略管理是高层管理人员最重要的活动和技能。首席执行官经董事会的授权和同意对组织的战略进行规划、加工和指引。然后，该战略在组织的最高领导团队或者高管的监督下执行。

❋ 学习目标

了解译前准备的意义和基本要求

熟悉译员译前准备的具体内容

了解战略管理的背景知识和相关文体的特点

掌握战略管理相关内容的常用口译句式

✲ 技巧讲解

要完成口译任务，译员除了要具备扎实的双语能力及娴熟的口译技巧外，做好译前的准备工作是口译顺利进行的保证。除了平时的积累和经验，译前准备工作是保证口译质量的重要一环。再有经验的专业译员，也不敢在对口译任务一无所知的情况下贸然接活，更不可能在毫无准备的情况下去进行口译。没有人拥有百科全书般的知识，面对未知的任务，多少都会有些不安和紧张，只有做好相应的准备，译员才能更有效地传递信息，也可以缓解心理压力。译前准备从时间上大致可分为长期准备、短期准备和临场准备。

长期准备

长期译前准备是指译员为了胜任口译任务而进行的长期的、日常的语言知识和语言技能积累、语言外知识的积累和素质训练。一名优秀的译员必须能够熟练地掌握双语或多语的语言知识和技能，具有完备的语言知识和丰富的词汇量。另外，译员还须根据时代的发展不断更新自己的词库，了解最新的语言现象。

同时，口译工作涉及的领域包罗万象，因此译员除了语言知识外还必须具备一定的语言外知识，才能更好地完成口译工作。这就要求译员在日常生活和工作中要扩大视野，注意收集归纳不同领域、不同专业的话题和专业术语，以应对可能的口译任务。因此，译员平时要有意识地进行口译技能的训练，积累各个领域的知识，从而扩展自己的知识范畴，加深理论深度，增强信息储备，以此来应对即将接受的各种口译任务。

短期准备

短期译前准备是指译员从接到口译任务到口译工作开始（包括开始前的现场准备）的一段时间内所做的准备。短期译前准备工作主要包括以下几个方面：一、发言稿件及相关内容的搜集；二、了解活动的内容和主要参与者，以及他们的姓名、头衔和职位；三、争取和发言人进行沟通，了解讲话的主要内容。

接到口译任务后，译员应与会议组织者或者活动主办方保持联系，索要会议或活动的有关资料。通常可以索要的资料包括：会议／活动议程、发言人名单及简介、发言主题或题目、发言大纲或发言稿。

在阅读相关资料的过程中，注意学习相关学科的基础知识、专业知识、最新发展动态。同时要利用图书馆或者因特网查找资料，掌握可能出现的新词汇、新短语、新缩略语等。在了解会议／活动主题的背景知识的过程中，要积极调动双语思考。阅读英文资料时，要考虑相对应的中文表达；阅读中文资料时，要考虑相对应的英文表达，充分做好语言上的准备。还要做专业术语的准备。专业术语要特别准备双语版本的表达。

会前尽可能了解发言人及听众的情况。会前争取与发言人见面，了解发言人的语音、语调、口音、说话的速度和风格。了解听众是技术专家、领导人，还是普通听众，以便有针对性地选择合适的目的语表达方式和风格。除此之外，译员对整个活动的流程、活动场地以及设备的使用也应有所了解，以便更快地适应工作现场，投入口译工作。

临场准备

无论短期准备做得多么充分，临场时译员仍有工作要做。译员要尽可能提前一小时左右来到会场或者活动现场，以免因会议日程或活动流程临时改变而措手不及。如果译员到达现场后发现可能有新的情况和变动，比如：发言顺序调整、有的发言取消、新增发言人或者临时拿到发言稿等，这就需要译员带好相关资料，以及笔、词典、笔记本等，充分利用会谈或者会议开始前和开始后的茶歇、用餐时间，主动与主办方和发言人沟通，及时更新信息。

有时还会出现在会前拿到的资料可能只是发言的背景资料，更多的信息则蕴藏在现场的发言或讨论当中，这时前面所听到的信息则是理解后面信息的最好准备，译员要靠平时的功底，尽量抓住发言人讲话的逻辑线索，进行口译。同时，在会议或活动进行中，译员要敏捷地捕捉信息，及时调整自己的用词和译文，从而能够自如地应对现场的口译任务。临场准备还包括译员的仪表和着装。译员的衣着打扮要视会议或活动场合而定。口译现场还要具备极强的自信心和临场不乱的心理素质。

另外，译员应在执行口译任务前调整好自己的生理和心理状态，保证充足的睡眠和营养，以充沛的精力投入口译工作。只要译员能够做好上述三个方面的准备工作，就可以从容地应对各种口译任务，顺利完成工作。

✽ 技巧练习

🎧 先根据以下段落的主题进行译前准备，再根据录音将下列段落口译成英语或汉语。

1. 京剧是中国最高雅、表现力最强，因而也是最受欢迎的剧种。京剧还赢得了很多外国戏迷的青睐，被看作是东方艺术的杰出代表。//

京剧同西方歌剧的相似之处在于它们都有唱段和道白，有悲剧，也有喜剧。但它们毕竟是很不一样的戏剧。//

西方歌剧的表现手法一般比较现实主义，而京剧则大量采用象征手法，对时空变化的表现极其自由。//

京剧的另一特色是脸谱。京剧脸谱象征着人物的性格，不同的颜色表示不同的性格。例如：黑色代表刚直，白色表示背叛和狡诈，红色则常用来表明忠诚。//

2. One of the most amazing tales of business success is the story of Hallmark Cards. As it is the festive season and everybody likes a happy family story with an even happier ending, this may seem appropriate on this occasion. // Hallmark Cards started as a two-person operation in a small office in downtown Chicago. And yet the business succeeded beyond the wildest hopes of its founders. //

It started as an insignificant firm with one person cutting out famous pictures from magazines making up sentimental verses to go inside, while the other person set the type—letter by letter—on an old-fashioned hand press and arranged the verses and pictures on the cards. //

Without really understanding it, these two businessmen had discovered a previously untapped market: the "mush" market. People just loved their cards. They loved even messages in them. Who cared if they were sloppy and sentimental? Who cared if the verses were childishly simple? // The important thing was that they expressed feelings in a way which the sender could understand. It was great to have someone else write a nice little poem for you and put it on a pretty card. After all, we can't all be poets or artists. This simple idea soon made Hallmark into a billion-dollar business. The company is now the world's leading manufacturer of greeting cards. //

主题口译

Text A　集团战略管理概述

主题导入

战略管理是指对一个企业或组织在一定时期内全局的、长远的发展方向、目标、任务和政策，以及资源调配做出的决策和管理艺术。以下段落是对集团战略管理涉及的几个方面的内容介绍。

请先熟悉列出的词汇与短语再听录音，并在录音停顿时将下列篇章口译成英语。

词汇与短语

战略管理	strategic management
前提	premise
打造	make

集团战略管理是解释企业获得超额收益和保持企业竞争力的关键性理念。所谓集团战略管理，就是对企业竞争、生存和发展的全局谋划进行科学的管理，主要包括价值战略、经营战略和文化战略。// 在 21 世纪，企业间的竞争已不是产品之间的竞争，而是战略管理之间的竞争。因此，许多集团公司将战略管理视为企业竞争、生存、发展的前提，把企业管理建立在战略管理基础上，集团战略管理融于企业管理中。//

在集团战略管理中，价值战略管理、经营战略管理和文化战略管理起着重要的作用。价值战略管理是企业主体依据自身存在作用、效应等，对社会需要及其发展一致性的管理。世界一流企业和二流企业的分野，不仅在于资源，更在于价值集团战略管理的高下。// 经营战略管理是经营主体自身具备的、有关经营管理方面的观念、意识和品质的设计与打造。

它贯彻于企业经营管理活动的全过程,并起着主导作用,直接影响着企业经营战略的制定和经营方式的运用。// 除了价值战略管理和经营战略管理,还要注重文化战略管理。文化战略管理是一种文化管理,更是战略管理的体现,是整个战略管理中的一种精神物质产品的打造,它具有文化自身的本质规定性和特殊性;同时,它又不同于一般的企业文化,它对提高管理水平、管理效率起着潜在作用。//

Text B The Sundown Rule—A Story of Management in Wal-Mart

主题导入

沃尔玛百货有限公司由美国零售业的传奇人物山姆·沃尔顿先生于1962年在阿肯色州成立。经过五十多年的发展,沃尔玛公司已经成为世界最大的私人雇主和连锁零售商,多次荣登《财富》杂志世界500强榜首及当选最具价值品牌。以下是对沃尔玛"日落原则"这一管理策略的介绍。

请先熟悉列出的词汇与短语再听录音,并在录音停顿时将下列篇章口译成汉语。

词汇与短语

Arkansas	阿肯色州
Harrison	哈里逊
pharmacist	药剂师
diabetic	糖尿病患者
insulin	胰岛素
the Sundown Rule	日落原则
Sam Walton	山姆·沃尔顿

One Sunday morning, Jeff, a pharmacist at a Wal-Mart store in Harrison, Arkansas, received a call from his store. A store associate informed him that one of his pharmacy customers, a diabetic, had accidentally dropped her insulin down her garbage disposal. // Knowing that a diabetic without insulin could be in grave danger, Jeff immediately rushed to the store, opened the pharmacy and filled the customer's insulin prescription. This is just one of many ways your local Wal-Mart store might honor what is known by our associates as the Sundown Rule. //

It's a rule we take seriously at Wal-Mart. In this busy place, where our jobs depend on one another, it's our standard to get things done today—before the sun goes down. Whether it's a request from a store across the country or a call from down the hall, every request gets same-day service. These are our working principles.//

The Sundown Rule was our founder, Sam Walton's twist on that old adage "why put off until tomorrow what you can do today". It is still an important part of our Wal-Mart culture and is one reason our associates are so well known for their customer service. // The observation of the Sundown Rule means we strive to answer requests by sundown on the day we receive them. It supports Mr. Sam's three basic beliefs: respect for the individual, customer service and striving for excellence. // At Wal-Mart, our associates understand that our customers live in a busy world. The Sundown Rule is just one way we try to demonstrate to our customers that we care. //

 **Text C** 中久集团总裁在公司年会上的发言

主题导入

企业年会是企业在公历年末通常举办的一场活动，在年会中一般会进行一年的工作回顾，进行总结并为下年的工作提前奠定基调。以下是中久集团总裁在年会上的讲话。

请先熟悉列出的词汇与短语再听录音，并在录音停顿时将下列篇章口译成英语。

词汇与短语

资产	asset
净利润	net profit
销售收入	sales revenue
制药业	pharmaceutical industry
基本类药物	basic drug
进入壁垒	entry barrier
融资渠道	financing channel
瓶颈	bottleneck
激励机制	incentive

各位同事：

经过十年的艰苦奋斗，中久集团已具备了坚实的竞争实力和根基，正在向更高的层次发展。目前，集团总资产 2 亿元，年销售收入 3 亿元，年净利润 1000 万元。销售收入和利润正以年均 15% 的速度递增。//

制药业和轻工业是集团的两大支柱产业。制药公司设备先进，拥有数个基本类药物专利权，利润稳定，但目前缺乏新、特药品种。轻工方面市场需求增长很快，产品严重供不应求，但该行业市场进入壁垒较低，生产厂商众多，竞争激烈。//

集团目前的困难直接体现在：一、融资困难。集团基础雄厚，现有项目市场前景广阔，但作为民营企业融资渠道缺乏，资金问题已成为集团发展的瓶颈；二、人员问题。集团的创业元老有待进一步提高现代企业管理能力，集团目前的人才引进、培训、激励机制有待进一步完善。//

当今的市场竞争越发激烈，我们必须在短期内完成集团向现代企业的转型，确立更明确的战略发展思路，迅速壮大集团的规模，为此集团将从以下三个方面入手：一、制定集团发展的新战略、新方法和新框架；二、构建完善的人力资源系统；三、在符合集团资本

运作实情的基础上进行企业变革，使集团向更高层次进一步发展。

同事们，让我们携起手来，为集团的下一个十年共同努力！谢谢大家！//

Text D The L'Oreal Group

主题导入

法国欧莱雅集团是世界上最大的化妆品公司之一，创办于 1907 年，也是财富全球 500 强企业之一。欧莱雅集团是化妆品行业中的领导者，经营范围遍及 130 多个国家和地区。以下是对欧莱雅集团商务战略方面的介绍。

请先熟悉列出的词汇与短语再听录音，并在录音停顿时将下列篇章口译成汉语。

词汇与短语

strategic plan	战略计划
to cater to	满足；迎合
customer satisfaction	客户满意度
a whole gamut of	全方位的
affluent	富裕的；丰富的

The L'Oreal Group is known for their continuous innovation in order to improve the quality of their products and the services they have to offer to their consumers. Part of their strategic plan is to cater to the best interest of their consumers, in other words, customer satisfaction. // Through giving a wide variety of products, consumers have a whole gamut of products and services that they can choose from, which best serves their preference. The range of their prices caters to the demands of women, from the younger ones to the aging, from the affluent to those with lower budget for cosmetic products. // Through constant research and passion for innovation, the L'Oreal Group best caters to the demands of women of different cultures. The company also sees to it that they know the latest trend, or better yet, set the trend in the market as to attract more consumers. //

Text E 通用汽车战略目标

主题导入

通用汽车公司（GM）成立于 1908 年 9 月 16 日，自从威廉·杜兰特创建了美国通用汽车公司以来，通用汽车在全球生产和销售包括雪佛兰、别克、GMC、凯迪拉克、宝骏、霍顿、欧宝、沃克斯豪尔以及五菱等一系列品牌车型并提供服务。以下是对通用汽车公司未来发展战略目标的简介。

第 14 单元　译前准备 / 战略管理

> 🎧 请先熟悉列出的词汇与短语再听录音，并在录音停顿时将下列篇章口译成英语。
>
> Ⓦ 词汇与短语
>
> | | |
> |---|---|
> | 斥资 | to spend |
> | 深化 | to push into |
> | 成长型市场 | growth market |
> | 重塑 | to recast |
> | 新兴经济体 | emerging economy |
> | 接近饱和 | near its peak |
> | 乏力增长 | anaemic growth |
> | 新兴市场 | emerging markets |
> | 通用汽车 | General Motors |
> | 中国上汽集团 | SAIC Motor |
> | 雪佛兰 | Chevrolet |
> | 丹·安曼 | Dan Ammann |

　　通用汽车将斥资 50 亿美元打造一个全新车型系列，在全球成长型市场中推出，同时深化与中国上汽集团的合作关系。这家世界第三大汽车制造商一直在重塑其针对新兴经济体的战略。//

　　通用汽车与其中国合资伙伴上汽集团将联合为一系列车型研发车辆架构与发动机，这些车型将在中国、巴西、印度和墨西哥以高度利用当地配件的方式进行生产。// 这系列配有雪佛兰车标的车型预计将在 2019 年上市销售，计划年销量 200 万辆。这些车型会被出口，但目前并无在美国或欧洲销售的计划。//

　　通用汽车总裁丹·安曼表示，该公司的目标是在驱动未来汽车销量增长的市场获得一种"致胜公式"，因为目前汽车制造商面对的是被认为接近饱和的北美市场以及增长乏力的欧洲市场。//

　　据通用汽车预测，从现在到 2030 年，约 88% 的全球汽车销量增长将来自新兴市场。//

Text F　SWOT Analysis of Vodafone

> **主题导入**
>
> SWOT 分析是基于公司内外部竞争环境和竞争条件下的态势分析，就是将与研究对象密切相关的各种主要优势（Strength）、劣势（Weakness）、机会（Opportunity）和威胁（Threat）等，通过调查列举出来，并依照矩阵形式排列，然后用系统分析的思想，把各种因素相互匹配起来、加以分析，从中得出一系列具有决策性的相应结论。以下是对英国沃达丰公司简要的 SWOT 分析。

词汇与短语

to roam	漫游
acquisition	收购
at the expense of	以……为代价
subscriber	用户
subsidiary	子公司
to nominate	提名
handset	手机
procurement	采购
to saturate	饱和
sofistication	精明
alliance	同盟
customized	定制的

请先熟悉列出的词汇与短语再听录音，并在录音停顿时将下列篇章口译成汉语。

Vodafone Group is a global telecommunication company with headquarters located in Newbury, Berkshire United Kingdom. It is the world's largest mobile telecommunication company with around 341 million users worldwide. It operates network in over 30 countries and has partner networks in over 40 additional countries. //

The following is the SWOT analysis of Vodafone.

First, its strengths. Vodafone has its brand image and its ranking is second in the world. So one thing is confirmed that Vodafone has good network and outstanding services. That's why its users are most after China mobile. It can offer international roaming facility more than any network in the world. Financially, Vodafone is strong and is able to invest heavy amount in the world. //

Second, its weakness. The expansion of Vodafone has been completed at the expense of direct control of its operations. The company grew through a process of acquisitions of telecommunications companies rather than organic growth. This increased its subscriber's base quickly, offering direct market knowledge and immediate additions of customer bases at the expense of direct effective control of the subsidiaries. // At the same time, though, it implicitly imposed a centralized operational structure for the group, nominating the UK headquarters as the leading business unit running a much centralized marketing and handset procurement at group level. This has resulted in the neglect of local market and local differences, allowing market share to be gained by smaller local competitors. //

Third, its opportunities. The telecommunication market, even though highly saturated in some regions, offers great potential due to the ageing population and the sophistication of the consumers. It offers great opportunities through a careful market segmentation and exploitation of particular profitable segments. // Different strategies should be pursued—simple phones and simplified pricing plans to the ageing population and more updated, sophisticated solutions for younger generations. // The expanding boundaries of the market could provide further opportunities by allowing Vodafone to enter more aggressively into fixed line service and to better enjoy the benefits of its high investment in 4G technology. Moreover, the company has undertaken its first steps in establishing strategic alliances to develop customized solutions for end-users. //

Finally, the threats that Vodafone is confronted with. The European part of Vodafone's market is characterized by existing high levels of competition. Major brands are exploiting the price sensitivity of customers. And in this way, they are building a stronger image and presence in the market. Indirect competition is also increasing further, through the presence of Skype and other related Internet based services. //

✱ 情景口译

提示：
学生三人或四人一组，根据下面的主题提示进行模拟口译，注意使用本单元介绍的技能和句型。

主题一　某团购网的发展战略

参与人： 1. 陈默先生，某团购网市场总监
2. 参加信息产业大会的海内外嘉宾
3. 译员

地　点： 信息产业大会展示厅

内　容： 1. 陈先生讲述该团购网的研发背景
2. 陈先生通过数据分析该团购网目前的发展状况及市场占有情况
3. 陈先生展望该团购网的未来发展方向和各地区的市场定位及战略

主题二　某品牌汽车女士款的市场战略

参与人： 1. 舒尔特先生，某品牌汽车（中国）营销总监

2. 参加大连国际汽车博览会的中外嘉宾

3. 译员

地　点： 大连国际会展中心多功能厅

内　容： 1. 舒尔特先生介绍该款女士汽车的产生背景

2. 舒尔特先生通过幻灯片演示该款女士汽车的卓越性能及技术支持

3. 舒尔特先生分析该款女士汽车定位的目标人群及主要营销策略

❋ 句式扩展

1. I want to thank Frank Clegg and Microsoft Canada for bringing us all together for this second summit on business leadership issue, and particularly for giving us the opportunity to discuss the issue of innovation.

   感谢弗兰克·克莱格和微软加拿大公司邀请我们大家一起参加第二届商务管理事务峰会，尤其感谢他们给我们提供了一个讨论创新问题的机会。

2. Competitors to the House of Dior include the fashion houses of Chanel, Louis Vuitton, Yves Saint Laurent, Gucci, Versace, and Prada.

   迪奥公司的竞争者包括：香奈儿、路易·威登、伊夫·圣罗兰、古驰、范思哲和普拉达等时尚品牌。

3. Very often companies will use SWOT to carry out the analysis. SWOT means strength, weakness, opportunity and threat of the company.

   公司最常用的分析方法是SWOT。SWOT是指对公司优势、劣势、机会和威胁的分析。

4. In the field of business administration it is useful to talk about "strategic alignment" between the organization and its environment or "strategic consistency".

   在商业管理领域，对组织和大环境之间的"战略协同"或者"战略一致性"的谈论是很有效的。

5. It's particularly important for them to understand advanced management techniques and something about cultural nuances for the sake of organization harmony and efficiency.

   为了增进公司内部的和谐、提高工作效率，对他们尤为重要的是要了解先进的管理方法以及中西方文化上的一些差异。

6. Making tough personnel decisions doesn't come easily for Chinese managers. They find it hard to

give written warnings to employees, and even harder to fire them.

中国管理者在人事方面做出强硬的决定不太容易。他们觉得给雇员书面警告很难，要解雇他们更难。

7. In the first half of this year, Noble's revenues almost doubled to 19.9 billion USD, producing a net profit of 290 million USD. Year-on-year gross profits at the company's agriculture division increased more than four folds to 209.3 million USD.

今年上半年，来宝公司的收入翻了将近一番，至 199 亿美元，净利润 2.9 亿美元。公司农产品业务的毛利润为 2.093 亿美元，同比增长三倍以上。

8. The U.S. management philosophy gives each manager a great deal of responsibility. For example, managers in the U.S. firms generally have some degree of spending autonomy.

美国的管理理念赋予每一级经理很多的职责。比如：美国各级经理都享有一定的费用支出自主权。

9. In my view, what really makes our company tremendously successful are our management philosophy and understanding of information. I hope we can make some of these assets available to you.

在我看来，我们公司得以取得巨大成功的真正原因是其经营管理的指导思想以及对信息的掌握。我希望能与你们共享这些使我们得以成功的经验。

10. Taobao is a Chinese language web site for online shopping, similar to eBay, Rakuten and Amazon, operated in the People's Republic of China by Alibaba Group.

淘宝网是由阿里巴巴集团在中国经营的一家从事网上购物的中文网站，和易趣、乐天以及亚马逊相似。

11. 我想向各位介绍我公司的市场营销策略和未来 5 年的发展战略。

I would like to say something about my company's market strategies and development strategies for the next five years.

12. 我公司经营方式灵活多样。我们的产品有着最好的性价比，所以有稳定的消费群。

Our company adheres to its policy of flexible and varied business operations. Our products enjoy the best price versus performance ration and therefore, have a stable consumer group.

13. 战略管理能为组织的发展掌舵，它是一门类似于组织学的学科。

Strategic management provides overall direction to the enterprise and is closely related to the field of Organization Studies.

14. 众所周知，中国汽车市场的快速发展同中国经济的快速发展密不可分。

    We all know that the rapid development of China's auto market is closely associated with the robust growth of its economy.

15. 战略管理的目的是有效协调和整合企业内务职能部门的活动，以实现企业的长期组织目标。

    Strategic management seeks to coordinate and integrate the activities of the various functional areas of business in order to achieve long-term organization objectives.

16. 战略管理是企业为了实现其长期目标而制订、执行和评估跨部门决策的艺术、科学和工艺。

    Strategic management is the art, science and craft of formulating, implementing and evaluating cross-functional decisions that will enable an organization to achieve its long-term objectives.

17. 许多人都知道，中国人一般回避在公众场合或在公开会议上处理冲突和矛盾。丢面子在亚洲国家是一个大禁忌，丢面子被认为是很可耻的事情。

    As many people might already know, managing conflict in public or open meetings is largely avoided in China. In Asia, the loss of face is major taboo. Losing face is viewed as something quite shameful.

18. 为了让人们能够更有效地合作，必须明确他们的任务、目标、责任与权力，这就需要设立一个正式的组织来规约他们相互之间的种种关系，为决策的交流与沟通提供方便。

    In order to let people cooperate effectively, they must know their roles, their objectives, their responsibilities, and their authority. This requires a formal structure to define relationships and to facilitate the communication of decisions.

19. 平安的愿望是成为国际一流的金融保险集团，成为世界金融保险企业中的百年老店。

    The vision of Ping An is to grow into a world-class finance and insurance group, becoming one of the shops of a century's standing among international finance and insurance players.

20. 在当前的情况下，我们一定要居安思危，一定要看到可能要出现的危机。

    In times of prosperity, we have to be prepared for adversity. We have to be alert to danger.

第 14 单元 译前准备 / 战略管理

✱ 口译小贴士

口译面试

新手译员在接受口译任务之前通常要经历主办方或翻译公司的面试。在面试的环节中,应注意以下几个方面:

1. 充分准备。面试前,应该根据面试的口译项目搜索相关信息,增加对相关主题知识、技术术语等方面的了解。面试的试题一般不会具有很强的技术性,通常都为企业相关的演讲稿或报道,其中会涉及一些通用的术语。因此,要在这些方面做好充分的准备。

2. 保持自信。自信是口译的基础,只有保持自信才能够克服怯场、处变不惊,也有利于在面试过程中集中注意力,灵活处理口译中遇到的问题。作为门外汉,译员在面试中难免会遇到听不懂的地方,此时要敢于发问,切忌不懂装懂,胡翻乱译。但也要注意,发问不能过于频繁,更不能总以面试官说得太长太快为由不断询问。

此外,与面试官保持自然的目光交流也是自信的体现。如果自始至终地把头埋在口译笔记本里,很难会给面试官留下好的印象。

3. 表达流畅。译语的表达要具有条理性、逻辑性。即使在口译过程中遇到难点,也不要慌乱,吞吞吐吐、"这个……""那个……"说不停;而是可以稍作停顿,迅速理清思路,继续进行。面试中不可避免地会出现一些技术术语,目的在于考察译员的应变能力。如果一遇到术语就停下来,恐怕就会拖面试的后腿了。

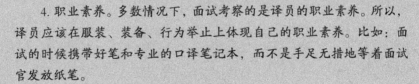

4. 职业素养。多数情况下,面试考察的是译员的职业素养。所以,译员应该在服装、装备、行为举止上体现自己的职业素养。比如:面试的时候携带好笔和专业的口译笔记本,而不是手足无措地等着面试官发放纸笔。

译后总结 / 交通物流

第 15 单元

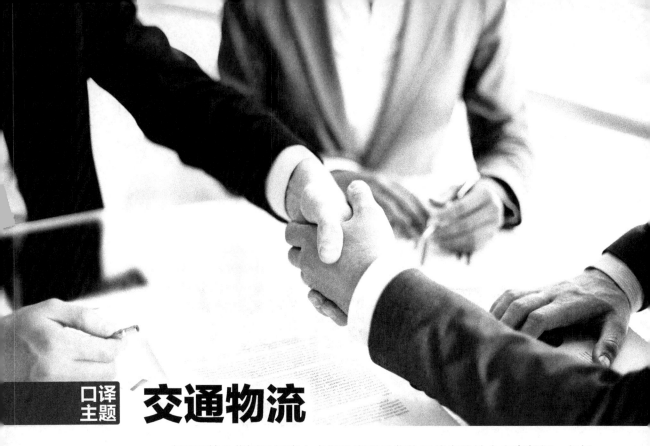

口译主题 交通物流

　　交通运输业指国民经济中专门从事运送货物和旅客的社会生产部门，包括铁路、公路、水运、航空等运输部门。物流是指为了满足客户的需要，以最低的成本，通过运输、保管、配送等方式，实现原材料、半成品、成品及相关信息由商品的产地到商品的消费地所进行的计划、实施和管理的全过程，物流由商品的运输、配送、仓储、包装、搬运装卸、流通加工，以及相关的物流信息等环节构成。

　　交通物流是指以交通运输（包括铁道、民航、公路、水运、管道运输等）为中心的物流运作程序。物流实际上是对运输概念的一种延伸，是通过现代先进的信息技术对以运输为核心的各项物流功能进行整合，是传统运输方式的一次革命性突破，是交通运输发展的高级阶段，也是发展现代交通运输业的重点内容。

✱ 学习目标

　　了解译后总结的必要性和基本要求

　　熟悉译员译后总结的具体内容

　　了解交通物流的背景知识和相关的文体的特点

　　掌握交通物流相关内容的常用口译句式

第 15 单元　译后总结 / 交通物流

✳ 技巧讲解

口译工作具有以下三个特点：工作时间上的即时性、工作内容上的随意性及工作环境上的孤立性。基于这些特点，我们不难看出口译工作是一个永无止境的学习过程。即便是从事了数十年口译工作的"老翻译"，也不敢说自己就能够应付各种类型的口译任务，因为口译实践所涉及的内容涵盖面极广，而且往往用到的都是各领域中最前沿的知识。因此这项工作就要求译员不但要做好详尽细致的译前准备工作，而且还要加强译后的自我总结工作，依靠译后的总结来修正自己在口译过程中无法弥补的不足甚至过错，以便自己在下次执行口译任务时不再犯同样的错误，不断地修正提高自己、完善自己。译员主要从语言因素和非语言因素两大方面来总结自己在口译活动中的临场表现。

语言因素

语言因素的译后总结主要包括词汇层面和术语、背景知识层面。现在大多数的情况下，主办单位都会对会议或者活动口译现场进行录音或录像，如有可能，译员在口译活动后可以向主办方索取本次会议或者活动的口译录音或录像。译员通过回听录音或回看录像来进行译后总结，首先要分析整场的译文是否达到"准""顺""快"的标准。然后再针对每句译文进行斟酌、推敲。

在听录音的过程中，译员应重点查看自己的录音中是否有语法错误或用词不规范的地方；然后对照资料和录音找出自己翻译卡壳的地方和译得不准确或者不理想的地方。找一个本子将这些问题记录下来，并加以修改重译，以便下次不犯同样的错误。同时将在本次口译实践中遇到的新词、专业术语和背景知识记录在本子上，过后加以分类梳理，编制成某个专业领域的词汇表。译后总结时编制的词汇表较之译前准备中制作的词汇表会更为完善，更具针对性，因为此时的词汇表涵盖的不仅是译员预测口译活动中将会出现的词汇，还包括实际在口译过程中用到的词汇，这些词汇很可能在将来的类似的口译实践中多次重现。

另外，要是有时间，译员可以对照录音自己再重新翻译一遍，以此来熟悉本次口译内容，提高口译技能。可以说，每一次口译实践内容都是全新的，而译员从每一次口译活动中总是可以学到不少新的知识。对于这些新知识，译员应该在口译活动之后做好总结梳理，这些新知识就能进入译员的知识库，成为熟悉的知识，进而帮助译员更好地完成下一次口译任务。

非语言因素

除了上述的语言因素方面，还有一些非语言因素也需要加以总结。首先，译员通过回听录音或回看录像，对自己在口译现场的音量、音调、语速等情况加以总结。回顾一下自己是否在口译现场运用了合适的音量、音调和语速，是否让听众感受到了诚恳和热情。其次，译员还要总结自己在此次口译活动中着装、仪表方面是否得体；临场时的姿态和手势是否合适。如发现有不得体、不合适的地方，应加以记录并确保以后要避免类似情况的发生，进一步提升自己的口译能力和素养。另外，译员在译后要主动向主办单位了解自己的工作质量，取得反馈意见。这样可以清楚自己的现场工作有哪些不足之处，并有针对性地改正错误，以达到提高自己、完善自己的目的。

总之，译员通过译后总结仔细地排查自己在临场中的种种不足，加以改正和完善，处理得好的地方加以发扬提炼。译后总结是对译前准备和现场实践环节的加固和补充。通过译后总结，译员加强了对所译内容的理解，完善了自身的知识结构。译前准备、现场实践和译后总结构成了口译活动的"学习连续体"，这几个环节相辅相成，共同成就高质量的口译表现，也是打造优秀译员的必备之法。

❋ 技巧练习

🎧 **请根据录音将下列段落口译成英语或汉语，请在口译后进行总结。**

1. 丝绸之路，简称丝路。是指西汉时，由张骞出使西域开辟的以长安（今西安）为起点，经甘肃、新疆，到中亚、西亚，并联结地中海各国的陆上通道。因为由这条路西运的货物中以丝绸制品的影响最大，故得此名。// 丝绸之路，在世界史上有重大的意义，这是亚欧大陆的交通动脉，是中国、印度、希腊三种主要文化的交汇的桥梁。// 丝绸之路的开辟，有力地促进了东西方的经济文化交流，对促成汉朝的兴盛产生了积极的作用。这条丝绸之路，至今仍是中西交往的一条重要通道。//

敦煌是丝绸之路上的一座重镇。因为当时有了丝绸之路，也就有了传播佛教的路线和敦煌财富的聚集，也就有了敦煌石窟的开凿，才会有窟内的壁画，才会有如此灿烂的敦煌文化。//

2. Ladies and gentlemen, we've commenced our descent in the Sydney Airport and we'll arrive outside the terminal building about 30 minutes from now. //

For those of you visiting the city for the first time, I have some information for you. The distance from the airport to the center of Sydney is approximately 10 kilometers. Taxis are available. You'll find taxis right outside the terminal building. The cost of Taxi trip to the city is about 12 AUD. //

There is the coach service available and the cost of the journey to the city and major hotels is 6 AUD for adults, and 2.5 AUD for children. There is also the open yellow bus No. 300 to the city at a cost of 3 AUD for adults or 1.5 AUD for the children. //

Banking facilities are available outside the Customs Hall. Hotel booking facilities can be found at the Travelers Information Service. I'd like to remind you when you leave Sydney Airport on the next international flight, you'll be required to pay a Departure Tax of 10 AUD. Thank you.//

第 15 单元　译后总结／交通物流

❋ 主题口译

Text A　顺丰速运

主题导入

快递又名速递,是兼有邮递功能的门对门物流活动,即指快递公司通过铁路、公路、空运和航运等交通工具,对客户货物进行快速投递。除了较快送达目的地及必须签收外,现在很多快递公司均提供邮件追踪功能、送递时间的承诺及其他按客户需要提供的服务。以下是对顺丰快递公司进行的介绍。

🎧 请先熟悉列出的词汇与短语再听录音,并在录音停顿时将下列篇章口译成英语。

Ⓦ 词汇与短语

专注于	to be committed to
信息采集	information collection
物流配送	logistics distribution
拓展	to expand
基础设施	infrastructure
作业自动化	automatic operation
优化	to optimize

　　1993 年,顺丰速运诞生于广东顺德。自成立以来,顺丰始终专注于服务质量的提升,不断满足市场的需求,在中国大陆、香港、澳门、台湾地区建立了庞大的信息采集、市场开发、物流配送、快件收派等业务机构及服务网络。//

　　与此同时,顺丰积极拓展国际件服务,目前已开通美国、日本、韩国、新加坡、马来西亚、泰国、越南、澳大利亚、蒙古等国家的快递服务。//

　　截至 2015 年 7 月,顺丰已拥有近 34 万名员工,1.6 万台运输车辆,19 架自有全货机及遍布中国大陆、海外的 12 260 多个营业网点。//

　　22 年来,顺丰持续加强基础设施,积极研发和引进具有高科技含量的信息技术与设备,不断提升作业自动化水平,不断优化网络建设,实现了对快件产品流转全过程、全环节的信息监控、跟踪、查询及资源调度工作,确保了服务质量的稳步提升。//

商务英语口译

Text B High-Speed Train in China

主题导入

高速铁路在不同国家、不同时代有不同规定。中国国家铁路局的定义为：新建设计开行 250 千米/小时（含预留）及以上动车组列车，初期运营速度不小于 200 千米/小时的客运专线铁路。以下是对中国高速铁路的简要介绍。

请先熟悉列出的词汇与短语再听录音，并在录音停顿时将下列篇章口译成汉语。

词汇与短语

high-speed network	高速铁路网络
from scratch	白手起家；从头做起
showcase project	示范项目
sleek	圆滑的；井然有序的
rival	竞争的
terminus	终点；终端站
touted as	追捧为
intermediate stops	沿途停靠站

The heart of China's national railway policy has been the pursuit of speed. And having built the world's longest high-speed network from scratch, this week the country proudly launched its showcase project, the 1,318 kilometers Beijing-Shanghai line. Running at speeds of over 300 kilometers an hour, the sleek electric train cuts the travel time between China's two most important cities by nearly half, to 4 hours and 48 minutes. //

The service is designed as a rival to air travel. Indeed, at Beijing South station, the ultra-modern facility resembles an airport. The other terminus, meanwhile, actually is at Shanghai's domestic airport. But that means travelers lose the benefit of a downtown arrival, often touted as an advantage of trains. Even on intermediate stops, stations are far from urban centers. //

Text C 马士基航运公司

主题导入

马士基集团成立于 1904 年，总部位于丹麦哥本哈根，在集装箱运输、物流、码头运营、石油和天然气开采与生产，以及与航运和零售行业相关的其他活动中，为客户提供了一流的服务。集团旗下的马士基航运公司是全球最大的集装箱承运输公司，服务网络遍及全球。以下是客户对马士基航运公司物流服务的评价。

第 15 单元 译后总结／交通物流

🎧 请先熟悉列出的词汇与短语再听录音，并在录音停顿时将下列篇章口译成英语。

Ⓦ 词汇与短语

集装箱	container
拖车	trailer
储藏罐设备	tank equipment
马士基航运公司	Maersk Line
客户体验	customer experience

中国国际海运集装箱有限公司（CIMC）是集装箱、拖车、储藏罐设备和机场设施等全运输设备全球性的制造商和供应商。//

将这类大型产品运输到世界各地时，大多数 CIMC 的产品需要特殊设备。在大多数情况下，马士基航运公司都是这类运输需求的首选。//

马士基航运公司被认为是市场上最可靠的航运公司。马士基航运公司的一大优点就是其"单一窗口"的服务模式——无论在全球哪个港口，客户只与固定销售或客服代表联系，他／她直接在内部为客户提供服务或者帮助客户进行协调。相比其他公司，他们提供的客户体验更好。//

Text D　The Channel Tunnel

主题导入

英吉利海峡隧道也称为英法海底隧道、欧洲隧道，是一条连通英国英伦三岛和欧洲法国的铁路隧道，位于英国多佛港与法国加来港之间，于 1994 年 5 月 6 日开通，也是世界上规模最大的利用私人资本建造的工程项目。以下是对英法海底隧道概况进行的介绍。

🎧 请先熟悉列出的词汇与短语再听录音，并在录音停顿时将下列篇章口译成汉语。

Ⓦ 词汇与短语

Folkestone	福克斯通
Coquelles	科凯勒
Pas-de-Calais	加来海峡省
Strait of Dover	多佛尔海峡
Seikan Tunnel	青函隧道
Eurotunnel Shuttle	欧隧穿梭
to disrupt	干扰
refugee camp	难民营
Sangatte	桑加特

　　The Channel Tunnel is a 50.5-kilometre rail tunnel linking Folkestone, Kent, in the United Kingdom, with Coquelles, Pas-de-Calais, near Calais in northern France, beneath the English Channel at the Strait of Dover. // At its lowest point, it is 75 meters deep. At 37.9 kilometers, the tunnel has the longest undersea portion of any tunnel in the world, although the Seikan Tunnel in Japan is both longer overall at 53.85 kilometers and deeper at 240 meters below sea level. //

The tunnel carries high-speed Eurostar passenger trains, the Eurotunnel Shuttle for road vehicles—the largest such transport in the world—and international freight trains. The tunnel connects end-to-end with the LGV Nord and High Speed 1 high-speed railway lines. //

Ideas for a cross-Channel fixed link appeared as early as 1802, but British political and press pressure over the compromising of national security stalled attempts to construct a tunnel. // The eventual successful project, organized by Eurotunnel, began construction in 1988 and opened in 1994. At 4.65 billion GBP, the project came in 80% over its predicted budget. // Since its construction, the tunnel has faced several problems. Both fires and cold weather have disrupted its operation. Illegal immigrants have attempted to use the tunnel to enter the UK, causing a minor diplomatic disagreement over the siting of the refugee camp at Sangatte, which was eventually closed in 2002. //

Text E 世界一流的铁路服务

主题导入

港铁是香港最大的铁路运输系统，泛指能够通过一张港铁单程票通行的9条路线，广义上包括一条连接香港国际机场及香港市区的机场快线、拥有12条路线的轻铁系统等贯通香港岛、九龙及新界及多座新市镇的铁路网。以下是对港铁服务情况的介绍。

请先熟悉列出的词汇与短语再听录音，并在录音停顿时将下列篇章口译成英语。

词汇与短语

港铁	MTR (Mass Transit Railway)
九龙	Kowloon
新界	New Territories
屯门	Tuen Mun
元朗	Yuen Long
轻铁网络	Light Rail network
接驳巴士	feeder bus
机场快线	Airport Express
亚洲国际博览馆	Asia World-Expo
城际客运服务	intercity railway service
调校	to regulate
最适当的	optimal
滑行速度	coasting speeds

港铁被公认为全球首屈一指的铁路系统，以其安全、可靠程度、卓越的顾客服务及高成本效益见称。//

公司在香港营运九条铁路线，网络覆盖香港岛、九龙及新界，同时在屯门及元朗为当地社区提供轻铁服务及接驳巴士。//

公司设有机场快线，为海外旅客提供高速铁路专线，连接市中心和香港国际机场以及香港最新的展览及会议中心——亚洲国际博览馆。//公司的城际客运服务，为往返广东省、北京及上海的旅客提供方便的铁路运输。//

港铁列车与其他交通工具不同，极少受路面交通或天气影响，每天由清晨 5 时 30 分至 6 时不等至翌日凌晨 1 时提供约 19 小时快捷可靠的服务，让你准时到达目的地。//

为了维持最高的安全及可靠程度，列车装有自动保护及控制系统，可自动调校行车时列车与列车之间的距离，决定最适当的加速及刹车速度，以及在不同轨段的滑行速度。//

Text F　Cathay Pacific Airways

主题导入

国泰航空有限公司是香港最主要的航空公司，在香港注册，是在香港交易所上市的综合企业。旗下的子公司包括港龙航空及香港华民航空，是"寰宇一家"航空联盟的重要成员。以下是对国泰航空有限公司的介绍。

请先熟悉列出的词汇与短语再听录音，并在录音停顿时将下列篇章口译成汉语。

词汇与短语

Cathay Pacific Airways	国泰航空
legend	传奇；传说
Manila Hotel	马尼拉酒店
Swire Group	太古集团

American Roy C. Farrell and Australian Sydney H. de Kantzow founded Cathay Pacific Airways on 24 September, 1946. Initially based in Shanghai, the two men eventually moved to Hong Kong and established the airline. // Legend has it that Farrell and a group of foreign correspondents thought up the airline's unique name in the bar at the Manila Hotel! //

The new company began to operate passenger flights to Manila, Bangkok, Singapore and Shanghai. Expansion was fast and, in 1948, one of Hong Kong's leading trading companies, Butterfield & Swire (today known as the Swire Group) took a 45% share in the company. Under the leadership of John Kidston Swire, Butterfield & Swire became wholly responsible for the management of the airline. //

情景口译

提示：

学生三人或四人一组，根据下面的主题提示进行模拟口译，注意使用本单元介绍的技能和句型。

主题一　现代物流业简介

参 与 人： 1. 帕金斯先生，某国际知名大学的教授

2. 参加国际物流研讨会的中外嘉宾

3. 译员

地　　点： 某大学科学报告厅

内　　容： 1. 帕金斯先生介绍现代物流业的特点和发展方向

2. 帕金斯先生提及物流企业目前的运营模式和发展方向

3. 帕金斯先生分析物流业的竞争趋势

主题二　某市地铁的建设及运营情况的介绍

参 与 人： 1. 李淼女士，某市地铁有限公司运营公司总经理

2. 参加中国城市交通规划年会的中外嘉宾

3. 译员

地　　点： 某市国际会议中心

内　　容： 1. 李女士介绍该市地铁运营公司的基本情况

2. 李女士通过幻灯片演示该市地铁线路规划和提供的服务

3. 李女士介绍目前开通的线路及运行情况

4. 李女士通过数据分析地铁运行对整个城市交通情况的影响

第 15 单元　译后总结 / 交通物流

✻ 句式扩展

1. We saw that Canada-U.S. trade and trade with Mexico were growing. The trucks were handling most of that growth. We wanted more of the action.

   加拿大和美国之间的贸易以及美国和墨西哥之间的贸易过去一直在增长。在贸易流通中卡车运输起到了主要的作用，但还满足不了我们的需要。

2. In the 19th century, railroads were the big innovation. Perhaps nothing matched their economic impact until the advent of the personal computer.

   在 19 世纪，铁路是最大的创新。在个人计算机出现之前，它对经济所产生的影响或许无与伦比。

3. Our goal is to create a transportation service that offers customers a competitive advantage—a service so superior that customers think that a premium price is reasonable.

   我们的目标是为顾客提供一种具有竞争优势的运输服务，即给顾客一个物超所值的优质服务的感觉。

4. The traditional railroad franchise is bulk commodities that are too heavy to be carried cost-effectively by truck—coal, potash and grain, for example.

   传统的铁路经营特许，指的是那些沉重而难以用卡车进行节约成本运输的大宗货物，比如：煤炭、碳酸钾和粮食。

5. Customers can click onto our website and order a car, send us shipping instructions, ensure that we pick up their delivery as scheduled, track the shipment to its destination, receive an invoice, clarify any questions, and pay the bill.

   顾客可以点击进入我们的网站，订购汽车并给我们发送装运要求，这样保证我们按时发运、从头到尾地跟踪运输情况、收取发票、澄清问题和付账等。

6. Scheduled service also provides a foundation for innovation in our e-business solutions.

   定时运输服务为我们在电子商务解决方案方面的革新提供了基础。

7. Products of Western Canada's farms, ranches, forests, coal mines, and industries are sent by rail to Vancouver and then by water to the ports of the world.

   加拿大西部的农产品、畜牧产品、木材、煤炭和工业产品，通过铁路运往温哥华，然后经水路运往世界各地的港口。

8. As we know, logistics is that part of supply chain that plans, controls, and carries out the efficient and effective forward and reverse flow and storage of goods, services, and related information between the point of origin and the point of consumption.

   我们知道,物流是供应链的部分环节,包括由商品的产地到商品的消费地的计划、控制、运输货物、存储以及相关服务与信息的全过程。

9. Modern logistical activities are no longer limited to passive storage and transportation. It involves systemic operations, including transportation supports, warehousing, packaging, loading, distribution and processing, which will all contribute to the overall performance.

   现代物流活动已不限于被动的储存和运输。它涉及一系列系统化的操作,包括运输支持、仓储、包装、装货、分配和加工,所有这些都将影响物流的总体运行状况。

10. As for air transportation, Odessa International Airport is one of the largest airports in Ukraine and is connected by its air lines with a lot of Ukrainian cities, and the countries of the CIS, Western Europe, Asia and Africa.

    在航空运输方面,敖德萨国际机场是乌克兰最大型的机场之一,与乌克兰许多城市、独联体国家、西欧、亚洲和非洲等都有直达航线。

11. 我们为顾客提供外汇兑换、托运、保险等服务项目。

    We provide our customers with services of foreign currency exchange, exchange, shipping and insurance.

12. 天津滨海新区凭借着得天独厚的地理条件,即拥有海港、空港及保税区三大功能优势,发展现代物流业,这成为必然的选择。

    It has become a necessary choice for Binhai New Area to develop the modern logistic industry by making use of the advantages of seaport, airport terminal and bonded area.

13. 作为中国北方最大自由贸易区的保税区,天津港保税区以其良好的区位及海运、陆运、空运条件,构成了国际货物多式联运系统,形成了便捷的交通运输网络,成为名副其实的物流国际绿色通道。

    As the biggest free trade area in north China at the bonded area, Tianjin Bonded Area has formed a thorough traffic system by making use of its good location and navigation, land-carriage and aviation conditions. It is worthy of the name of the international green channel of logistics industry.

14. 中国在交通领域实行积极的对外开放政策,促进了对外交流与合作,不仅引进了资金、技术,而且提高了我们的管理水平。

China has implemented a positive reform and opening-up policy in its transportation sector, which has promoted exchange and cooperation with foreign countries. All these efforts have not only attracted capital and technology for development, but also improved our management efficiency.

15. 我们在多式联运、物流组织、智能运输、交通工程、电子商务等方面也进行了有益的探索。

We have also conducted profitable trials in the fields of multi-modal transportation, logistics, intelligent transportation, transportation engineering and electronic commerce.

16. 交通运输是中国重要的基础性产业之一，也是重要的服务业部门。中国 90% 以上的对外贸易货物是通过海运完成的。

Transportation is not only one of the very important infrastructural industries, but also a major service sector. Over ninety percent of China's foreign trade goods are shipped by sea.

17. 上海是世界上最大的海港城市之一，也是中国最大的工业、商业、金融、航运中心之一。

Shanghai is one of the world's largest seaports and among China's biggest industrial, commercial, financial and shipping centers.

18. 新西兰是一个活跃的贸易国，通过定期的海上和空中运输服务与主要的贸易伙伴保持联系。

New Zealand is an active trading nation, linked to its principal trade partners by regular sea and air services.

19. 本次会议的主题确定为"海港的作用——内陆与海运连接的桥梁"，这充分体现了联合国欧经委对海港在国际贸易运输及经济发展所起的重要作用的高度重视。

We have decided on the theme of this meeting, that is, "The Role of the Harbor—a Bridge to Connect the Inland and the Sea Transportation", which fully demonstrates that the UNECE attaches great importance to the important role the harbors have made in the international trade and economic development.

20. 中国铁路四年来通过技术改造，三次大幅度地提高旅客列车速度，取得良好的效益，并为提升高密度运输创造了条件。

In the last four years or so, the technical innovation has brought about three increases in the running speed of locomotives, which has produced considerable profits and prepared necessary conditions for realizing high-density transportation.

口译小贴士

口译工作中的人际关系

译员在工作中通常需要处理与雇主、服务对象、听众以及同行的关系。处理好这几个方面的关系，保持良好愉快的合作会为译员的准备工作以及现场翻译提供极大的便利。

1. 译员同雇主之间的合作

译员的雇主可能是公司、活动组织者、翻译公司或者中介，也可能是发言人或听众。译员需要认真对待雇主的要求，同时要以职业化的态度积极督促雇方提供必要的信息和背景资料，熟悉流程和要求等。译员在工作准备期间，要定期与雇主保持联系，让雇主了解你所做的准备，同时了解雇主方可能发生的各类变化。这也是专业性、敬业精神的一种表现。

2. 译员同服务对象之间的合作

在口译工作中，译员同服务对象之间的合作尤为重要。通常服务对象会把翻译服务的看法反馈给雇主，并影响雇主对译员的看法。理论上讲，服务对象为了达到预期的讲话效果，会尽量向译员提供信息、及时交流发言的变化。但现实工作中，有时服务对象是国际要员、企业高管等，译员不能与他们直接接触；有时服务对象因为忙碌或不了解译员的需求，没有提供相应信息，或及时沟通发言内容。通常情况下，译员需要主动争取机会，与服务对象在会前进行沟通，或者与服务对象方面接待部门的负责人进行沟通和联系。积极的沟通也是职业性的一种体现。

3. 译员同听众的关系

尽管译员与听众之间没有直接的接触，但听众是译员译文的接受方，因此译员有必要对听众进行必要了解，如听众的人数、社会背景、听众可能关心的问题。并在翻译的过程中预测听众的兴趣和困难，用听众最能接受的方式进行翻译。

有些场合，译员会面对来自听众的反馈。对于听众给予的正面反馈要不骄傲，面对负面评价，也要不气馁、不慌张，并根据反馈做适当的调整。有时，听众或服务对象自认为对目的语有所了解，认为译员有翻译不当之处，并给予纠正。只要不是由于发言人不当的批评，妨碍了翻译工作，引起听众对译文准确性的质疑，译员可以表示接受，不去争辩。但是如果引起在场人员对翻译的质疑，译员应进行恰当地辩驳，如对方有原则性错误，译员应及时指出，使他及在场其他听众了解他的问题所在。

4. 译员的同行合作

在工作场合,有时有两名译员同时在场,双方服务对象不同。一般惯例是,双方译员把己方语言翻译成对方语言,如译员为中方雇主服务,就需要把中文翻译成对方的语言,如英文。而英方/美方译员把英文翻译成中文。两位译员彼此之间要互相尊重、互相体谅,并尽量协助。既不要抢着译,两人一起说话,也不要都不张口,等着对方翻译。如果宴会上,宴会主办方为译员准备了食物,两名译员可以轮流工作,另一方可以转身吃一点东西。如果是同传,更要分工协作,帮助对方完成好同传工作。

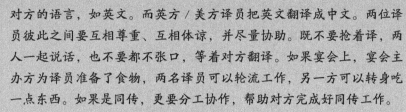

附录 1　AIIC Code of Professional Ethics

Version 2012

I. Purpose and Scope

Article 1

a) This Code of Professional Ethics (hereinafter called the "Code") lays down the standards of integrity, professionalism and confidentiality which all members of the Association shall be bound to respect in their work as conference interpreters.

b) Candidates and precandidates shall also undertake to adhere to the provisions of this Code.

c) The Disciplinary and Disputes Committee, acting in accordance with the provisions of the Statutes, shall impose penalties for any breach of the rules of the profession as defined in this Code.

II. Code of Honour

Article 2

a) Members of the Association shall be bound by the strictest secrecy, which must be observed towards all persons and with regard to all information disclosed in the course of the practice of the profession at any gathering not open to the public.

b) Members shall refrain from deriving any personal gain whatsoever from confidential information they may have acquired in the exercise of their duties as conference interpreters.

Article 3

a) Members of the Association shall not accept any assignment for which they are not qualified. Acceptance of an assignment shall imply a moral undertaking on the member's part to work with all due professionalism.

b) Any member of the Association recruiting other conference interpreters, be they members of the Association or not, shall give the same undertaking.

c) Members of the Association shall not accept more than one assignment for the same period of time.

Article 4

a) Members of the Association shall not accept any job or situation which might detract from the dignity of the profession.

b) They shall refrain from any act which might bring the profession into disrepute.

Article 5

For any professional purpose, members may publicize the fact that they are conference interpreters and members of the Association, either as individuals or as part of any grouping or region to which they belong.

Article 6

a) It shall be the duty of members of the Association to afford their colleagues moral assistance and collegiality.

b) Members shall refrain from any utterance or action prejudicial to the interests of the Association or its members. Any complaint arising out of the conduct of any other member or any disagreement regarding any decision taken by the Association shall be pursued and settled within the Association itself.

c) Any problem pertaining to the profession which arises between two or more members of the Association, including candidates and precandidates, may be referred to the Disciplinary and Disputes Committee for arbitration, except for disputes of a commercial nature.

III. Working Conditions

Article 7

With a view to ensuring the best quality interpretation, members of the Association:

a) shall endeavor always to secure satisfactory conditions of sound, visibility and comfort, having particular regard to the Professional Standards as adopted by the Association as well as any technical standards drawn up or approved by it;

b) shall not, as a general rule, when interpreting simultaneously in a booth, work either alone or without the availability of a colleague to relieve them should the need arise;

c) shall try to ensure that teams of conference interpreters are formed in such a way as to avoid the systematic use of relay;

d) shall not agree to undertake either simultaneous interpretation without a booth or whispered interpretation unless the circumstances are exceptional and the quality of interpretation work is not thereby impaired;

e) require a direct view of the speaker and the room and therefore will not agree to working from screens except in exceptional circumstances where a direct view is not possible, provided the arrangements comply with the Association's appropriate technical specifications and rules;

f) shall require that working documents and texts to be read out at the conference be sent to them in advance;

g) shall request a briefing session whenever appropriate;

h) shall not perform any other duties except that of conference interpreter at conferences for which they have been taken on as interpreters.

Article 8

Members of the Association shall neither accept nor, a fortiori, offer for themselves or for other conference interpreters recruited through them, be they members of the Association or not, any working conditions contrary to those laid down in this Code or in the Professional Standards.

IV. Amendment Procedure

Article 9

This Code may be modified by a decision of the Assembly taken with a two-thirds majority of votes cast and, if appropriate, after having sought a legal opinion on the proposals.

附录2 翻译服务规范 第2部分：口译

2006-09-04 发布 2006-12-01 实施
中华人民共和国国家质量监督检验检疫总局
中国国家标准化管理委员会
GB/T 19363.2-2006

1. 范围

GB/T 19363 的本部分确立了口译服务方提供口译服务的过程及规范。

本部分适用于翻译服务口译业务。

2. 规范性引用文件

下列文件中的条款通过 GB/T 19363 的本部分的引用而成为本部分的条款。凡是注日期的引用文件，其随后所有的修改单（不包括勘误的内容）或修订版均不适用于本部分，然而，鼓励根据本部分达成协议的各方研究是否可使用这些文件的最新版本。凡是不注日期的引用文件，其最新版本适用于本部分。

GB/T 19000—2000 质量管理体系 基础和术语（idt ISO9000：2000）

ISO 2603：1998 同声传译室一般特性及设备

ISO 4043：1998 移动式同声传译室一般特性及设备

3. 术语和定义

下列术语和定义适用于本部分。

3.1 口译 interpretation

口头将源语言译成目标语言。

3.2 口译服务 interpretation service

提供口译的有偿经营行为。

3.3 口译服务方 interpretation service provider

具备提供口译服务资质的组织。

3.4 顾客 customer

接受产品的组织或个人。[GB/T19000-2000，定义 3.3.5]

3.5 口译对象 source speaker

源语言信息。

3.6 口译语言 interpretive language

源语言和目标语言。

3.7 交替传译 consecutive interpreting

当源语言使用者讲话停顿或结束等候传译时，口译员用目标语清楚、准确、完整地表达源语言的信息内容。

3.8 同声传译 simultaneous interpreting

借助专用设施将听到的或看到的源语言的信息内容，近乎同步地准确传译成目标语言。

注1：耳语同传可不借助专用设施。

注2：同传设备要求参见ISO2603：1998和ISO4043：1998。

3.9 口译现场 interpretation site

译员的服务场所。

3.10 纠正措施 corrective action

为消除已发现的不合格或其他不期望情况的原因所采取的措施。[GB/T19000—2000定义3.6.5]

4. 要求

4.1 口译服务方的资质

口译服务方应具备以下资质：

—具有符合本部分4.3要求的译员；

—具有相关的专业知识；

—具有履行合同的能力。

4.2 业务接洽

4.2.1 接洽场所

作为口译服务方的窗口，应清洁、明亮，在明显的位置展示翻译服务方的营业执照、税务执照、行业资质等相关证照。

4.2.2 接洽人员

应熟悉口译服务过程、服务范围、收费标准等诸方面内容，着装得体、语言文明，解答顾客的询问。

4.2.3 接洽内容

4.2.3.1 短期业务

约期不超过一个月的为短期口译业务。双方应签订书面合同或协议书，内容应包括：

—顾客的全称；

—联系方式（电话、传真、地址、邮编、电子邮箱等）；

—联系人；

—翻译语种；

—专业领域；

—收费价格；

—工作期限和时限；

—预付的翻译服务费；

—加班费用；

—交通费用、食宿费用等其他有关费用；

—安全措施及可能发生的工伤善后；

—口译质量纠纷仲裁；

—保密要求；

4.2.3.2　长期业务

约期超过一个月的为长期口译业务。双方应签订书面合同或协议书，除 4.2.3.1 中的条款外，合同或协议书还应包括以下内容：

—口译服务内容（翻译语种、项目、每周工作日、日工作时间）；

—口译质量要求；

—口译现场安全防护要求；

—意外事故保险要求；

—可能发生的工伤善后责任方；

—休假及其待遇；

—收费内容（口译服务费、加班费、食宿费、交通费等）；

—计费方式（按月计费、按工作日计费、加班计费等）；

—结算周期和付费方式；

—违约和免责条款；

—变更方式；

—其他。

4.2.4　计费

—按工作日计费。不足半个工作日的按半个工作日计；超过半个工作日，不足一个工作日的，按一个工作日计。工作日以外按加班计酬。

—按月计费，每月工作天数与顾客约定，约定以外工作天数按加班计酬。

注：同声传译（组）工作日按 6h 计。

4.2.5 其他事项

合同规定以外的服务，双方商定另行收费。

4.3 译员

译员应符合以下条件：

— 有国家承认的有关部门颁发的口译资格证书或有相应的能力；

— 接受培训和继续教育；

— 具有职业道德。

4.4 顾客支持

4.4.1 顾客应向口译服务方介绍：

—口译涉及的专业；

—服务的范围；

—口译对象。

4.4.2 顾客应向译员提供：

—所涉及的相关文件、资料和专业术语；

—背景材料；

—为观看现场或实物提供方便。

4.4.3 顾客应提供安全培训或必要的安全知识。

4.5 业务管理

4.5.1 译员资质管理

—对译员的职业道德教育、安全教育；

—对译员进行业务培训和考核；

—掌握译员的业务经历、水平和工作绩效。

4.5.2 译员安排

根据合同的协议，选配合适的译员。

4.5.3 标识

每批次口译业务应用数字、字母或文字记录标识。作为追溯性标识，应有以下一项或数项记录内容：

—顺序批次编号；

—日期；

—翻译语种；

—口译人员和口译对象；

—口译涉及专业及项目内容；

—顾客。

4.5.4 档案管理

口译服务方应建立和保存：

—项目档案；

—顾客档案；

—译员业务档案等；

—业务记录档案等。

4.6 口译服务过程控制

4.6.1 工作流程

4.6.1.1 译前准备

译员要认真查阅相关资料、熟悉词汇、了解口译对象和双方相关人员，以及熟悉工作现场或设施情况。要做好必要的准备，携带必备的证件和有关资料，按要求着装，提前到达工作现场。

4.6.1.2 口译过程

在口译过程中应做到：

—准确地将源语言译成目标语言；

—表达清楚；

—尊重习俗和职业道德。

4.6.1.3 在口译服务过程中出现问题，口译服务方应与顾客密切配合及时予以处理。

4.6.2 译后工作

口译结束后，口译服务方应听取顾客的意见反馈，必要时对顾客反馈意见予以答复。

4.7 保密

口译服务方应按照合同或协议为顾客保守秘密。

4.8 一致性声明

每个口译服务方都可以自愿履行本部分各项条款并自负责任地声明是根据本部分提供口译服务。

附录3 口译服务报价规范

2014年9月18日发布

1. 适用范围

本规范规定了口译服务报价的内容与方式。

本规范仅适用于口译服务业务。

2. 规范性引用文件

下列文件中的条款通过本部分引用成为本部分条款。凡注有日期的引用文件，其随后所有修改单（不包括勘误内容）及修订版均不适用于本部分，然而，鼓励根据本规范达成协议的各方研究是否可使用这些文件的最新版本。凡未注明日期之引用文件，其最新版本适用于本部分。

GB/T 19363.2-2006 翻译服务规范 第2部分：口译

ISO 2603: 1998 同声传译室一般特性及设备

ISO 4043: 1998 移动式同声传译室一般特性及设备

3. 术语和定义

下列术语和定义适用于本部分。

3.1 交替传译

当源语言使用者讲话停顿或结束等候翻译时，口译员用目标语清楚、准确、完整地表达源语言的信息内容，简称"交传"。

3.2 陪同交传

译员陪同客户参与涉外活动，并随行为其提供交替传译服务。

3.3 会议交传

译员为客户举办或参与的涉外会议提供交替传译服务。

3.4 远程交传

译员及会谈各方借助通信设备提供交替传译服务。

3.5 同声传译

借助专用设施将听到的或看到的源语言的信息内容，近乎同步地准确翻译译成目标语言，简称"同传"。

3.6 耳语同传

译员在服务对象身旁耳语为其进行同声传译。

3.7 会议同传

译员在国际会议现场借助同声传译设备为服务对象进行同声传译。

3.8 远程同传

译员及会谈各方并非全都同在一地时，译员借助通信设备为服务对象提供同声传译服务。

3.9 跟会人员

口译服务方派至会议现场负责协调、保障的人员，主要负责在现场与客户方的沟通与协调，保障译员的翻译工作。

4. 口译服务工作内容

4.1 口译服务工作类别

口译服务由交替传译（简称"交传"）和同声传译（简称"同传"）构成。

交替传译主要包括陪同交传、会议交传和远程交传。

同声传译主要包括耳语同传、会议同传和远程同传。

4.2 口译服务工作内容

4.2.1 与客户沟通

—主要包括：确认工作语种、时间、地点、所需译员数量、客户联系人信息、所译内容的背景信息及资料。

4.2.2 内部准备

—确定译员人选；

—安排译员研究学习相关背景材料，做好译前准备。

4.2.3 现场服务

—译员按约定时间到达工作现场，提供所需翻译服务；

—技术人员按约定时间，提前完成会议现场同传所需设备的安装与调试；

—发放同传接收器，做好领取接收器的登记工作。

（注：与翻译不相关的其他服务，另行酌情收费。）

4.2.4 远程服务

—**远程交传**：技术人员提前完成通讯设备调试工作，保证通话质量。

—**远程同传**：技术人员按约定时间到达工作现场，提前完成远程同传设备的安装与调试；发放同传接收器，做好领取接收器的登记工作。

4.3 报价方式

4.3.1 费用构成

—口译费（译员人数 * 工作时间）；

—工作天数；

—加班费（超过约定时间按加班计）；

—交通费；

—食宿费；

—设备使用费、通信费；

—其他相关费用（如，跟会人员费用等）。

4.3.2 计费方式

—工作时间以天为单位，不足半天按半天计；超过半天按 1 天计；

—长期项目可另议（具体周期须经双方协商确定）。

4.3.3 计价公式

总价 = 口译费 + 交通费 + 食宿费 + 设备使用费（需要时）+ 其他相关费用（需要时）

4.3.4 报价一览表

口译类型	报价方式
陪同交传	总价 = 口译费 + 交通费 + 食宿费 + 其他相关费用
会议交传	总价 = 口译费 + 交通费 + 食宿费 + 其他相关费用
远程交传	总价 = 口译费 + 通信设备使用费 + 其他相关费用
耳语同传	总价 = 口译费 + 交通费 + 食宿费 + 其他相关费用
会议同传	总价 = 口译费 + 同传设备使用费 + 译员及跟会人员交通费 + 译员及跟会人员食宿费 + 其他相关费用
远程同传	总价 = 口译费 + 同传设备使用费 + 通信设备使用费 + 其他相关费用

5. 一致性声明

每个口译服务方都可以自愿履行本规范的各项条款，并自负责任地声明是根据本规范提供口译服务报价。